PARIS
MY BEAUTIFUL MADNESS

A Hedonistic Journey in the City of Light

A Memoir by **KRISTA BENDER**

Copyright © 2022

Graphic art done by Lily Davis
Summary and Author Bio by Zoe Quinton
All wine quotes (unless otherwise stated) at the beginning of the chapters are referenced from Karen MacNeil's *The Wine Bible Copyright 2001, 2015 Hachette Book Group.*

ISBN 978-1-66786-174-6 (ebook)
ISBN 978-1-66786-173-9 (Paperback)

Disclaimer

This is a work of nonfiction. Names of people have been changed to protect the privacy of the characters in the memoir. All of the stories here are written from my memory and perception of events. I drink wine sometimes, so it is entirely possible that none of this is true.

This book is dedicated to
my ultimate muse and inspiration.
… the city herself, Paris.

Acknowledgements

Thank you to all of the people who played a part in helping this book come to print and made my dream possible.

Jessica Hatch, my editor, you made this book that much better. You got me and the message of my work from day one, and it was such an enjoyable part of the process receiving your feedback and edits. The collaboration was meant to be.

Zoe Quinton with your literary strategy, you helped me see that this book was worthy of publishing and a sellable product.

Thank you to the entire publishing team that corrected and perfected every last detail and who helped me along the way with the smoothest publishing process from start to finish.

To all of my readers and everyone who has read my early blog PastryinParis or has followed the excerpt releases on my website kristabender.com.

To every person in the book, whom I met in Paris and beyond who made my world a movie set, and made writing about it so fulfilling.

To France for making life interesting, adventurous and the ultimate playground.

Finally, to my family who have been nothing but entirely supportive. Mom and Dad thank you for your encouragement and understanding and believing in me. Love you lots.

Immense Gratitude! MERCI

ONE

Champagne is my downfall. While other people
might spend money on really nice clothes, the latest technology,
or exotic travel, I spend money on bubbles.

I t was February 2015. I was fast approaching my thirtieth birthday, living in LA, and miserable at my corporate job. My intuition told me I was playing it small and safe, and I was constantly fighting against my own beliefs. Why had I wanted to become a chef in the first place? Certainly not to create food in a factory or, even worse, to be a part of an industry that relied heavily on chemical preservatives. I felt like a fraud. Sure, I was paid a decent salary, put up in hotels, and taken to fancy restaurants all over America on my company's dime, but after a while the feeling of entrapment makes a person want to scream from the rooftops for something new, to escape and start over. I longed to wake up excited, rejuvenated, and ready to dive into my work with full force. I was working as an innovation chef for a company that mainly specialised in creating frozen appetizers to stock in major grocery chains. I had a fancy title, and great pay, but felt completely empty inside.

I was planning to throw in the towel, though I didn't know what I'd do next. Maybe turn to my savings and open a French bakery in LA? My bakery would have chandeliers and crown moldings like those of eighteenth-century buildings, and the charm and essence of Paris, my favorite city in the entire world, would be with me every day. I could stay up until the wee hours of the morning making fresh croissants and sip coffee at sunrise as the smell of *pain aux raisins* wafted from the deck ovens.

Or I could just go live in Paris.

My phone buzzed, knocking me back into reality.

Hey. Call me, I miss you.

A text from Eddie, the man I'd been dating on again and off again for the past five years.

Eddie and I had first met when I was twenty-five and he was thirty-three and we both worked for a gourmet food emporium in Northern California. I had been given the incredible opportunity to manage the entire operation while he was the talented executive chef that my boss and I had hired to oversee *Le Bistro*. Eddie, being half Hungarian and half Filipino, had the most gorgeous olive skin, deep brown eyes, and the most charming dimples I had ever seen. He had perfectly formed muscles, and when he rolled his sleeves up to his elbows, it was hard not to imagine what his forearms could handle besides the sauté pan. His voice was butter to my ears—deep, scruffy, and manly with a slight, mysterious accent.

I will never forget the first dish he cooked for me. In order for Eddie to be promoted to executive chef, my boss, Jules, asked him to make us lunch. Twenty minutes later he came to the table with a smoked, almond-crusted chicken thigh, topped with a sweet, dark-cherry gastrique, and the most delicious shallot-confit mashed sweet potatoes whipped to creamy perfection. Wow. Jules and I gaped at each other over each salivating forkful. Eddie was given the title of executive chef with a generous salary that afternoon. It had been forever since a dish was able to transport me to the *plats du jour* I had eaten in Paris, but Eddie's did.

From that day on I knew I had an attraction to Eddie, but I promised myself I would operate on a business level with him and keep the flirting to a minimum. I was single and free and, at the time, loved the feeling of being needed and important to my boss. I felt I had been given the stars, so why on earth would I want to ruin it? That was then, but now, nearly five years later, Eddie was still in my life. Some people would call it fate, some people would call it passion, lust, immense attraction, but whatever it was, I knew it had been meant to be. Eddie and I had beaten all the odds. We had met when he was on the cusp of a divorce, staying together only for his kids, and through it all, his marriage ending, me moving to LA for my corporate job, we had stood the tests of time.

I miss you too, I texted back. *Busy at work right now—Cheryl's on my case. Call you tonight? I can't wait for you to come visit!*

I was doing my best to be optimistic. With Eddie in Sacramento and me in LA, we didn't get to see each other as often as we used to, but he would be coming down for my birthday the following weekend. This was a hard time in my life, though, as I felt zero connection to my job and was pretty miserable going to work every day, not to mention the fact that Eddie's and my relationship had reached the ultimate snarl of complications. As our relationship unfolded, it became apparent that substance abuse was a battle Eddie encountered on a daily basis.

"Actually, I don't drink," he had told me the first New Year's Day that I knew him, when we were still in a flirtatious, racy borderland between friendship and something more. "I—um. I can't really. I am now eight months sober."

I had set the bottle of Veuve Clicquot back down on my kitchen counter. This was news to me.

"Oh. Really? Well, in any case, good for you." I didn't really know how to respond at the time. I was a little shocked. I had never met someone with such extremes as *I cannot take a sip of wine.*

"Is this going to be a problem for you?"

Eddie had sounded ashamed, so I rushed in to soothe him. "Absolutely not. No, sorry for not knowing this and offering you a drink." This was new territory that I didn't quite know how to handle. Enter the second biggest red flag ever, which I was perfectly fine ignoring at the time.

That flag had nearly worn itself out waving ever since. His last relapse had been six months before, and we were still limping back from the damage it had caused.

A marriage can end, but addiction is a disease one needs to face for the rest of their life, and once you're in the life of someone with addiction issues, you are jolted into a different reality. I stayed with Eddie year after year because I loved him and he was my best friend. I also believed in his potential and his talents. He was a beautiful person inside and out, a great father, a talented artist and chef, and he had a wonderful personality. He was a charmer, a smiley guy, a person passionate about food and life, and someone who could make me laugh on a whim. His hot arms, smile with dimples, and amazing food got me in the beginning, but his soul captured me in the end.

I smiled at his reply text, then put my phone down and got back to work.

I had given Eddie permission to celebrate with me in LA, despite my better instincts, but was that what I wanted? How did I want to celebrate this next chapter of my life?

I was mulling this over as I walked into what I called my sanctuary loft that night after work and opened the fridge. Wonderful, a nice, cold bottle of Miraval rosé from Provence; my prayer had been answered. It was a gorgeous evening, and I was looking forward to dining on my terracotta balcony, with its blue-and-white tiles, which I had fully furnished with comfy wicker patio chairs and a stone fountain. I sliced the heirloom tomatoes that were starting to wrinkle on my counter, then tore apart some buffalo mozzarella and sprinkled the tomato slices with sea salt. I grabbed some basil from my herb garden on the terrace. *Parfait*. A little olive oil and balsamic vinegar and we have a meal. I defrosted a hunk of rosemary baguette from the freezer. Just eating baguettes with my meals made me feel a twinge of Frenchness. It's a meal staple rarely absent from the table in Paris.

It was in these moments—ones that were enjoyable and simple and in which I was by myself—that I pondered what exactly I was doing with my life, with my time. Eddie had become a serious disappointment. This latest slip-up was supposed to be the final straw and he had been warned, so the letdown, when it came, felt ten times worse. The fact that I still was allowing him to come down for my birthday seemed to contradict my words, to be the opposite of what I wanted. What did I want, though? Something nice for myself? A consolation prize?

That night, I sat on my terrace and watched the sun set over the palm trees. What a pleasant sight; it was almost as if I were in the South of France enjoying my rosé and tomatoes. I took my last bite of baguette and slowly chewed it, relishing the turn from salt to sweet on my palate. I picked up my glass, and as I watered my herbs, I took a fresh whiff of my lavender. Heaven must be a chilled glass of rosé and the scent of lavender... A thought popped into my head. What if I celebrated turning thirty in the South of France? I felt a jolt of euphoria. I had never been to Provence, but its alluring countryside is complete with acres of lavender, vines growing grapes that will soon be turned into wine, and old villages full of Roman ruins. There must be organized tourism trips, winery tours, and cooking classes in Provence, right?

I raced inside and frantically googled "Vacations in Provence." The options were endless, so I narrowed my search to "Cooking in Provence." It felt like it had been ages since culinary school, and I was constantly traveling and eating meals in restaurants and hotels. I longed to cook classic French cuisine again. I was intrigued as the Patricia Wells Cooking Class popped up on my screen. I clicked on the link, and beautiful photos of food and the French countryside appeared. I read the description, and it sounded divine. Leisurely preparing meals at a chateau daily, cheese and wine pairings, visits to a winery in the region of Gigondas, a farmers market visit where fresh fish of the day would be selected... If anything has ever been more up my alley, I would be shocked. I looked at the calendar and selected a week at the beginning of June when the weather would be perfect.

I am going to Provence! I danced around my apartment. I needed to share my excitement with someone. Though I was still feeling grumpy toward him, I dialed Eddie's number, my fingers shaking in excitement.

His phone was off. That was odd. Maybe he didn't have service? I dialed again ten minutes later. Now it was ringing, though it went straight to voicemail. I left a message stating it was urgent that he get back in touch with me. When I hadn't received a call back an hour later, I started to panic. I sent multiple texts and called several more times to no avail. This feeling within me unfortunately was all too familiar. Eddie and I spoke at the end of the day without fail. It was our thing and always had been. When Eddie didn't answer his phone, this was most definitely a sign that he had relapsed, that a serious drug or alcohol binge had occurred.

Tears formed in my eyes. Why now? Why right after the slip-up? And why right before my birthday? He had sounded so healthy the last few days and seemed really into his AA program. He had received his six-month coin and sounded happy.

Many of my close friends and family members could not understand why a girl like me would want to be wrapped up in an unstable relationship, a relationship that could descend into pure terror based on Eddie's daily decisions. Every time this pattern replayed itself, I told myself *this* time I would leave. This was it; it was over for good. Usually I would break up with Eddie. Then weeks would go by; he would be sober again and beg me back with intense romantic gestures. I longed for him and missed him, and I would always give in. It was a sick cycle that I just didn't know how to break. The good times were so good they were pure ecstasy. The bad times were so bad that life was hell. It feels like pure cliché, like I should have known better, but I wanted so badly to fix him. I wanted to take this addiction away. I thought if I could love him enough and make him happy, he wouldn't need to turn to drugs and alcohol. However, as I learned more and more about addiction, I realized it really was not this simple. It was a struggle every day for Eddie, for any addict. One decision, one wrong choice, can ruin their lives. I had witnessed Eddie lose wonderful jobs, completely destroy his friendships, and his children—that was the saddest of all of it—they suffered through this emotional turmoil. We all asked why he kept doing this. To me it felt like the ultimate betrayal.

Looking back, I can see that Eddie's addiction to drugs and alcohol ran in parallel to an addiction I had, an addiction to the roller coaster itself, to the drama of its highs and lows. It was a cycle that I was participating in, hoping one day I would be enough for it to go away. The idea of how I would feel, if I could change it, was powerful. Every time he turned to drugs and alcohol, I felt like he chose something over me. Why didn't he want *me* more? It was worse than catching him with another woman because not only was he ruining any trust that had been built between us, but more importantly he was ruining his own life. Not only did our relationship turn to dust when he did this, but I also had to worry about him and ask myself if he was even alive.

What had started as a glorious night, followed by pure joy over my Provence trip, turned into crying myself to sleep in utter despair. Eddie was hopeless.

TWO

The range of red Bordeaux is astounding. At the most
basic level there are scores of utterly simple Bordeaux stacked,
by the case, on the floor of any large wine shop.

H*i Anne. Is he okay? Alive?*
Within five minutes Eddie's aunt Anne responded.

Yes, he relapsed. He is resting up today and will attend a meet-
ing tonight. He called his sponsor. He feels ashamed. He has been
tearing up thinking that he has done this to you again.

In true Eddie fashion, I would hear from him tomorrow. He always took a day to sober up and get his head on straight. Then he would call and cry and beg for my forgiveness. This had been happening roughly twice a year since I had been with him. One year we had a great run where he only fell off the wagon once. Five years later, this would be my ninth time experiencing this.

Soon after I got home from work that night, my phone rang. "What do you want?" I answered abruptly, predicting the exact conversation that was about to unfold.

"Please, Krista. I am so sorry." Eddie's voice was shaking. "Just hear me out. Please."

"Eddie, I really can't keep going through this. You are an addict, and you will never change. It rips me apart, affects my work, and I just can't. It's torture."

"I love you. I love you more than anything, Krista. I am really, really trying for us. You have to believe me on this."

I stayed silent.

"Krista, I made a mistake. And yes, this is the ninth time— trust me, I counted. But I know I can beat this. The thought of losing you kills me. Please. You didn't hear from me for a day; yes, I drank. But I promise I am back in the program and I will stay strong. For you. For us."

"All you did was drink? No drugs this time? Really?" I asked aggressively.

"I promise. Not that it excuses any of it, but I did not touch drugs this time. I want to come for your thirtieth. Everything is booked, and I wouldn't miss it for the world. Please. I will make it up to you. I will take you to whatever restaurant you want and hold you all night. Plus, I already talked to your mom and was going to surprise you… but I am bringing Simba."

Simba was our beloved three-year-old teacup Pomeranian. He was seriously the cutest dog I had ever seen, a total cuddle bug, and made my day every time I was with him. Due to my packed travel schedule in LA, Simba rotated among my parents' home, Eddie's, and LA with me when I had lighter months of travel.

I sat on the couch and stared at a picture of me, Eddie, and Simba. They were all I had. Yes, I had friends, but my closest friends were not in LA. They were living in different cities across the country. No one would make my birthday weekend on such last-minute notice. Besides, I could not bear to tell my parents that once again Eddie had fallen off the wagon and we had broken up. It was becoming humiliating. I was going to choose to believe he only abused alcohol this time, even though I could only take his word for it.

"I don't know. I need time to think. I am hurt, sad, and most of all, I am very, very disappointed, Eddie."

"I know. I know this isn't fair to you. Krista, you are all I want, and all I think about. Please consider forgiveness. I will let you be and call you first thing in the morning. I love you. So much."

"Good night."

I loved him, too, and at that moment, I knew I would stay with him. However, I also felt that once I left my job, I would make a different decision. The timing of his relapse was really the only reason I stayed. I didn't want to be sad on my birthday. My emotions went through waves of anger to sadness for Eddie. While I could feel bad for myself, I could always erase this from my life. He couldn't. This disease would live in him forever.

I distracted myself by checking emails before bed, and was excited to see a message regarding my Provence cooking class. *Wine Tasting in Gigondas.* It was an email describing the day of the cooking program on which we would head to the vineyards and taste wine. It gave a list of the vineyards, the wines, and the Michelin-starred restaurant we would be dining at for lunch.

My current life was a struggle, but at the end of the day, I had this trip to look forward to. I clicked on the link in the email with the winery's information. The photos made the vineyards look so dreamy.

The bottom of the winery's website listed its affiliates and write-ups. *Sommelier School in France* was a bullet point on the list. Wow. Now that would be the ultimate life, I thought to myself. Studying wine in the best wine-producing country in the world— what kind of person gets to do that? I was suddenly curious. I clicked the link to find a full review of a day in which wine students from Le Cordon Bleu came to the vineyard to practically test their knowledge. There were several paragraphs from different students about their experience.

My curiosity grew, and I pulled up the Le Cordon Bleu Paris website. I had attended culinary school at their sister institute in San Francisco, though I did not remember there being a wine program available. I clicked the caption listing the different programs offered at the Paris campus. Sure enough, Wine Consulting and Management was listed.

Oh my goodness. Studying wine in Paris—is there such a thing? I had fallen in love with the city on my first trip there nearly ten years before. Its food culture, from my first flaky bite of *pain au chocolat*, had changed my life, driving me from my planned course as an accountant for my dad's commercial construction company to culinary school in San Francisco. I sought out cafés in my home state of California that served crepes, omelets, and onion gratinee soup. I wore oversized scarves and listened to Édith Piaf on my iPod. I eventually started a blog called Pastry in Paris, capturing all my passion and excitement for the French culture. In a word, I was obsessed.

What if I could make a go of living in Paris? *Okay, Krista,* I told myself. *Focus. How long is the program? Is it even offered to people who do not speak French?* I read through the entire online brochure. It was an intensive ten-month program centered in Paris, with several trips to the different wine regions of France. The course was taught in French, but everything was translated into English. Twenty students maximum were accepted each year from around the world. Requirements: high school diploma, college degree desired, resume of work experience, several interviews with faculty board members, a passion for wine and food, a visa, and, of course, tuition. The next program would start in September 2015. I reread the brochure five times. Was this a real program? It sounded like a ten-month vacation.

Students will enter a wine immersion program where 30-hour-per-week lectures and practical work will begin in September.

Students will spend time on a vineyard learning the intricacies of the wine making process, and also a short internship will take place at a restaurant in Paris where they will practice their sommelier skills. Different regions of France will be explored and multiple vineyard visits are included in tuition, as well as regional accommodations and transport.

Apply to be one of the lucky few that receive top-notch training in the food and wine center of the world—Paris.

Oh, Paris. In my gut, I knew I needed to experience life there. It had been a dream, but I guess I never had the courage to make the dream come true. I worried that I needed to build my career, that it would be irresponsible to live abroad in my favorite city. Instead, I worked my tush off for years in the restaurant business, which included regularly working holidays, weekends, and grueling ten- to twelve-hour shifts. At least I was stable in my career and making good money, I would tell myself. I don't even speak French—that was one of my many excuses, along with: I love my boyfriend; I can't just leave someone I love. But I got a strong sense that I had run out of excuses. There was nothing holding me back. I wanted out of my job. I wanted a better relationship with someone stable whom I could trust. The decision was now or never.

It was the first time in my life that I knew going to Paris would not be running away. Rather, it would be running toward something. Paris would open doors; it would change me as a woman. I had read about women doing this—leaving corporate environments and whisking themselves off to a land of buttery croissants, crunchy baguettes, and wheels of Camembert. Could I be one of those women? Leave California, where I had lived for nearly thirty years? The mere thought felt expansive. I envisioned a new world, and it felt empowering. I wanted mystery to wrap its arms around me and for certainty to disappear. I had nothing to lose, which essentially meant I had freedom. True and pure freedom.

Typically, when something feels right in my bones, I am quick to pull the trigger. I have an impulsive personality that takes the leap and welcomes the risk. I bookmarked the Wine and Management page and told myself I would make a list of everything I needed to apply tomorrow. I went to bed in a joyous state, much different than the crying mess I had been the night before.

Another workday ended, and I pulled into the parking lot of my local market on the way home. I had decided I would send in my application to Le Cordon Bleu Paris's wine program that evening, but first I needed to purchase a bottle of French wine to set the tone. For the past few days I had been gathering everything I needed to send in a complete application. My resume was up to date; I had gathered and scanned my birth certificate and my official diplomas. I had made photocopies of my passport and written an essay on why I would be a good candidate. I had not told a soul I was doing this undercover work. Until I got accepted, I would keep quiet. I was sure hundreds of people applied and that my chances of acceptance were slim, but something in my gut told me this was absolutely meant for me.

I perused the wine display, looking at every label. To think that I could potentially study and understand what each one meant, what cryptic terms like *appellation* signified; that I could become an expert on French wine. The thought was almost too intoxicating. Wine was a major part of the culinary world, and attending a top wine program would only enhance my already paved career path. I selected a bottle of Bordeaux, Château Beau-Séjour Bécot, from Saint-Émilion. Any Bordeaux must be fabulous, right? I grabbed a fresh baguette and some cheese, as well as a bag of lettuce. I remembered eating green salads in Paris dressed with oil, vinegar, and Dijon mustard, giving it a refreshing tang. Oh, and some 70-percent dark chocolate. I wanted to feel that I was already French—law of attraction, *peut-être* ?

I got home and poured myself a glass of the Bécot. Exquisite. This was a different and highly welcomed taste compared to the California cabernets I was used to. French wine has that sense of the earth. At first it is an acquired taste, as California wines are a little richer and more fruit-forward. I closed my eyes and envisioned the French countryside before assembling the documents of my application into email attachments. I felt confident and had also written two paragraphs in the email that I hoped would at least catch the application committee's attention. I said a little prayer and dragged the arrow to the send button.

THREE

An intimate knowledge of anything necessarily begins with
the fundamentals of that thing. With wine, I'd even go
one step further and say that the capacity for pleasure—
the capacity to be thrilled by wine—is ineluctably tied
to understanding it in all its most basic details.

A *lemon layer cake with clouds of swiss meringue.* It was my thirtieth birthday, and this was presented to me with a single pink candle. It may not have been *tart au citron,* one of my favorite Parisian delicacies, but my boss Cheryl personally baked a lemon pound cake, layered with lemon curd and covered in sweet, marshmallowy clouds of meringue. I was touched. As if that wasn't enough to satisfy my taste buds, we also munched on *Salade Niçoise* for lunch that day at the office. Everyone adhered to the French theme in my honor, and it was a lovely, memorable afternoon.

Eddie would be landing around five o'clock that evening, and then he and Simba would jump in a taxi and come straight over. He was taking me to Bäco Mercat to celebrate. It was a new chic and trendy eatery located in downtown LA, with a rising chef at the helm. I had browsed the menu earlier that day and started dreaming up my order. Eddie had picked well. While his addiction was an unwanted third party in our relationship, Eddie was nothing but kind and considerate. He was always spot on about where to take me. He knew me so well and did his due diligence to make sure everything was perfect.

I ran the bath and lay my dress on the bed. I had purchased a sleek, black lace dress, and this would be the perfect occasion to wear it. I grabbed my phone to place on the charger—Eddie had just texted.

Landed. Be there soon! Can't wait until you're in my arms.

I instantly had butterflies in my stomach. I was glad I had forgiven him, and I was full of adrenaline, as it had been almost a month since I had seen him. We had endured a long-distance relationship ever since I accepted the job in LA. He remained in Northern California, where his life and children were. We had decided to make it work, as I could not have passed up this opportunity. He was very supportive of my choice, and I felt he wanted the best for me, even if it made things harder on him.

An hour later Eddie was at the door. I opened it, and he smiled at me with a look of awe. "Hello, gorgeous birthday girl..." He always made me feel like the most beautiful woman in the world.

He grabbed me and kissed me. Simba was yapping, whining, and squirming, practically leaping out of Eddie's arms at the sight of me. I quickly picked up the bundle of joy and got a million licks all over my face. I couldn't tell who was happier to see me, Eddie or Simba. I felt so full of love. After the near one hundred kisses from Eddie and Simba combined, I freshened my makeup, and Eddie and I set out for our romantic dinner.

Bäco Mercat was absolutely amazing. We indulged in an array of culinary creations including homemade pasta with pork belly; yam; spiced beef and goat cheese flatbreads; caramelized cauliflower with mint and pine nuts; and semolina pudding with cinnamon, maple, and apple butter. It was a flawless meal with the ideal company. Eddie and I could not keep our hands off of each other; even when the food was placed on the table, our handhold did not break.

After dessert, and my festive glass of Champagne along with Eddie's sparkling apple cider, we headed back to my apartment, where we cuddled with Simba on the couch and I opened my gift. In addition to chefdom, Eddie was also a talented painter and was always painting me pictures. This one happened to be a painting of two old French doors resembling an actual photo I had taken in Nice, France, the last time I had been there. Eddie had stolen the photo and recreated it in the painting. "This is so you can feel as though you are in France. Place it somewhere where you will see it every day." He smiled and kissed my cheek.

My mind raced to my possible acceptance into Le Cordon Bleu Paris and the second relocation of my entire life. I felt overwhelmed; I had not voiced a peep to Eddie about my thought process lately. How would he respond to my move not just farther down the West Coast but all the way across a continent and an ocean?

"It's beautiful. I am speechless. How thoughtful." I could feel tears welling up in my eyes, not only because of the special gesture and lovely painting my boyfriend had just given me, but also because I was secretly planning another life, another chapter. He was in the dark. I felt a strong pang of remorse.

Eddie wiped my eyes, perceptibly believing the former, not the two combined, caused the tears. He then reached for a chocolate and fed it to me and gently started kissing my neck. I could feel myself starting to be entranced in passion.

"But I still need to… to open my card from you," I said in between kisses.

"Yes, you will. Once you're in your real birthday suit. Come here. I want to kiss every inch of your body." He grabbed my hand, pulled me up, led me into the bedroom, and shut the door.

The next morning I watched Eddie sleep for a few minutes before deciding not to wake him. He was so handsome, I recall thinking. I scooped up Simba and proceeded out to the terrace to enjoy a cup of coffee. *You can feel like you're in France.* I remembered the pang of guilt that hit me when Eddie spoke those words last night. When should I tell him? I couldn't wait until after I had gotten accepted, if I did. I had to let him out of the dark.

With my mind turned to Paris, I inevitably wondered if the school had received my application. It had been a few days. I reached for my iPad to check my email.

> *Bonjour Krista,*
>
> *We have received your application. While it is under review by our administration, can you participate in a Skype interview at any of the following times?*
>
> *Monday 9:00 AM (Paris time)*
> *Tuesday 5:00 PM (Paris time)*
>
> *Please let us know. This is the next step in the process. The interview will last approximately one hour, and you will speak with several faculty members with your final conversation being with Mr. Laurent Lavigne, the professor of the wine program.*

Thank you, God! I was officially in the process of making this dream a reality. I immediately, without much thought, responded that I could be available for the Tuesday time slot. Just then, Eddie appeared out of the bedroom and wiped his eyes with a yawn and stretch. "Good morning, babe. Wow. What a night, huh?" He smiled and grabbed a toothbrush. I quickly looked to confirm that my email had been sent regarding the Skype time slot, and then I stood up to give Eddie a big hug.

Eddie started making one of my all-time favorites, French toast. I sat and sipped my coffee and read through a travel magazine. I loved lazy mornings with Eddie—him cooking something delectable and allowing me to relax and speak when I wanted to, to watch him, or to stare at a book or the TV.

But my eyes gazed past the pictures of Mediterranean vistas and blurred over interesting headlines. I had just set up a Skype interview. This conversation needed to happen.

"So, you know I am pretty miserable at my job," I began. "I have been thinking a lot."

"Yeah. So, what are you thinking? What are you going to do about it?" He took the spatula and flipped the egg-drenched, perfectly caramelized oval slice of bread, and the pan sizzled.

"What do you think about me going back to school? Like, not working for a bit? I feel burned out." I looked at him in anticipation.

"I think, I mean, honestly whatever makes you happy. I know it's cliché, but that's all I want for you." He started to dip more bread in the custard.

"So, okay… I. um. I was looking at schooling abroad. Just, y' know, because I can't imagine doing something basic. It would have to be worth it," I said hesitantly.

"Oh yeah. Really? Abroad where?" He stopped dipping the bread.

"Well, actually, I was looking at schools in Europe. In Paris."

There. I had said it.

"Paris? Meaning you would move there? What programs are you looking into? How long is the course of study?" I could tell he was speaking on autopilot, not having fully processed what I had said. Eddie had this calm, nonchalant attitude he deployed anytime he felt hurt or any negative emotion. It was his way of protecting himself, I was learning.

"Eddie, I'm serious. I need a change. It's a wine school where I would get to study French wine for ten months. It would basically be a sabbatical where I would have the chance to live in my dream city." I needed to declare it, get it out in the open.

A long pause ensued, and then he responded. "Honestly, Krista, that sounds like you. It sounds phenomenal. You should apply and see what happens." He plated my French toast and vigorously shook the tin of powdered sugar over it. "Enjoy, love."

The irony of me applying for a *wine* program, when my boyfriend was a true alcoholic, was not lost on me. Our lives were a complete contradiction: him attending AA meetings, trying not to engage in a single sip, while I would be drinking away, tasting bottle after bottle on a vineyard. It was moments like this when I realized life is not fair.

"Thanks for the support, babe. We can discuss more as it happens. For now, it's just an idea. My next step, though, is going to be resigning from my job." I cut a piece of the eggy, fried, deliciously sweet bread, and immersed it in the pool of maple syrup. I fed a bite to Eddie as he finished making his plate. "You continue to amaze me," I stated with a smile.

This whole visit, I hadn't wanted to punish him for his latest relapse. I had empathy and immense love for him, and I wanted to support him, so I never brought it up. We spent the next two days relishing every minute together. I could not have asked for a better birthday weekend. Monday came, though, and Eddie needed to fly home to his work and family obligations. I was sad but also had a lot I needed to accomplish. We said our tearful goodbyes, and I watched him disappear through the airport's sliding glass doors. I wondered how our story would play out. I loved Eddie, but I also loved Paris. I longed for both, but I had the strange sense that they could not coexist.

On Tuesday afternoon I prepared for my Skype call with the Le Cordon Bleu Paris administration. I was nervous but also excited. I had put on a black blouse, a strand of pearls, and tried to look ultra-professional, then sipped *un demi-verre* of Chardonnay to ease my nerves. This was a big step, a big interview that could lead to my next chapter.

Suddenly, my computer screen was lighting up and humming with the Skype incoming-call ringtone. *Here it goes,* I told myself as I clicked to answer. *Give it your best.*

I spoke with a lovely Parisian woman named Clara, who was head of student services, and a man called Nicholas, and then the head of the wine program, Mr. Laurent Lavigne, sat down. He was wearing a suit, and his hair was combed perfectly. He smiled and told me to relax; I guess he could feel my anxiousness through the computer screen. The professor wanted to know my history with wine, my culinary school experience, what I knew about French

26

culture and Paris in general, and two of my favorite French dishes, to which I embarrassingly muttered beef bourguignon, as well as croissants, both in an attempted French accent. I quickly added duck à l'orange, realizing that croissants are a breakfast pastry, not a French dish. How stupid of me! I laughed at myself, and so did he. After a lively fifteen-minute conversation, he said they would continue reviewing applications and should know decisions of acceptance within two weeks. Then they would ask for tuition payments, and we students would begin the visa application process. Both of the latter were the students' sole responsibility. I felt a sense of extreme exhilaration. The call had gone so well, better than expected. I had a feeling I would be accepted; they had all been not only kind but had seemed impressed with me.

I now had to think about how I was going to fund not only my tuition but my year in Paris. I would want to savor every minute, every restaurant, and live like a true Parisian. I did not want to sleep on a lumpy twin mattress in student housing at age thirty! I saw myself living in a charming flat in the swanky Saint Germain des Prés, shopping the open-air markets on Sundays, and meeting friends at trendy restaurants. I wanted to go big or go home, and I knew this would take a sacrifice and a great deal of planning.

For the next few days I was obsessively checking my email, praying to see a letter of acceptance or a *Congratulations* subject line. The wait was grueling.

Finally, the email I was anxiously anticipating arrived in my inbox.

Dear Ms. Bender,

We thank you for your interest in Le Cordon Bleu Paris. We are pleased to inform you that your application for the Wine and Management Program has been accepted. Please find attached the Admission Proposal to return within 10 days, the tuition payment form, as well as information regarding applying for your student visa. A mandatory deposit is due within the 10 days to hold your spot. Please do not hesitate to contact the admissions office with any questions you may have. We look forward to hearing from you.

I read this and literally pinched myself. The decision was made. I was moving to Paris.

I recognized that I was setting all of this up, checking off the steps, without having even put a phone call in to Eddie. Deep down I knew. This wasn't a conversation or decision we were arriving at together. Not anymore. This was a decision that would impact my life, first and foremost, and somewhere deep down, I knew I had to make it alone.

FOUR

Sitting in a café, you could drink the best wines of Provence all day long.
They are mostly not intellectual wines, but wines of pleasure...
wines that remind us of the time when reaching for a gulp of wine was
as natural and common as reaching for a hunk of bread.

It was a beautiful spring evening in 2015, and I had a lovely bottle of Sauvignon Blanc chilled in the fridge. I decided I would bake a quiche from scratch and serve it with a nice, crunchy green salad. Quiche always reminded me of Paris as I frequently ordered a slice at bistros *pour dejeuner*. I had remembered to get some pie dough from my sample fridge before I had left the office. All I had to do was prepare the filling and let it bake up. I decided on goat cheese, sun-dried tomato, and kalamata olives for the flavor. The goat cheese would pair wonderfully with the Sauvignon Blanc, as the acidity of the white wine would cut through the tanginess of the goat cheese. I figured before I began wine school in France I better start educating myself on proper food and wine pairings. I turned on some café tunes and got to work on my quiche filling. I poured myself a splash of Sauvignon Blanc while I mixed and chopped away. Once the quiche was safe in the oven, I would call Eddie.

This would not be out of the blue, I reminded myself. I had already mentioned the possibility of Paris on the last weekend we had spent together, but I still knew this would be a hard talk to have. I took a deep breath and dialed.

"Hey, babe, I miss you. So glad you called!" Eddie sounded like he was in a great mood.

"Hi, you sound great. You must be having a good day?" I loved when he was in a good mood, and I hated the thought that I might dash it with my news.

"Yup. Just had a great workout, hanging out and swimming with the kids. I just got out of the pool when I heard the phone."

"Oh wonderful, I love a nice sunset swim. Hey, listen, I need to talk to you. Remember on my birthday weekend when I mentioned going back to school? And you had said apply and see what happens? Well, I did and—"

"And you got accepted to the wine school in Paris?" he asked with knowing anticipation.

"Yes. Yes, I did."

"Krista, that's so great! I knew you would. Hey love, I am happy for you, but I need to get these kids back inside and fed. I will call in a little while—I want to hear all about it."

He sounded genuinely happy. This was where we differed dramatically. To Eddie, everything was about living right now, in this moment. In fact, the AA program encouraged him to stay in the present and *not* worry about the future. Me, on the other hand, I was always wondering what this present decision or moment could mean. What would it change? What would it stand for?

His reaction to my news had been a normal, work-a-day response, the same as, "Sure, I will take another cream for my coffee." I recognized that in this moment he was supporting my Paris dream, but I was now surprised and a little confused by the lack of confrontation I was receiving from him. In the grand scheme of things, I knew he wasn't fighting me on this because we both understood it was best for me. I felt a sudden pain in my stomach. I knew my time with Eddie was dwindling. I tried not to think about it, but soon I would be leaving my comfortable life and, with it, a man who loved me. I jabbed my fork into the last bite of the quiche crust. The crust was moist, buttery, and flaked apart as I chewed it, with the slightest remnants of creamy goat cheese.

The next two months were a whirlwind.

I endured the long and stressful process of gathering my documents for the visa application, and was now just waiting on the embassy's approval. The days at work were long, longer than usual. Once I knew I was leaving the company, I think my brain naturally checked out. I could not help but find myself daydreaming about my new life in France. Would I make friends with Parisians? Would I do well in the world of wine? What about the language? Would I become fluent in French just by living there? There wasn't much advertised about this wine course online, nor did they say much during the interview. It felt like a mysterious program, only offered in Paris, and it seemed odd that there wasn't much in the way of an itinerary or listed syllabus. I was nervous thinking about this, but my enthusiasm usually took over, placing the fear in the back of my mind. I would find out all about the program soon enough!

Eddie was set to fly to LA one weekend in May to help me pack up the loft. I had arranged for a moving company to put my belongings and furniture in storage, and I would move into my parent's home for the summer before I relocated to Paris. I was also getting extremely excited, as I would venture to Provence in a week! I had booked an Airbnb in the village of Vaison-la-Romaine. From the pictures, it seemed so charming, and the chateau I would go to daily for cooking classes was a ten-minute walk through the village. I would fly into Paris and immediately take a train to Avignon. Then an arranged taxi would take me to the little village. I had also decided to stay a few days in Paris after my vacation to tour my future campus and secure an apartment for my move in September. All of my efforts seemed to be coming together.

It was Friday afternoon, and Eddie would be arriving any minute. We would spend the weekend mostly packing up, staying in, and ordering pizza. When Eddie was with me, he was someone

I could count on, and so I felt a twinge of guilt, thinking of how he would do the dishes, help me clean the house, pack boxes, and then I'd just say, "See ya later!" to him by way of thanks. I had to remind myself that I had endured my fair share of unpredictable futures and difficult moments at his hands. When he was away from me, even if he hadn't relapsed, he made my life harder even in the most subtle ways because I never knew what he was doing. For once, I was the one making a change he'd have to adapt to. Guilt or no guilt, I knew I was making the right decision to be packing up my life and leaving, but I still couldn't help but wonder how many weekends we had left together.

Just before I left for vacation in Provence, I secured a visa appointment. If everything went smoothly at the embassy, I would be given my student visa in a month. It had been a tedious process, but completely worth it in the end.

I could not believe my trip to Provence had arrived. I was absolutely elated. I threw my final pair of shoes into my suitcase and zipped it up. I don't know which I was more excited for: a week of wine tasting and cooking in Provence or my two-day stay in Paris afterward. Knowing I would be back in Paris in September for good was nothing short of surreal.

The next morning, after having barely gotten a wink of sleep, Eddie dropped me off at the airport. I was Provence-bound.

"Have an amazing time," he said. "I love you. Text when you land in Paris."

We wrapped our arms around each other in a tight embrace, and Eddie kissed my forehead.

"Bye, I will miss you," I said, looking up with a smile. I would miss Eddie. I always did. Our relationship was untraditional in the sense that we were never in the same place for long. There was always an ending, and back to our lives we went. In hindsight, it was good that we weren't inseparable. It allowed for a sense of freedom within me, and I was able to make decisions on my own without the real feeling of being tied down. It also made things between us magnetic. The spark never faded because we only received small doses of each other and could never take anything for granted. Our time spent together was sacred.

After twenty hours in airports and on planes, I had finally landed. Whenever I got off the plane at Charles de Gaulle, a special feeling would come over me. I knew I was in Paris, and a small part of me weirdly felt like I belonged.

On this trip, I would wait at the airport train station for an hour before my train to Avignon departed. After barely eating and sleeping, I was running low on energy. I desperately needed my first croissant. I stood in line at the train station café and smiled. It was such a different experience than being in line at Starbucks in the States. Everyone here was ordering *un petit café*. At Starbucks, grande Frappuccinos towering with whipped cream seemed to be the drink of choice. I was next in line and decided to do as the French do: *"Je vais prendre un petit café, s'il vous plaît... et un croissant."*

I sat and relished my breakfast. I looked up at the large screen hanging from the ceiling and realized my train would be there in twenty minutes. I had never traveled on a train in Europe. I would be venturing to the South of France by myself, and while it mostly excited me, it definitely felt out of my comfort zone. I grabbed my luggage and went to the platform A4, where my train was set to depart.

Four hours later, I arrived in Avignon.

Susan, the lady who owned this charming flat I had rented for the week, welcomed me with a big hug. Susan was originally from Napa, had come to France to study, and had married a French man. Now divorced, she had received this property and decided to make it a rental while she lived in a neighboring village. She had also experienced a week in the Patricia Wells Cooking School I was about to attend, and said it was nothing short of remarkable.

Susan had purchased some delicious cheeses and local wines as a hosting gift for me. I was overwhelmed with joy—I had a wonderful lady greeting me; a charming, spacious, and beautiful flat; and two of my favorite things on this earth: cheese and wine. I had planned on arriving in Provence, taking a shower, settling in, and resting. However, pure adrenaline took over, and when Susan suggested heading into the village to visit the local chocolatier, I could not resist. *I'm in France, I will sleep when I am dead*, I remember telling myself.

Susan and I spent the afternoon popping into all her favorites including the chocolatier, cheesemonger, butcher, and pottery store. We ended the afternoon at the boulangerie, where they had just pulled their second round of bread from the oven. The smell upon entering the boulangerie was intoxicating. This is what I loved about France: all of my senses were captured and I was so present, taking in every detail of every moment, from the perfectly shaped chocolate squares painted with gold specks, to the layered and refined pastries, to the hams hanging in the *boucherie*, and now the smell of fresh-baked bread. Here, I could live in the moment, not a care for the future, the way Eddie was all the time. I walked out of the boulangerie with a warm, crusty baguette to accompany my cheese selection back at the flat, and a *palmier* for dessert.

After settling into my place, I sat on the stone terrace with a glass of local wine, slices of Comté, and a wedge of Camembert. I tore off a piece of baguette and chewed it slowly, allowing myself to taste the pure perfection of the crumb. I watched the sun drop in the sky and felt my eyes start to close. I retreated to my bedroom, lay down on the plush, violet quilt of my king-size bed, and drifted off into dreams of France. I slept for twelve hours straight.

The next morning I woke up feeling refreshed and rejuvenated. Eddie had texted to make sure I was safe, alive, and well. I responded with ten photographs, clearly already enthralled by southern France. I leaped out of bed and opened all of the doors to the apartment, allowing the fresh, Provençal air in. I dug into my palmier and made a cup of coffee.

Today was the start of the cooking program. I would head to the chateau on the hill at 3:00 p.m. to meet everyone and enjoy an aperitif followed by a lavish meal. I slipped into a black- and white-striped cotton dress, and strapped on my wedge sandals. I had called a taxi to take me for the first day. I wanted to wear something a little more fancy and avoid the walk up the hill. The next few days I had planned to walk to the chateau.

I arrived at three o'clock sharp. I walked down a gravel pathway, turned a corner, and saw a stunning masterpiece in front of me. There it was, the chateau, better known as the Clos Chanteduc, or Madame Wells' farmhouse. This massive property was breathtaking—a pale yellow mansion of a country house with mint-green shutters, surrounded by gardens and olive trees, overlooking a vineyard. Around the corner, there was a large, Roman pool with statues and fountains. Beyond the pool there were several open terraces with patio furniture, with multiple views of the plush, green landscape.

I heard voices and walked through a small courtyard to see everyone seated in a circle, glasses of Champagne in their hands. I approached and was warmly greeted with hugs from Patricia and her husband, Walter. Smiling faces were looking up at me, and I was handed a fresh fig stuffed with walnuts and fennel, seared and seasoned with sea salt, as well as a glass of Champagne. *Divine.* We all exchanged introductions and sipped our Champagne with heaven land as our backdrop. Turns out there were nine ladies mostly from the States, with two from Canada. I was the youngest, but as I had done, most women were there as a gift to themselves. It was one woman's sixtieth birthday, another was celebrating fifty, another her work promotion, and there was a mother there with her two daughters. The aperitif hour turned into a sunset dinner on a large terrace overlooking the vineyard. As the five courses were revealed over several hours, I listened to stories about how Patricia and Walter had acquired this magnificent property, and how Patricia had been close friends with none other than my idol, Julia Child. It all felt like a devastatingly beautiful dream. I made it back to my flat that evening and could barely sleep anticipating my next fun-filled day at the chateau.

Upon arriving at the chateau the following morning, I was given the task of making a cherry clafouti. This is a typical French dessert, essentially a thick pancake embedded with whatever fruit was in season; this would serve as our lunch dessert. After preparing the clafouti, I would assist the others in making traditional *soupe au pistou*, a white bean and vegetable stew topped with fresh pesto. The premise was that we would cook dishes together under Patricia's instruction and using her recipes, and then we would spend two hours dining on our creations for lunch and dinner. We were given aprons and recipe books with our names on them. The wine was opened at 11:30 a.m., and we were given a small glass to enjoy while cooking. If our recipes called for fresh herbs, tomatoes, or olives, we would search the gardens on the property to find them. This was a luxury retreat with a light cooking agenda mixed in, and it was my perfect form of meditation.

That day at the chateau I discovered that Julia Child had given Patricia one of her stoves years ago. It was located in one of the kitchens, and I was going to get to prepare a meal on it! What? This was music to my ears. I walked into the kitchen dedicated to Julia and was overcome by emotion. Pictures of Julia lined the walls, and there was even a letter from her addressed to Patricia. Julia Child was one of my greatest inspirations. She moved to Paris at fifty years old and started a career in food that would vastly change how Americans viewed French cuisine. I was somewhat taken aback by how Patricia described their friendship as she would her friendship with anyone else. I felt a deep sense of history, and chills formed at the back of my neck.

The next few days were divine. I had gotten close with the ladies and had shared over lunch one day my next chapter and the thought of moving to Paris. I vividly recall Patricia Wells turning to look at me across the table and saying, "Go to Paris. If you even have to ask yourself, 'Should I go?' You don't deserve to. The answer is an absolute *yes.*"

I knew she was right. *An absolute yes.*

Our days were filled with cooking, baking, sipping wine, visiting outdoor markets, educational presentations from local cheesemongers, and five-hour dinners with tantalizing conversation. We also went on a trip to the town of Gigondas, known for some of the best wine in the region. I remember experiencing utter enchantment that day, after walking around the vineyards, tasting wine, and thinking to myself, *I am about to spend a whole year doing this!* I knew now more than ever that wine school in Paris was the right decision. Now only if I could get my visa.

We spent our last day making fresh pizzas and roasting whole chickens in the wood-fired oven in the courtyard. We sipped wine and listened to jazz music, and it was a relaxed, all-day party. I had a flashback to the night on my terrace when I was holding a glass of rosé and smelling my lavender plant. *Who knew that would lead to this moment?* I thought. I was cooking on a vineyard in Provence with new friends, laughing and drinking wine… I felt strongly that this was a warm up to what my year in Paris would bring. I would meet new friends there, too, from all over the world, sip wine on vineyards, and be changed as a person forever.

The party lasted until midnight. All the ladies and I exchanged phone numbers and emails and promised to keep in touch. It was sad to see them go, but I was so grateful to have experienced the sheer bliss of that week with them. I left with a recipe book that included all the dishes we had cooked together. This would serve as a great memory for this fabulous vacation. Any time I wanted to reminisce, I would whip something up in the kitchen and be transferred back to this chateau in Provence.

I needed to get to sleep. I would take the train back to Paris the next morning. Out of all the euphoria of this week, that was the most comforting thought I had had in a long time.

FIVE

A glass of Syrah has always reminded me of a guy
that wears cowboy boots with a tuxedo.

Manly, yet elegant.

Watching it, it's like a performance. The Parisian café scene. Small circular tables are perfectly placed next to each other facing the streets. The pin-thin waiters dressed in black pants and white button down shirts whirl around balancing their trays as if it were a choreographed dance. The energy of their movement stands in the exact opposition of the relaxed europeans at each table inhaling their cigarette, or bringing their glass slowly up to their lips to take a sip of wine. I found this scene, the "pulse" of the city absolutely intoxicating to not only watch, but rather be a part of on a daily basis.

The few days I spent in Paris were magical. I spent my days exploring, sitting in cafés, and taking in the city's beauty. I even managed to squeeze in a food tour of Le Marais district, where I tasted the best croissants, chocolates, wines, and cheeses of the neighborhood.

While strolling the city, I had browsed the different *arrondissements* and decided that I wanted to stay in the Fifth. It had an innate charm, it was practically the city center, it was close to the river, and the metro stops to my future campus were all easily accessible. I looked around, met with a lovely landlord, and secured a flat near the Pantheon. The flat was a tiny apartment that had been an attic in the eighteenth century and had exposed wooden beams. It had old hardwood floors, and an architect had just refinished the place to maximize efficiency. Without thinking too much about it, I had signed a lease. It was affordable, and in the district I wanted. Apartment searching in Paris is unequivocally very competitive, and I wanted to relieve the stress and worry of not having a place to live. The apartment was not available to rent until the end of September, so I figured I would rent a short stay for my first three weeks in Paris to punctuate my arrival. Then I would move into my little attic.

Before, when I had visited Paris, I had felt lost and used a map frequently. Not this time. I impressed myself with my ability to get around, walking everywhere and starting to recognize the streets and routes between destinations. In essence I felt like I had been living there already. I boarded my flight to California and relished the fact that I would be "home" in Paris in a short six weeks.

Back in California, I spent as much time with my family, friends, and Eddie as possible. I didn't want to take a moment for granted, as I would soon only be calling them from afar. My younger sister, Kaley, was getting married, and I was so happy for her. I kept busy in the beginning of the summer trying to do my best at being her maid of honor.

On the flight home from Paris, I had written my speech for the wedding and sobbed. I could not believe my little sister was getting married. While I was so thrilled by the fact, I couldn't help but mull over how differently our lives were playing out. We were close in age, and had always dreamed up our futures together. As girls, we picked out our houses in the neighborhood where we would live, talked about our babies' names, and even imagined who our husbands would be. Kaley was getting married to a wonderful man, and was going to have a house, babies, and a life full of love. I was the older one, leaving all comforts behind and moving to Europe at thirty. Life is so crazy, and I could not have imagined this as a little girl planning future lives with my sister. Hadn't I wanted to get married, to have a dream wedding and live a traditional life? I had thought so, but my recent actions had led me very far away from that. I was now leaving old-fashioned dreams behind for an international world of becoming anonymous, meeting people from all walks of life, and sauntering through this earth with only myself by my side. Even though Paris felt so right, it begged the question: *Will I be able to have it all?* Will I be able to meet someone, have a baby and a secure life? Is Paris a dream, or is it a sacrifice I am making, trading one life for another?

At my age, I had to wonder about this. I was choosing the unknown, mystery, and adventure over security, comfort, and certainty. I figured fate, the universe, God's hand, whatever you want to call it, was at work here. The invisible breadcrumb trail that had led me from my college boyfriend, who left after seven, surely-headed-down-the-aisle years; to Eddie having too many of his own issues to allow for a future; was now pointing me toward France. You cannot change people, and you cannot change desires; my desire for nearly a decade had been Paris.

One morning in late July, I received my visa in the mail. I took ten pictures just to make sure it was real and then jumped around screaming. This was the final stamp of approval: I could now go to Paris and legally reside there for a year. I was in disbelief and at the same time elated. In a short period of time I had applied and gotten accepted to a prestigious sommelier school, left my job, secured an apartment in Paris, and received a stamp of approval from the French government to live there. It was an *absolute yes!* This entire time everyone in my life had been so supportive; in fact I had yet to hear anyone try and change my mind, even Eddie.

I had decided that Eddie and I would leave things open and just see what happened. There would be no official breakup at this time, nor would there be a firm commitment that we were staying together no matter what, that at the end of this year I was hopping on a jet plane headed straight for him. I was embracing the mystery. Intellectually and rationally I knew that living abroad would eventually call for a final decision on our relationship. Eddie had children and a full-time job, and could not just spend weeks in Paris with me. In fact, I wasn't sure he could come visit at all.

It was the night before I would leave for Paris, and Eddie had just finished cooking a cornbread-stuffed duck to celebrate. We sat by the fire at his condo and laughed, talked, and fed each other bites of the fabulous meal he had prepared. He had surprised me by cooking duck, my favorite, and by saying, "You are going to eat a lot of duck over there, but none of those French assholes can cook it as good as me!" We laughed hysterically.

I still had not seen Eddie shed one tear about my move; it surprised me, as I had spent a few nights crying myself to sleep at the thought of everything changing between us. He remained positive and kept his emotions hidden. I took my last scrumptious bite, and as I was chewing, Eddie gently grabbed my chin and stared into my eyes. "I am going to miss you terribly." He looked down, then back up, and tears had started forming in his beautiful, brown eyes. Seeing him emotional overtook me, and I started to sob.

We lay down by the fire under a blanket and held each other. We were lying there, just breathing deep breaths together, smelling the scent of each other's skin, and letting the tears tremble down. I had not felt pain like that since the day my first love and college boyfriend of seven years Alex, had walked out on me. In fact, this pain was worse because it was my own doing. I had control over this, and I had grief in my heart over seeing someone I loved hurting from a decision I was making. I also felt sadness for myself, for us, and for all that we had been through the last five years, all that we had invested emotionally and built together. I felt like I had just taken a hammer and slammed it down, cracking our foundation.

We made love, and a tear fell with every touch and kiss Eddie gave me. I had never been so emotional during sex before; it was a new experience, almost too overwhelming. I felt so safe and loved in Eddie's arms. I could not imagine another man touching me. It felt so right with Eddie, as if I could never ask for anything more. Just like his paintings or the meals he cooked, his lovemaking was perfection, surreal, natural, and complete.

I literally cried from my last bite of duck, through sex, and up until that last kiss goodbye. Eddie stayed strong for both of us and reserved his emotions as best he could. We hugged each other so tight, and I got in my car. I drove away and watched Eddie waving to me through the rearview mirror. I remember feeling like that would be the last time I ever saw him. I was closing a chapter without having said it. I trusted my body, my overwhelming tears, and the pain surging through every inch of my being. I understood what had just occurred.

That night I barely slept a wink. I was moving to Paris the next day; I kept repeating this fact over and over again in my thoughts. I had a one-way ticket and was going to land in France and have to adjust and "make it work." No turning back. I think I went through every emotion in the book.

Suddenly, my alarm clock started to buzz. I jumped out of bed, showered, and put on my jeans and a striped, navy-and-white T-shirt. I was going to tamp down my sadness from the night before and focus on being French in all ways from day one: from appearance, to lifestyle, and hopefully to speaking the language.

After more tearful goodbyes with my mom, dad, and Simba, I was in the airport, all checked in and ready to board my flight. I thought about what I would do for my first couple of days in Paris. I had rented a stunning one-bedroom flat complete with a full kitchen and balcony for the first three weeks until my attic near the Pantheon was available. I envisioned daily walks through the Luxembourg Gardens, sitting at a café for two hours feasting on *salade chèvre chaude* and duck confit, strolling the open-air markets, and retreating into a museum in the late afternoons. I would spend the first several weeks taking it all in, and then school would commence and I would be on my way to becoming a wine expert. My last emotion as I boarded my flight to Paris and flew out of California was pure excitement.

I am so lucky.

SIX

La vie est trop courte pour boire du mauvais vin.

('Life is too short to drink bad wine.')

Tellingly, the French were the first people to assert
this new common bit of wisdom.

My taxi drove down rue de Berthollet, and I gaped out the window at the entrance to my flat. It was a charming eighteenth-century building on a bustling street in the Fifth Arrondissement. I looked around at Parisians out on their balconies, watering pots of flowers; French women walking down the street with their children on scooters, getting them off to school; some on the way to work with baguettes sticking out of their backpacks. Is this *real*? I get to live here? There was a boulangerie on the corner of my street, as well as a traiteur, a takeaway store that actually has a chef who prepares simple French dinners to go, as well as meats, cheeses, combination salads, wine, and desserts. Yes, I had been dropped at the point on earth where food is the central focus. I was instantly happy. I paid the taxi driver and entered the code to the large, old, wooden, pine-green door.

Upon my arrival Genevieve, the quintessential French woman from whom I had rented the apartment, greeted me. She was very welcoming and showed me around the charming place. I thought I was enchanted from the outside, but once inside, I was even more enthralled. The flat was complete with two sets of large doors that opened up onto the balcony; it had a fireplace, a full kitchen, and several windows allowing the place to feel light, airy, and bright.

I noticed Genevieve had a style about her that seemed simple yet sophisticated. She had a bohemian look, wearing violet jeans and an ivory blouse. Her hair was a bit messy but still fashionable; she wore very little makeup, letting her natural beauty shine, and immediately pointed out the bubble gum I was chewing would ruin my palate. How embarrassing! I guess I needed to break my gum-chewing habit while in Paris. It was apparently *non-chic*.

I was a bit delirious from my travels, but when Genevieve offered me a cup of tea at her residence upstairs, I could not resist. There was something about being invited to "hang" with a Parisian woman that was fascinating to me. I had always been told that Parisian women are very cold, too cool for school, and it takes a very long time to "unpeel the onion," so to speak. To get to know them or, dare I say, build a friendship seemed impossible. But she made a delicious cup of tea for me, all loose leaf as she said she despised "the bags," mumbling something about quality. We started talking about my upcoming program, and Genevieve's face lit up. Turns out, her father was from Bordeaux, and so wine had always had a strong presence in her life. We had a lovely conversation, which lasted about an hour and ended with Genevieve showing me maps and writing a list of the best boulangeries, restaurants, and butchers on the block. After my enchanting introduction, I came back down to my flat and settled in. I unpacked my suitcases, set up my room, and took a nice, long bubble bath.

Refreshed and ready, I took a short stroll down the street to a small market. The sun had painted the clouds an effervescent, rosy pink. I arrived in the store and immediately greeted the shop owner, "Bonjour, monsieur," to which he gave a nod and said, "Bonsoir, madame." Oh yes, I had forgotten around 6:30 p.m. everyone switched to *Bonsoir*, which means good evening. I grabbed a basket and bought whole-milk yogurt, sparkling mint water, wine, cheese, and jam. I then stopped at the boulangerie Genevieve had recommended and picked up a baguette and some croissants for the morning. I also purchased a beautiful slice of Quiche Lorraine, which I planned to devour for dinner. I was exhausted but in complete rapture being out and about in *my neighborhood*, attempting the French language and picking out my daily baguette. I sat on my balcony that evening and watched Parisian life pass me by. For the next week, until my wine program started, I would get to "just be" in Paris. I was ecstatic. My first day in Paris had been a success, and I went to sleep dreaming of what tomorrow would bring.

The clock next to my bed said 10:00 a.m. I turned to face the window and smiled. Yep, still in Paris. That day I was planning to explore more of my neighborhood and the Saint Germain des Prés, which was a short walk away. I also planned to Skype with Eddie and my parents separately. I wanted to give them a virtual tour of my apartment. I was so excited about my new life and desperately needed to share in my enthusiasm. I started into the kitchen and toasted some baguette, which I slathered with strawberry jam, as well as a torn-off piece of croissant. I also took the petite cup of Bonne Maman yogurt from the fridge.

As I was enjoying my *petit dejeuner* on my balcony, feeling the warm sunshine on my back, Madame Genevieve spoke to me from above, which sounded more like music to my ears. *"Bonjour, mademoiselle. Comment-allez vous? As-tu bien dormi?"* Just someone asking how you slept in French sounds so romantic and beautiful. We spoke a bit from our balconies, and five minutes later she came down to my flat to go over the best routes to my future campus. They say a French woman will never leave her home without "putting herself together." I made note that she had changed out of her silk robe, put on lipstick, and spritzed on perfume. She was wearing the same lavender jeans as yesterday with a black blouse and her hair pulled back. She once again looked effortlessly chic. After writing down the best route and practicing some French phrases with Genevieve, I set out for my day. I was about to meet Paris on a more intimate level.

For the next six days I challenged myself to stay out in Paris for hours at a time, occasionally retreating to the apartment for an afternoon nap. I attempted the metro system whenever I was not walking, explored every arrondissement, and did the more obvious activities such as walking to the Eiffel Tower and sitting on a bench eating a Nutella crepe in front of Notre Dame. I wanted to feel comfortable after the week and well-adjusted in my new city. I sat in cafés for two-hour lunches complete with wine and then would pop into the Louvre or whatever museum I fancied. Some days I would walk to my campus and, on the way back, explore every open-air market I came across.

The Sunday before the program began, it rained. I decided I would spend several hours indoors cooking *coq au vin,* the traditional French dish of chicken cooked in wine. I wanted a celebratory, home-cooked meal, and I figured nothing could be better than a wine-inspired dish on the eve of wine school. I strolled the open-air market on Rue Monge and waited in the long line to purchase my whole chicken. It was finally my turn, and the butcher stared at me, waiting for me to speak. *"Ici, poulet roti... grande."* I pointed to the whole chicken. The butcher smiled as he understood what I wanted, but with the undertone that that was absolutely not how to ask for it. I probably sounded like a two-year-old, but oh well. I aspired to channel my inner Julia Child on this rainy afternoon. I returned to the flat and spent the next few hours preparing my coq au vin. I broke down the bird, something I had not done since culinary school, chopped my vegetables, and let it all marinate in a bottle of Bordeaux while I set out to try the rumored best savory crepe in the city at Breizh Café in Le Marais.

In addition to Breizh Café, that first week I discovered many other exceptional eateries. Erik Kayser, the fourth-generation baker with over fifty varieties of bread, became my go-to boulangerie. Café Delmas had a definite Parisian scene, and I went there a few nights during the week to enjoy their delectable French

onion soup and to people-watch. Jacques Genin, a talented chocolatier, became a frequent stop as I could not resist his mint ganache
or passionfruit chocolate squares.

That first week settling into Paris had been the equivalent to
the most perfect feeling of alignment where it felt as though nothing in the world was ever going wrong. I couldn't help but wonder
when I would start to feel lonely or when emptiness would ensue. I
had read that this bliss was not a sustainable feeling for a foreigner,
and I was bound to experience severe alienation. I had Skyped
with Eddie several times, as well as friends and family, telling them
stories about my daily rendezvous. I felt so satiated in Paris; it was
an adventure, and seemingly I had prepared myself for the energy
it took to endure the adjustment. The first week had been a victory,
as I felt very comfortable with the city itself, my neighborhood,
and just being able to function in France. The next day I would
start sommelier school, and I was nervously pondering questions
like, What had I gotten myself into? Who would my classmates be?
Do we start tasting French wines on the first day of school? I was
about to enter unknown territory. Paris and I now had an intimate
relationship, but this wine program was a shot in the dark. My
entire kitchen smelled of roasted chicken, herbs, wine, and any
delicious, savory scent you can think of. I plated up my coq au vin
with giddiness and sat on the balcony. It was Sunday night, and I
felt so content to be dining on my first home-cooked meal in my
new home.

I arrived at Le Cordon Bleu about ten minutes early for orientation. I walked into a jury of French administrators standing at attention in the lobby to guide me to my class. Leading me back into the classroom was Jane, a girl from the States who had taken a job in the administrative department as a way to stay in Paris. In the room, where several other students had already arrived, I was given a stack of papers to fill out. I could not yet tell if anyone else was from America, or at the very least spoke any English. Even at my age, there was still this nervousness about starting anything new, the "first day of school" feeling where you are on observation mode and a million thoughts are running through your head.

As I started to fill out my Parisian address, I was lightly bumped from behind. "Oh, excuse me." I looked next to me as the girl who had bumped into me sat down. She smiled. "Hi, I am Sarah. How are you—please tell me you speak English, a little?"

Phew. We exchanged a few sentences, and I found out she was twenty-eight and from Seattle. Instant comfort, an American girl like me. I privately wondered if she had decided to come here for reasons like mine. Two other women introduced themselves. Anna was from Greece, specifically the island of Rhodes. Suzette was from Bordeaux and spoke perfect English as her father was American and hailed from Virginia. I already had a good feeling about the course. These girls were nice and seemed to feel the same uneasiness as I was experiencing. We took our seats, and I counted fourteen women and six men. *Bon*—it would be a woman's world here in France attending sommelier school.

A few moments later, our professor, Laurent Lavigne, waltzed in. Alongside him was our British translator, Jonathan Porter. I made note that both were dressed to the nines, wearing none other than Hermès belts with the signature H at the buckle. Their suits must have been Gucci.

"Wine is an integral component of gastronomy," Professor Lavigne began. "Wine has a place at the table. It is the heart of the meal. We are going to be following the Latin module for tasting. We are going to be experts at expressing the emotion and the sentiment of a wine to allow others to enjoy the pleasures of the mouth."

This was said in French as an opening statement and quickly translated by Mr. Porter. The entire course would be taught in French, then translated into English. I was captivated. Professor Lavigne went on to recite a few more poetic sentences about wine. I didn't know I could feel so consumed and taken with words, and I suddenly realized with great affirmation wine was a latent passion for me. I sat intently listening to the entire class. After introductions and details about the program, the professor told us the experiences we would undertake for the next ten months here in Paris, things like working large events at the Four Seasons Hotel George V alongside some of the top sommeliers in the world. Or… participating as guests at private multi-course, food-and-wine-paired dinners. *Seriously?!* Or… staying on a vineyard in Bordeaux for two weeks, making wine. All of this, as well as the fact that we would be traveling together to the regions of Champagne, Cognac, Bordeaux, Rhône, and Alsace. My mouth dropped in disbelief, as did everyone else's—none of this had been advertised during initial enrollment!

I found this comical. If it had been a program in America, these details would have been broadcast everywhere and priced at a pretty penny because of it. An American institution would have milked every last detail for every last dollar. As Professor Lavigne stated these things, he acted blasé about it—"no biggie." Sarah turned around at a certain point and gave me an inquisitive, puzzled look, and I smiled. We both were like, "What in the actual hell?" As Americans, we had an understanding we had just arrived in a dream life, whereas to the French this was, as we would learn was a favorite statement, "C'est normale." As the French say this statement, they shrug. Again: "No biggie." The cultural difference was already setting in. France and in particular Paris had a beauty and sensuality about everything, but *Ce n'est pas important*. It was a way of life; to be expected, even.

So, in true American fashion, I was stunned when bottles of Louis Roederer were brought into the classroom on ice. It was then announced we would be concluding the orientation day with a glass of Champagne to kick off our year of adventure! This felt like a vacation, but ironically it was my first day of school. I had never experienced the first day of school being so exciting. Was it just because I was attending school in France?

I graciously took my glass and held it up in the air. *Santé*, we all toasted each other's health, and the clink of glasses progressed through the room. I spoke with several other students during our Champagne sipping. Sebastian was a prim and proper gay man from Hong Kong who had a strong sense of fashion and sported a navy cape. He had dreams of getting into the import-export business in Hong Kong, specifically for French wine. He and I bonded immediately over our love of food and wine and started to talk about restaurants we wanted to check out in Paris. Pearl was from the States like Sarah and me, and she had visions of working for a famous marketing house such as LVMH. Sarah and I spoke more about the loveliness of living on the Rive Gauche, the Left Bank, and how we adored our flats and neighborhoods. I met others from India, China, Venezuela, and natives to France as well. Most of my classmates spoke a minimum of two languages, and I felt immensely proud to be on this journey with such cultured individuals coming from all over the world. We all shared a passion for wine, and more than that, everyone was ecstatic to be living in Paris.

I instantly felt like I had found my long-lost tribe. Visions of dining in Parisian restaurants with other food and wine lovers crossed my mind. I had not only moved to Paris, but I was going to be surrounded by people who shared my passions. It was riveting. As the Champagne dwindled and we could feel the school administration cleaning up the napkins and rinsing glasses, we all decided to carry on this cocktail hour at the rooftop bar of a nearby hotel. It is an addicting feeling to feel instantly connected with strangers in a foreign land. *Maybe I will never feel emptiness in Paris,* I remember thinking as we rode the hotel elevator to the top. *Maybe I will instantly be immersed with fellow partners in crime and have a packed social calendar.* I had come here for an adventure, a sabbatical from life in America, sure, to learn a little about French wine, but maybe this journey would have a bigger purpose. I felt like I was exactly where I was supposed to be.

Once at the rooftop bar, several bottles of wine were ordered, and the twenty of us gathered around concentrated conversation and laughter. We had all just moved to Paris, even the six French people in the class. Everyone had their vision of what they wanted to experience by living in Paris, and there became lists and lists of things to do. Picnicking beneath the Eiffel Tower, a crepe food crawl, hitting up the top ten wine bars of Paris, dining at Michelin-starred restaurants, attending the chocolate festival in October, exploring the city's largest flea market in Montmartre. It all sounded outright fabulous, and to think that we would all be in this together? *Magnifique.* It also turned out that Pearl, Sarah, and Sebastian lived within a ten-minute walk of my apartment, so we started discussing restaurants in our area to try and the idea of dinner parties rotating among each others places.

Had I come here for a career change? Had others? Sure. But more importantly, we all loved life, were passionate about wine and food, and adored Paris. I walked home as the sun set that evening feeling like I was on some luxury galaxy far away. They say the reality is not nearly as good as the dream, but my current reality was exceeding any prior vision I had created in my brain. Joy was pulsing through me, and I knew in that moment the next ten months would change my life.

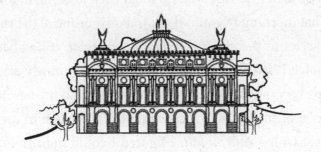

SEVEN

The name Bordeaux derives from au bord de l'eau, meaning
'along the waters.' Bordeaux lies within the French region of Aquitaine,
a word whose Latin roots mean a well-watered place.

H*i, I feel you are distant. I am having a hard time without you.*
Please send me some sweet nothings.

"Sweet nothings" was Eddie's and my term for sending random, loving messages to each other throughout the day. The whole time I had been in Paris, I had fallen short in the sweet nothings department. It made me feel sad that I was so captured by Paris that Eddie often slipped my mind.

Being in your arms is one of the best feelings, I typed. *I love you. XO*

I pressed send. The thought of being in his arms made me happy, but then I quickly wanted to go back to being in love with Paris. That morning I ventured out to Poilâne, one of the rumored best bakeries in the city, for a *pain au chocolat*. It had been two weeks since I had started school, and I was genuinely excited to wake up every morning. Today was Saturday, and my new idea for Saturday mornings was to locate a pastry and relish in my delectable treat with a *café au lait*. I figured I could indulge in a pastry once a week and my jeans would still fit the same. *The French women do this right? They stay elegantly chic and slim with a patisserie on every corner.*

I had always had this curiosity about French women, with the underlying question of how they manage to enjoy food and stay slim and fashionable. My mother was thin and beautiful, but there was a deprivation attached to it, more of a restrictive punishment, and I will never forget her telling me as a teenager that I would be overweight if I "ate that" or "didn't get on the treadmill." French women didn't view food as good or bad, it seemed. They didn't punish themselves for indulgences. They ate for pleasure just as much as for nutrients, and I found I resonated with this so much.

Poilâne's location in Saint Germain des Prés was a tiny boulangerie, probably only the size of my soon-to-be attic apartment. Inside, there were tall, wooden shelves that held perfectly formed loaves of bread, and the smell permeating the space was intoxicating.

I ordered my pain au chocolat and half a baguette from a man wearing a pressed, white apron. I felt like I should have selected a few more items, but instead made a note to myself that I would be back to sample other delights. I paid, took the warm, parchment-wrapped treats, and wished the man a good day.

My phone vibrated.

I miss you. Please Skype when you can. I want to see your beautiful face.

I dug into my pain au chocolat and pondered love. I was in love with a man, but I was also in love with a new life in a new city. Could they coexist? For the last twelve years, I had been consumed by my relationships, first with my college boyfriend, Alex, and then with Eddie. I was feeling increasingly connected to Paris, but not necessarily connected to Eddie or to any other person. I could feel a shift within me. I felt like I was finally living for me and my decisions. Would this feel lonely eventually? Time would tell, but I felt ready to welcome the discomfort.

In class, Professor Lavigne had told us that we would be individually staying on separate vineyards in Bordeaux. I envisioned waking up at the crack of dawn to the sound of roosters, putting on my rain boots and setting out into the grapevines, but really we had no idea what to expect. The next day we were all assigned our prospective chateaus, addresses, and winemakers' names. We were instructed to google and gather information on our new homes for the multi-week stay in Bordeaux.

I would be staying on mine, Château Gaillard, for two full weeks, with a French family of winemakers, helping them harvest grapes and make wine. A flood of emotions came over me. *Did these people speak any English?* I thought nervously, as my French was still elementary at best. It was one thing to think of visiting multiple vineyards with a guide and a translator over the ten-month course, but another to contemplate living on a vineyard. While out living the vineyard life, I would not be able to Skype with Eddie or my family, much less call them. I was told it was the countryside, and therefore it would be fairly desolate, with little in the way of cell phone or internet reception.

That week in class I had distracted myself from my vineyard fears by practicing my first blind tasting. As sommeliers we would need to analyze the wine with the end goal being to accurately guess the region, appellation, and grape varietal of the wine. My first go at this had been a success, and I was amazed at how much information I was retaining. I recognized that I had cracked into a passion here.

Wine. Who doesn't want to drink it? It is a pleasure, delicious, and relaxing. But this program was very intense, and drinking wine was the least of it. In lectures daily, we were highly discouraged from swallowing the wine. We tasted each wine, and then we spit it out. We also entered into deep analysis, investigation, and critique of each pour. Analysis to wine people in a professional setting can last for ten minutes—ten minutes, that is, describing one solitary wine. The study of wine, I was finding, was complicated; it combined multiple subjects into one, including history, science, and geography. It required an intense amount of concentration, and I felt extremely productive and increasingly knowledgeable by the end of each class day.

Beyond the program, I noticed a difference in France's general drinking culture. The French view wine as an addition to the meal, and it is almost always consumed with food. There is a great deal of respect for wine, and though more American-style cocktail and tiki bars had sprouted up around Paris, I had yet to see a French person get wasted or even tipsy off wine itself. In California, I had frequently ordered a glass of Chardonnay or Sauvignon Blanc purely as a cocktail, with no intention of eating anything alongside it. In France, this was odd; even at aperitif hour there is always food brought out to nibble on.

That didn't stop me or my cohort, though, from having the occasional tipple.

"Here ya go, a whole lotta cheapness." Pia, one of my classmates, set down a mini plastic bottle holding six ounces of red wine and a plastic cup on the tray table in front of me.

"Cheers!" Everyone twisted the screw caps of their plastic wine bottles and poured. Apparently we were drinking our last mediocre wine on the train ride to Bordeaux.

Halfway into my cup, I stared out the window on the train, thinking about the rather gloomy discussion Eddie and I had had the night before. Eddie voiced that he was feeling depressed, and this was really becoming hard on him, the distance between us. I understood, but short of him coming here, to Paris, I could not offer him any comfort. The sad part was, I was so busy and had been living such a full life that I doubted I would even have the time to enjoy Paris with him if he were to visit.

I knew the inevitable was approaching. We would grow apart, and things would end. My mind flashed back to three weeks before, to my last night with Eddie and the pain of the last hug, the thought of the last time his strong arms would be wrapped around me. My eyes were beginning to swim, and I felt a tear roll down my cheek. I turned my head abruptly, not wanting my classmates to notice.

Four hours later, we arrived in Bordeaux. The weather was rainy and damp, and I was feeling relaxed and a bit sleepy from the red wine. We all departed the train and gave hugs, wishing each other luck.

I was met at the station by Catherine, the owner of Château Gaillard. Catherine spoke a little English, and on the car ride over, she explained that she runs not only Château Gaillard, but two other vineyards as well. All of her vineyards and land are located in the Saint-Émilion region labeled "Grand Cru" by French appellation control standards. In France as well as in most of Europe, there is a classification system built to mark the quality of wine. Saint-Émilion is a region known for having great terroir and producing wonderful wines. However, the winemaker's skill and ability to produce a great wine is also important. Catherine had been awarded the Grand Cru, the highest and most well-respected classification in France's Appellation d'origine contrôlée (AOC).

As we drove along the narrow roads, with the rain sprinkling down on the windshield, I started to notice the charm and the juxtaposition of the old stone buildings next to the vast rows of grapevines. Saint-Émilion was picturesque from all angles. Each vineyard plot had what appeared to be a castle on it, but these were essentially large chateaus housing all of the wine vats. The chateaus were also equipped with bedrooms, kitchens, cellars full of old bottles, and open common areas.

After a twenty-five-minute drive, Catherine took me to one of the vineyards to introduce me to her team of winemakers. She explained that they were just finishing a day's work. At this point in the year, it was harvest every single day. Harvest, which I would soon learn, consisted of a full day of picking grapes, sorting and removing stems and debris, as well as pumping the grape juice into a temperature-controlled vat. A vat was essentially a large tank where the grape juice would transform itself to wine over the course of roughly two weeks.

I was introduced to everyone, and quickly noticed their magenta-stained hands from the constant handling of the juicy, ripe purple grapes. All of the workers, there were seven of them, looked up and gave a smile and a nod. There was a confused look on some faces, and I sensed they were wondering, *Who the heck is this American girl, coming to this remote French vineyard?*

I suddenly felt a surge of embarrassment, realizing I was wearing Coach sunglasses and diamond studs. I was in a land of new territory where English was not easily understood, much less spoken, and it felt massively different than what I had become accustomed to in Paris. *Oh man, this is going to be a long two weeks*, I thought to myself.

Catherine carried on speaking to her team in French. I could not understand exactly what they were saying, but I picked up the subject matter with the few words I was able to string together. Apparently, there was a problem with the harvest schedule due to the rain coming in. Catherine wore her emotions all over her face; she seemed stressed, hurried, and had this underlying nervous energy. She glanced at me with a forced smile, after the gloomy reality of the conversation she had just had with the workers, and told me to get in the car. Once in the car, she mentioned we were heading to Château Gaillard, the main vineyard, where she would show me to my living quarters, but first, we would go into town to check on her restaurant. Then we would go to the town bakery to pick up baguettes and pastries for the morning.

This was my first glimpse not only of the vineyards of Bordeaux, but also into the town center of Saint-Émilion. We drove past an old church and down a cobblestone pathway. I was instantly enchanted by the stone buildings, the colored ivy creeping over the brick archways, and the family-owned boutique shops. I loved the feeling here, and I secretly hoped I would be able to come into the town more frequently.

Catherine abruptly pulled into a public parking space near the village's glorious old church, and told me to come with her. We walked a few minutes in silence, and I unexpectedly got a whiff of baked bread. We had come upon the only bakery in town. Once again I was reminded of the importance of freshly baked goods. They were not only supremely valued in Paris; it was a French custom. These people ate bread with every meal. I was starting to be convinced it was some form of law in France. The term "breaking bread" was taken to literal standings, and no meal would be complete without it. Catherine purchased a selection of lovely pastries including a delicious almond crumble cake with nougatine on top. I had never seen this dessert in a patisserie, and it not only looked beautiful, but Catherine mentioned it would pair perfectly with coffee in the morning. She handed me the fresh baguettes as if they were fragile babies, and I held them as such. The baguettes were warm in my hands, and I had to seriously talk myself out of ripping a hunk off and digging in. Geez, the French have such discipline.

Next, we were en route to my living quarters, where I would finally see the main vineyard of Château Gaillard. Despite the light drizzle of rain, the sun was setting over the grapevines, and I felt a twinge of emotion. The sheer beauty and rarity of my experience in that moment was priceless: grasping warm baguettes tightly, staring over hundreds of grapevines, witnessing the sun set over the vineyard hills, in a foreign, sought-after destination—the wine country of France. Chills ran up my spine, and I had to swallow the lump in my throat.

We pulled up to a massive chateau with cypress trees surrounding the entrance. *Château Gaillard* was painted above the doors in large, red lettering. I stared out to the rows of grapevines surrounding the chateau with no other homes, chateaus, or outbuildings for miles around. Catherine explained to me that this would be my home for the two weeks—not just a bedroom within the chateau, but I would actually have this entire place to myself, complete with a kitchen, bedroom, main living area, office, wine cellar, barrel room holding aging wine, and a large, open area with the commercial storage tanks of wine. I glanced up at the arched windows, stucco walls, and terracotta roof tiles, and felt a little bit like I was living in a movie. Just a small-town California girl, you know, with a chateau in Bordeaux for two weeks; no big deal. Surreal was a good word to describe it.

Just then three cars pulled up and parked in the gravel lot in front of the chateau. Catherine explained that every night at nine o'clock we would eat dinner together at the main chateau with all of the workers. Marcella, one of the winemaker's wives, would cook for us. Dinner would end around eleven, and everyone would return to their home, get some sleep, and gear up for the next day of work.

After touring the chateau, which was massive and intimidating, Catherine suggested I take some time to myself before dinner. I looked at my watch. It was 7:30 p.m.—I was starving and dinner wasn't for another hour and a half. I pondered tearing off a large piece of baguette but decided against it. I would do as the French do and not be tempted to snack. I also didn't want to experience the embarrassment of Catherine witnessing this. I went to my bedroom and shut the door. I opened the arched windows out to the vineyard and took a deep breath, inhaling the crisp night air. This felt so unreal. I unpacked and took a shower, anticipating my first meal on a vineyard.

I met Marcella, a plump firecracker of a woman, an hour or so later as I walked into the kitchen. She only spoke French of course, but was very warm and gave me a giant hug—very un-French, or at least not very Parisian. She gestured for me to take a seat at the large farm table. She poured me a glass of the table wine, pouring it almost past the top of the glass, forcing it to drip down the stem.

I welcomed this intense, warm greeting from a French woman, instead of the aloof, calm coolness I had become accustomed to.

The other vineyard workers were slowly trickling in, taking their seats. I was like a little mouse, quiet and observing everything. All I could say was *Bonsoir* and *Ça va?* They all smiled but got along with their conversations, which seemed to be very passionate. There was a boisterous energy among everyone, and I could tell they were happy to be relaxing and drinking wine, legitimately exhausted after a long day.

Catherine came in and took a seat next to me, and the pâté and cornichons, little French pickles, were passed around. The men were tearing baguettes, ripping them into pieces, and slathering butter and pâté on each slice, much like I had envisioned doing two hours before. The red wine was being consumed like water. These men were larger than the skinny Parisian men I had observed. They had muscles and bellies, and I quickly realized the countryside French wine makers were a little different than the poised, elegant Parisian males.

Catherine informed me that the wine we were drinking was last year's harvest, Cabernet Franc from the Petit-Gravet vineyard, which I would discover tomorrow. The wine was balanced and delicious with the perfect amount of tannins. As simple as the pâté was, the wine was the perfect pairing. Next, a garlic soup was served. It was unique, given the egg cooked into it, so that it almost resembled a savory porridge. Catherine mentioned that her great-grandmother had passed this recipe down, and she had been eating it since she was little.

Only French was being spoken, and while I understood bits and pieces, I loved perceiving the banter and conversation, and just being able to enjoy my meal. Marcella set down two piping-hot ceramic dishes of cauliflower gratin and a large bowl of carrot salad. The gratin was layered with a béchamel sauce and tons of fresh herbs. This was served alongside roasted chicken leg. So simple, yet so delicious. After the main course, a large platter of *fromage* was passed around and more baguettes were sliced. I took a sliver of Camembert, recognizing my impending fullness. The conversation lingered over the cheese course, and I looked at the clock, which read 10:35 p.m. Just when I thought everyone was going to retreat home, a pot of coffee was made and dessert was presented. Dessert for the evening was mini vanilla rice puddings and warm apple tarts. I couldn't resist either, so I took a sampling of both. I made a note to myself to take smaller portions tomorrow; this was so much food and I would need to seriously pace myself. I was in heaven: a long, drawn-out French meal, just as I had envisioned it; true vineyard living. I felt delightful and extremely lucky that I was able to experience this.

When dinner was finally finished, everyone wished me a *bonne nuit* and made a dash for their cars, including Catherine.

The large doors slammed shut, and a deafening silence fell over the chateau. I slowly walked up the stairs to my bedroom; the creaking of the wood made itself heard with every step. Night one, alone in a chateau, on a vineyard, in France…

Dorothy was not in Kansas anymore.

EIGHT

A winemaker is a farmer first and foremost. The tiny town of Pomerol
encompasses the square around the small church and not much more.
In general, a winemaker here owns a vineyard less than
4 acres in size, and eighty percent are less than 2 acres.

Aloud noise, followed by a wooden door shaking. Then male voices.

Oh my God, oh my God… Where is my French cell phone? My hands were trembling fiercely as I reached over to the nightstand to grab it. My fingers touched the screen of the phone, trying to land on the contact icon. *Catherine's number… shit, where is it?*

I sat straight up in bed, sweat dripping down my spine and sucking in air trying to catch my breath. My eyes did a once-over of the bedroom, and everything was exactly in its place as it should be. A few more deep breaths, and I slowly came to my senses.

A nightmare. It had been a dream. A fatal thought of people trying to get me, knowing I was alone on this large plot of land in this old historic chateau. I was alive, and no one was banging down the door. I glanced at the window and noticed the sun rising over the vineyard. I was safe.

I set my phone down. No need to dial Catherine's number, not that it would have saved me in that kind of situation. I had fallen asleep terrified the previous night; terrified after the deafening silence had fallen over the chateau. All I could think about was being brutally murdered or being all alone in this large, empty place, with evil spirits coming to haunt me. I wiped the sweat from my back and comprehended how I had turned those nasty, conscious thoughts into a nightmare.

This was going to be the longest two weeks of my life if I didn't feel safe going to sleep here. I would talk to Catherine today about my concerns. Were there even police in this village? What if someone was stalking me? I realized these were horrible thoughts to be having in this magical land, but the reality was, I felt uncomfortable enough during the day with the foreignness of it all. Then to be left on my own every night as a single woman on acres of open land in a small village possibly lacking police did not sit well with me. I realized this was mostly likely a reaction to the change and discomfort I was experiencing. Even though this at moments felt like a surreal and beautiful dreamland, it was an *incredibly* foreign experience, and I could feel it changing me on a molecular level. This nightmare was my brain trying to scare me into backing out of this unknown territory.

I heard voices. This time I was relieved, as it was the vineyard workers arriving outside the chateau. Catherine had mentioned that every morning I would need to open up the chateau at eight o'clock. This is when everyone would show up, have coffee, and meet about the vineyard plans for the day. I unlocked the large, wooden doors and pushed them open. Pierre, Emmanuel, and Jean, three of the winemakers from the day before, immediately greeted me. Bonjours were exchanged and of course the ever-famous *bisous*. The French literally give men and women a kiss on each cheek as a standard greeting for each new day. Four more workers arrived and poured coffee—bonjours and bisous again. Next, I saw Catherine walking toward the entrance with a man I had not been introduced to or seen the previous day. They seemed deep in thought and conversation; the gravel created a cloud of dust with each step they took.

Just as Marcella was pouring me a cup of coffee, I heard Catherine's voice. "Bonjour, Krista, did you have a good sleep?"

I quickly smiled and said, "Yes." I could not bring myself to sound like a paranoiac who had watched too many episodes of *Cops*. Plus, in the daylight my situation seemed less dramatic, and I felt that my scared feelings would pass. I quickly chalked it up to the natural adjustment I would need to my environment and decided not to mention it for the time being.

"Krista, this is Cedric. He is the head enologist, the scientist who makes all of the wine decisions."

Cedric looked at me with a big smile and reached out to shake my hand. No bisous from him. "Pleasure to meet you, Krista. How long are you training here with us?" Wow. He spoke very good English; maybe things were about to look up.

"Nice to meet you, Cedric. I will be here for two weeks."

Catherine went on to explain that I would be spending a lot of my time in the cellar with Cedric learning the science behind making the wine. As Catherine and Cedric returned to speaking in French, I observed him. He was tall, sounded smart, and I got the instant feeling that Catherine relied on him greatly. He was probably in his mid-thirties if I had to guess, and quintessentially French—dirty blond hair, thin, and calm with an aura of relaxed confidence about him. Even though I could not make out what they were saying, I could tell by Cedric's body language that he was fundamentally the boss around here. I sat patiently listening to the French exchange about the strategy for the day, and then Cedric looked over at me and said, "Well, shall we get to work?" I nodded, grabbing my notebook and pen while thanking God that I would be spoken to in English. Catherine told me to stay with Cedric until lunchtime, when she and I would check back in. She was busy getting governmental paperwork signed for the van full of people from Spain who had just arrived. They had come to assist in the manual harvest. I could feel that the pressure was on to get those grapes picked and out of the rain.

Cedric and I made our way into the large cellar that housed all of the large tanks of wine. The tanks were made of giant, white cement, standing about twelve feet tall. He instructed me to take a temperature reading of all tanks and record this into a chart.

He gave an explanation of how important it was to have the tanks remain at the proper temperature for fermentation to occur. Cedric told me this would be my daily routine. After measuring the temperatures, I would gauge the alcohol levels with a special tool. Then he would make adjustments based on this information. He really was a scientist. To think that he was left in charge of all of these decisions was incredible. If the vineyard makes a wrong move, this could greatly affect the quality of the final product. Therefore, the wine would become unsellable and no money would be made from the batch. I could sense I would learn a vast amount from Cedric and became eager at the thought.

In between temperature readings and alcohol adjustments, Cedric and I had miniature conversations. It turns out his brother lived in Paris and had just had a baby. I quickly learned Cedric was married and had two sons. He had been working for Catherine for the last four years and had studied enology, the science of wine-making, in Burgundy. He loved his job and enjoyed living on the outskirts of Bordeaux. Next thing I knew, I found myself asking him about the police situation in the village. He chuckled and asked why. I explained my fears of being on open land with no protection, and he started mumbling something about gun control laws and saying because I was American I wouldn't feel safe without a gun under my pillow—*Ugh. So French to immediately start in on politics with a practical stranger.* I was not about to embark on the train of a political debate, and I felt he sensed this in my facial expression because he suddenly invited me to stay at his home with him and his family. I smiled and said I would take him up on the offer one of these nights. I secretly could not wait. I was utterly, perennially fascinated by French home life, and I was curious as to how a young French family living in Bordeaux operated.

After a full morning learning the tricks and trade of the wine cellar, Cedric led me to the harvest machine. I would spend the next two hours sorting and destemming grapes with a group of other harvesters. I was ready for my hands to appear shriveled up and purple by lunchtime. I gave a genuine smile to the other four people at the sorting table, and put my head down to the grapes with the intent of beautifying the grape bunches. As I removed the stems from the fruit, my mind drifted to Eddie. I had texted him the night before and in my lonely panic had even attempted to call him despite the outlandish international price of a phone call. My cell connection was weak, and I hadn't been able to reach him. I suddenly had a nervous thought: It was weird that I had not been able to get ahold of him and connect. He understood I was in a remote location, but something in my gut didn't feel right. In typical Eddie fashion, usually I would have received an email or text, but there had been nada—zilch, zero. He was usually good about figuring out a way to reach me. I would try calling him again after lunch. I felt anxiety creeping into my body. The last thing I needed was to have more unease here, and I was not going to let Eddie or a bad decision he made ruin my experience on a vineyard in France. This was also the problem with my relationship with him: It was never really over. It was like I had an addiction to him, to love, to the ups and downs, the emotional-drama roller coaster? Even though I was thousands of miles away in a foreign land, he still rented space in my brain.

It was 1:00 p.m., and my stomach was seriously grumbling. I was starving and running low on energy. Cedric came out from

the cellar and told me it was time for *dejeuner*, and I could not
have been more elated.

I took my seat at one of two long farm tables. There were
plastic, red-and-white-checkered tablecloths, and a water glass as
well as a wine glass marked each seat. Baguettes were placed in
the center of each table. I poured a glass of water and practically
drank it in one large gulp. Then I watched as people started to
tear hunks of baguette and place the hunks on the table next to
their empty plates. This is one rule that I had come to learn about
French dining culture: they always put their bread on the side of
the plate—directly on the table, never on the plate, unless there is
a distinguished bread plate just for it.

I was offered red wine to which I responded, *"Un petit peu,"*
meaning "just a little bit." For the main course we were eating a
baked egg-and-potato gratin, and it looked heavenly with caramelized onions and herbs sprinkled all over the top. I was served
a generous wedge of this. Then, there was a large, crispy green
salad to accompany the creaminess of the bake, and of course the
baguette. We had a starter of endive leaves topped with figs and
a little chèvre drizzled in balsamic vinegar. After the gratin came
the cheese course just like the previous night. Finally, coffee was
presented, as well as crème caramel for dessert. Lunch lasted an
hour and a half. Everyone sat relaxing and enjoying the several
courses, looking out to the beauty of the vineyards. This resembled pure utopia to me, and I felt lucky to be there. I also made
a note to myself that lunch was going to be as much food and as
many courses as dinner. Cedric confirmed that this was an everyday occurrence. He saw my eyes grow wide at the table when

the cheese was passed around after the heartiness of what I had already consumed.

Catherine instructed me to go with "the guys"—Cedric, Emmanuel, Jean, and Pierre—after lunch to the Petit Gravet vineyard. I knew nothing of what we were going to be doing at that vineyard or the purpose, other than that I was to go. I started to realize I was never going to fully understand what was going on during my stay here, much less the reason, until after it had happened. It was all part of this grand adventure!

I hopped in Jean's car, squished between Cedric and Emmanuel in the back seat, and Jean sped off down the narrow dirt road, driving like a bat out of hell. The next thing I knew, Pierre had turned around from the front seat and flashed a bottle of Calvados, taken a large swig and passed it to Emmanuel, who also took a large sip. *Oh dear,* I thought to myself. I flashed back to being five years old on Mr. Toad's Wild Ride at Disneyland. Hopefully we would not crash.

Two-hour lunches on a vineyard, race-car-driving down dirt roads for a little playtime afterward—boys will be boys, no matter what country. They were laughing and speaking French and then started calling me "zee belle Americaine!" and laughing more. Pierre turned around from the passenger seat, put his hat on sideways, and gave me a peace sign. "Am I COOL?" he asked. He emphasized the word "cool," as if to make fun of American slang. This was so funny, and I started laughing to oblivion.

After the crazy car ride, we arrived at the vineyard, and I wondered if the guys would actually be able to focus. They were acting insane and slightly tipsy from their recent Calvados shots. I was in complete observation mode and highly entertained by this behavior from grown French men. We got to work with me assisting, measuring the alcohol levels of the vats. Then we walked out to the rows and literally ate the grapes off the vines to check ripeness on the palate. Cedric and Catherine needed to make a decision if the Merlot grapes should be harvested at this vineyard tomorrow. If so, the troops would be called in. In addition to the van full of people from Spain that had crossed the border for work, the community of Bordeaux really participated in the two-week harvest season. Families with teenagers sent them for a day's work at the vineyards. It was equivalent to my summer hostess jobs in high school at neighborhood restaurants. It was a way for any resident in the French countryside to make a little extra cash. Cedric informed me that his wife, who mostly stayed home raising their boys, came for several days to help with the manual harvest every year.

After Cedric mentioned his wife, I realized I had forgotten all about trying to get ahold of Eddie that afternoon. I was really starting to worry now, though, every time my mind flashed to Eddie, and I needed to know what was going on. As soon as I was back to Château Gaillard, I would try to contact him again.

I heard Cedric on the phone but could not make out what he was saying. He snapped the phone shut. "Yes, these grapes are ready," he said sternly. Cedric had made the decision to go ahead with the manual harvest at the Petit Gravet vineyard for the next day. He then said we needed to go to the third and final vineyard and perform the *pigeage* there. Pigeage, or, in English, maceration is a technique in which grape solids are punched down into a wine vat several times to make sure all of the juice is coming into contact with the grape skins for better pigmentation and flavor development. I was excited that I was able to see all of the vineyards

Catherine operated. Going to each vineyard made the hours of the day fly by, and of course I enjoyed the car rides where I was able to see more of Bordeaux's vineyards and rolling hills.

That afternoon Cedric and I hung around Saint-Julien, the third more artisanal and tiny vineyard, and did maintenance there. All of Catherine's vineyards had the same winemaking technique, the same owner, the same winemaker, but different wines were produced at each. At Château Gaillard, more Cabernet Sauvignon grapes were present. At Saint-Julien, small batches of artisanal Cabernet Franc or Merlot boutique wines were made; these were the most coveted and expensive out of the three vineyards. At Petit Gravet blends comprising all three grapes—Merlot, Cabernet Sauvignon, and Cabernet Franc—were the stars of the show.

Pigeage, as Cedric had said, was always done on the smaller-batch boutique wines of Saint-Julien. I watched as he took a large rake and stood on top of the wine tank. He then pushed the large rake and all the grapes under it, allowing for them to mix with the grape juice, slowly bringing the rake up and pushing it back down until he felt satisfied that the grapes were mixed nicely and evenly with the grape juice. Next, after handling and adjusting the wine tanks, he took me down to the underground cellar that was housed below an arch of limestone. It felt like a cave. There, we drew wine straight out of the barrel to taste. This was wine from the previous year's harvest that they would now age for eighteen months in barrels before bottling. The wine was delicious and probably even more so because I had never tasted wine directly from the barrel before. We were tasting a Merlot. Merlot was one of the five grapes allowed to be produced in Bordeaux, and the intoxicating aroma of baked, ripe red plums mixed with smashed, macerated raspberry geared me up for the most incredible balance once the wine hit my tongue. A slight hint of baking spice was also present and a good indication of the oak aging. I was in a crisp, cool wine cave, barrel-tasting the most delicious wine in Bordeaux with a French enologist. Life was good.

At this point it was approaching 7:00 p.m., and Cedric declared we were just about finished for the day. We would head back to the Gaillard vineyard, and I could have some downtime at the chateau before everyone arrived for dinner. The sun was setting again over the grapevines, and I felt a rush of joy as I happily anticipated dinner.

Once back at the chateau, I called and texted Eddie but still had no response. I was about to contact his aunt Anne when he called.

"Hi, what's going on? How is Bordeaux? Are you safe?" Eddie sounded paranoid and guilty.

"Bordeaux is fine. Where have you been, and why have I not heard from you at all?" I was not in the mood for bullshit or to beat around the bush. I knew Eddie's tactics all too well.

"Um, you are in France. Do you get it? Why is this about me? I am living my life, thank you very much. What is the point of contacting you? You are so far away, and that was your decision, not mine." There it was. Eddie only treated me this way after a day spent drinking. The whole guilt game and writing me off so nonchalantly was my top clue that he was under the influence. The sober Eddie was always sweet and highly interested in my day and making sure I was happy, encouraging me to live my dreams.

"Eddie, you have been drinking. I can't talk to you anymore while I'm here. I need to stay focused on this vineyard. Let's call a spade a spade. Admit it." I said this sternly and was not about to play into his guilt schemes, in which he was trying to convince himself that I was the problem here, that I was the reason he had surrendered to substance abuse yet again. Eddie was very good at pointing fingers when he was drunk or high. He played the victim card, and if it wasn't me, it was his dad or his childhood or somehow everyone else's fault. I could not tolerate this here in Bordeaux.

"Goodbye, Krista." And with that, he hung up on me.

I suddenly felt sick to my stomach, and an intense feeling of loneliness washed over me. I knew this was the end of Eddie and me. I was going to be in France for many months to come, and I wanted more and I wanted better for my life. I knew I did not deserve to live in anxiety anymore over Eddie's instability. I had predicted this nearly four weeks before, when my body trembled in heartache while we kissed and made love up until our last tight hug goodbye.

I set my phone down and promised myself I would try not to think about him anymore. This had been my own doing, staying attached for so long to someone so unattainable. In Bordeaux at that moment I was aware that I had put myself in emotional pain by getting involved with troubled men, but I wasn't sure *why*. Did I somehow feel needed or important or worthy because the other person "had issues"? Eddie's and my relationship had gone on for years like this, and the feeling states, the hot and cold, the makeup and breakup, the fixing and striving to change it only to be let down in the end wouldn't be erased from my headspace easily.

Maybe I had held on so long because I just didn't want to be alone. Maybe I felt pressure to have a man in my life as everyone else around me was getting hitched and having babies. I wasn't sure it was so surface level, though. I felt there was a deeper psychological issue at hand.

I stepped into the shower and let tears flow down my face. For once, I would allow this surge of emotion to happen. It had been buried, stuffed down deep until this moment, I was realizing, for the entirety of our relationship. The real grieving pain, not just the pain from the addiction and the ups and the downs that came with it. This was the deeper pain of knowing it was done. Nothing else was left to do; I was finally at a point where I was not going to try to change or fix any of this.

The next morning I was relieved when I woke up and realized that I had slept through the night without a nightmare. The night before, prior to the guys leaving after dinner, they had put a large deadbolt lock in the front door, literally drilled it in so I would feel more secure. They also had checked out every room in the chateau, making sure no one was lurking in a corner waiting to pounce. I was also given each of their personal cell phone numbers, and was told to call if I was scared or heard a noise in the middle of the night. Pierre and Emmanuel only lived five minutes from the chateau and could be there quickly. All of this really helped, and I felt at ease and thankful that, despite some chuckling over my worry, they ultimately understood.

Downstairs in the kitchen, Cedric came in and poured a large cup of coffee. "Bonjour, Ça va?" he said with a smile.

"Très bien, merci. Et toi?" I responded intently.

"I'm good, thanks. We have a busy day ahead. As soon as I meet with Catherine, I will join you in the cellar. Why don't you go get started on temps?"

"Okay, no problem. See ya in there." As I was walking out the door, Cedric stopped me and mentioned that his wife, Claire, wanted to invite me for dinner and to stay at their home that weekend. I instantly responded that yes, I would love that.

"Oh, also… My friend Julien runs a vineyard in Pomerol. Would you be interested in going there with me and having lunch on Saturday?" Cedric asked hesitantly.

"Absolutely, sounds great, and thanks for all these invites!" I was so excited to have social plans lined up. My curiosity was sparked, and I could not wait to meet some other Bordeaux locals.

I spent the next few days feeling like I had structure and routine on the vineyard: eight-hour days, complete with sorting the grapes, walking out into the grapevines, and participating in the manual harvest, not to mention doing the scientific maintenance at all three vineyards with Cedric in the cellars. I was feeling a bit sore and realized making wine is extremely physical in addition to the scientific cellar work. Some wineries use machines to harvest all the grapes, but since Catherine was certified Grand Cru, her estate was really artisan and she relied on people to handpick the bunches.

On Friday, it was just a few hours before the weekend, and the *baba au rhum* that was served as lunchtime dessert helped to put a grin back on my face. Cedric had mentioned to Catherine that I would spend the weekend with him and his family, and Catherine had told me that I would have the weekend off. It felt a little bit like I was in a twilight zone, having these French adults deciding where I would be for the weekend. I appreciated them wanting to make sure I saw more of Bordeaux and that I would not be bored. I was greatly anticipating my social weekend plans and meeting new people.

Saturday arrived, and Cedric was on his way to pick me up to take me to Julien's vineyard where we would have lunch. I was just finishing my eye makeup and spritzing on a dash of perfume when I received an email from my parents.

Hello Krista,

Your vineyard seems lovely, and we adore the pictures.
We are so happy you are having a good time in Bordeaux.
Can Eddie watch Simba this week as we planned and
discussed? We have tried to get ahold of him, but he has
yet to call us back. What is going on? We have everything
booked for Hawaii. Please respond.

Oh God. I would need to break the news that Eddie was not reliable and that he was either drunk or high but definitely a mess again. I felt horrible, as my parents had lived this through with me year after year. I had finally given them an ultimatum that past Christmas that either they would accept Eddie or I would not speak to them anymore. They did accept it, and now I would have to disappoint them again. I responded right away. I explained what had happened and asked if their house cleaner could watch the dog. Zhanna was in love with Simba, and they had a special bond. As soon as I pressed send, I heard tires on the gravel pavement. I grabbed my overnight bag and locked the chateau door.

Pomerol was about a half-hour's drive away from Saint-Émilion, on the same side of the river known as the right bank of Bordeaux, and it produced quality, Merlot-heavy wines. I was excited to meet Julien and see his vineyard. Actually, Cedric told me it was Julien's grandparents' vineyard, but Julien was thirty-four, and he and his sister ran it nowadays.

We pulled up to the vineyard, and a beautiful Great Dane greeted us and gave some good barks alerting Julien that we had arrived.

Julien came out from around the corner, sipping a glass of pastis. Cedric and he greeted each other in French and gave each other bisous. I was introduced to Julien, and he gave me a half hug and two kisses on the cheek as well. *So French.* Julien was a little darker, suggesting more Mediterranean genes. I would have guessed he had Italian ancestry.

He invited us to sit down at a small table in the courtyard. I was handed a glass of pastis, and oysters were brought out with lemon wedges. Oh goodness. My favorite. *Was this really happening? Eating oysters on a vineyard in Pomerol with two French men in their thirties?* When I signed up for wine school in Paris, I knew

amazing experiences were awaiting me, but could not have anticipated this!

It did not stop with oysters. Next thing I knew, duck pan-
seared and sliced into medallions was being presented. Cedric
had brought along a bottle of Saint-Julien Merlot, and it paired
beautifully with the duck. I felt the universe was looking down on
me, making up for my crying and trembling chateau shower scene
the night before. I now had a French man who owned a vineyard
cooking me duck. We spent the afternoon drinking and eating
and talking about life—life in America, life in Bordeaux, and life
in Paris. Julien spoke fluent English as he had studied abroad in
Australia. I couldn't help but feel special with these two French
gentlemen showing me a good time and feeding me well. It was
a perfect Saturday. After lunch we toured the vineyard and spoke
a little about wine and the harvest. Cedric then invited Julien to
come with us to his home for the evening. Julien agreed and said
he would stop by later.

He walked us to the car, and as we were walking, he touched
the small of my back to lead me to the car. It was a subtle move,
but I felt an instant difference. He looked at me and smiled. It was
basically understood that at this point he was interested in me. He
was only coming to Claire and Cedric's home this evening for the
sheer reason of spending a little more time with me. I was flattered by this sudden realization, but also I instantly thought of
Eddie. I was technically still in love with another man. Julien was
attractive, yes, and French. But my mind hadn't even gone there,
until this moment, when I felt this delicate flirtation. I decided to
just shift my thoughts and not overthink something that hadn't
happened yet.

We arrived at Cedric's home and were greeted by Claire. She was beautiful and extremely thin, with a tan and a short, typical French bob. She was downright stunning with almost zero makeup, maybe a slight dash of mascara and lip gloss. She welcomed me and pointed out the French-English dictionary that she said we would be using throughout the evening. Claire was fluent in English and barely had an accent, which was not archetypal. She announced she was going to make pasta with tomato sauce and that we would have some charcuterie as well. It was not surprising at this point that the subject turned to food in a French home. Claire and I chatted as she started on dinner; Cedric took a shower, and Julien would be there at any minute.

"So, what do you think of French men?" Claire asked me with a smirk.

"I have only been in France less than a month, so I haven't had much experience yet," I responded.

"Well, look out. American women are very appealing to the French men." Claire's accent was adorable. Her English was perfect grammatically, but her pronunciation had French written all over it. I found this so charming. I felt that she was giving me a small warning regarding Julien coming over that night, and I instantly felt a little nervous. I wasn't ready by any means to date. I had just ended things with Eddie, and there wasn't even the proper closure on that relationship. I missed him. I didn't even want a man to look at me twice; I just wanted the pain around Eddie to go away. At the time I couldn't see how ultimately frustrating this was about my personality. I lingered in emotional pain over someone who wasn't worth it when right in front of my face there was someone who was.

Julien arrived. He was wearing a cream-colored sweater, dark jeans, and loafers, and his tanned skin looked great against the coloring of his clothes. He seemed very put together for a winemaker in the countryside. Everyone exchanged bisous, and I could tell instantly that Claire and he had a brother-and-sister banter. Claire made a joke that he was GQ, and he fired back that he was sorry she was jealous that he always looked better than her. I laughed at this and predicted this evening would be entertaining.

The wit and charm of these people was inherent. They analyzed the food like we were on the panel of *Top Chef*. I couldn't get enough. "This tomato sauce, Claire… is there oregano and shallots cooked down in this?" Cedric would ask inquisitively.

"No, it's actually my secret—marjoram. And it's simple white onion and garlic," she answered confidently.

We had a great dinner with flowing conversation on topics like American entertainment, French versus American culture, travel, and food. Once Michael Jackson, the Red Hot Chili Peppers, and the TV show *Breaking Bad* were brought up, I felt right at home.

They were all very curious about California. To them it seemed California was this palm tree paradise with celebrity sightings everywhere. It made me laugh when I had to break the news to them that there are many different parts to California, and my home state alone is almost the same size as their entire country. I remember Cedric quoting Proust at one point, and I felt I was around a sophistication I hadn't experienced before.

At a certain point I looked around the table, at the torn baguettes, the plated pasta, the Camembert wedge sitting on a wooden cheese board, and the faces deep in passionate conversation. I was in the countryside of Bordeaux, sitting at a dinner table with French people my age as a welcomed guest in their home. Seeing this from a bird's-eye view made me realize the power of manifestation. I had dreamed of one day being welcome at a dinner party in France, but I never thought it would be possible. Now here I was, experiencing this. My thoughts and dreams had been transformed into a reality that I could not have planned. There was no better feeling. I was living out my fantasy here.

NINE

*Anyone can drink good wines, and anyone wealthy enough
can drink super-expensive wines. But without knowledge,
the soulful, satisfying part of the experience is lost.*

I practically jumped out of bed the next morning. Our dinner party the night before had ended around 1:00 a.m., and two bottles of red wine, delicious pasta, and flowing conversation led me to doze off in utter bliss. Today, Claire and Cedric were taking me to the seaside village of Biscarrosse. This was a small town about an hour's drive from Bordeaux, almost to the border of Spain on the Atlantic coast. Claire's parents had a tiny cottage there on the beach. I was so excited. I had never seen the Atlantic Ocean. We would spend the entire day living it up there and basking in the sun.

My mind thought back to the previous night, when I had hugged Julien goodbye. He would not come with us to Biscarrosse despite being invited, as he had to tend to the harvest at his own vineyard. Unlike Cedric and me, he did not take days off at harvest. This was said very playfully to Cedric in front of me, in English. Before he left, he had asked for my number. Of course I gave it to him, as it was still innocent enough. I was happy there had not been any other advances. I knew in my heart I was not ready yet to face singledom. Yes, Eddie and I were over, but my heart was still with him. I was coming to terms with the brutal reality about breaking up when you are still in love, how painful it is and how it can take some time to be open and ready for someone new. It was as if my heart had turned to steel out of a sheer and innate impulse to protect itself.

Our breakfast consisted of pears and brioche drizzled in maple syrup. *Yum.* Claire had baked the brioche herself, and we had shared a conversation of pastry/kitchen talk over coffee that morning. There is nothing better than freshly baked, milky brioche. It brought me to a flashback of culinary school. I could still taste all of the freshly leavened breads we were required to make from scratch and bake daily. France was so true to my imagination. I was in the countryside and was witnessing this beautiful and chic French woman baking fresh brioche for her houseguest. Fantasy turned into reality once again. Claire had such an intent awareness about her and what she was doing. I noticed she treated *everything* with respect, especially the settings at the table, the plates, and the

94

food. For example, she brought out this beautiful coffee table book for me to glance through based on all of these French patisseries and famous French bakers, while we were eating and savoring our brioche. It added to the experience for me. It made me so aware of the sensual pleasure of the brioche because we were spending time with it. We were reviewing historical French bakeries. I think for me in that moment, I realized back in my American childhood, there was no nuance or specialness when it came to food and a meal. There was dinner on the table every night, and my parents were always present with us, but the attention to detail was lacking. Food was an afterthought, or not as important as our sports events the next day. France massaged thoughts around food that I reso-nated with. This was just one of the reasons I felt so aligned with France: the beauty, attention to detail, and the treatment of *food*.

After breakfast, we hopped in the car and we were off to the sea-side village, just me, Claire, and Cedric. I could not wait to spend the day with them. It had only been a short period of time, but I already felt completely comfortable around them. I couldn't help but think about fate. I was getting to embark on all of these amaz-ing experiences only because my professor had placed me at this vineyard. I had been in contact with several other classmates, and their experiences were not even close to comparable to mine. They definitely were not eating oysters with pastis and having lazy days, meeting locals, or traveling to seaside towns on the Atlantic. It was even rumored that some of them were straight-up miserable and felt like winemaking was essentially slavery, picking grapes in a hot field for twelve hours a day. Not my experience. I felt beyond blessed that my reality in Bordeaux was like a luxurious vacation.

I also felt that for some reason I was supposed to have met Claire and Cedric. I envisioned staying lifelong friends with them. Signs were everywhere; it was as if my ten-year fascination with France was being highlighted and rewarded. I had followed the proper path, I had received the universal clues, and I was exactly where I should be.

We pulled up to the cottage, which was exactly as I had imagined when Cedric had given me a description on the car ride over. The house was charming with white wood shingles and seafoam-green shutters. There was a screened-in porch complete with white wicker furniture. I got out of the car and could instantly smell the sea air. Claire gave me a short tour, and then we walked into the town where we would purchase lunch to enjoy on the cottage porch.

We stopped at the fishermen's port where we could select fresh seafood. This was where all of the marine catches of the day were sold in the town; the fishermen themselves made deliveries by the hour. We scooped up two dozen oysters, some fresh lemons, and a pound of large *gambas* or giant prawns with the heads still intact. We were told these had been caught that same morning. I remembered on my first trip to Paris I had ordered a big seafood platter, and when it was presented my eyes were drawn to the heads and beady, black eyes that remained on the shrimp. I hadn't a clue how to properly eat the suckers at the time, but the waiter dressed in his white, pressed shirt explained it to me in broken English. This was a fond memory, fonder still because perhaps it meant that today I wouldn't look like a fool and could eat them properly in front of Cedric.

A bottle of white wine, a baguette, and some garlic aioli, then all we needed was dessert. Being that we were close to the Basque Country, near a town called San Sebastián, we would need a traditional Basque pastry for dessert. We decided on *gateau Basque*, an almond pastry cake with black cherries dotted through its center. This sounded scrumptious, and my mouth started to water.

We returned to the cottage, and Cedric got busy shucking the oysters. He gave me a small lesson, but he was a pro at this, so I thanked him for teaching me and he proceeded to shuck them all. Claire and I set the table and chilled the wine. When the oysters and shrimp were ready, we sat down, and the sun was warm on our backs as we listened to the waves and ate our hearts out. There are moments in life that move you and you know you will never forget. Eating this meal with Cedric and Claire was one of those moments. I don't know if it was the French oceanside, the simple yet delectable meal of fresh seafood with nothing but a squeeze of lemon and aioli, the new friends I now had, or even our conversation. Or perhaps it was one of those unique experiences that cannot be put into words. Why I was so happy didn't really matter, but I was consumed by bliss, completely present in that moment, all my fears and sadness momentarily behind me. We took pictures, laughed, and finished everything on our plates. The gateau Basque was the perfect ending to one of my most pleasurable meals in France.

After we sat lounging in the sun with full bellies, we cleared the table and agreed that we were ready to go for a dip. I swam in the Atlantic, walked along the shore, and slept off the white wine from lunch in the warm sand. I collected a few seashells from the beach as a souvenir of that special day. Being in Biscarrosse taught me the importance of slowing down and savoring the simple things in life.

After our swim we stopped at a beachside bar and sipped kir blancs and admired the large and powerful ocean. My phone vibrated, and I looked down to see a text.

Bonjour Krista, ça va? How is the beach today? When you are back in Bordeaux I would like to take you to see the windmills and possibly share a meal. Yes?

This message was from Julien. It flattered me to know that he was still interested despite my shyness and guarded demeanor around him. I knew he understood on some level I was closed off from dating; if I could feel my own energy, I knew it was impossible for him not to. And yet, despite the things I was learning about myself, despite how I knew Eddie would take a long time to get over, I felt annoyed with myself that here I was with Cedric and Claire, enjoying all of these experiences; that I had a French man wanting to date me (the dream!) and that I couldn't take advantage of it. I did not understand myself. I was upset with my own feelings, especially with the fact that I did not have it in me to let anyone in.

I allowed myself to think about this on the drive home before I responded to the text. Was it Julien? Was I not attracted to him? That seemed almost impossible as he was cute, charming, and French. I suddenly felt that I was doomed. If it was so challenging for me to even accept a date with a cute French winemaker, how would I ever meet anyone or ever find love again?

Not wanting to trust my own feelings, I texted back, accepting his invitation. He quickly replied that he would pick me up from the Château Gaillard at noon the next day. I told myself to buckle up and get in the right mindset for a date. I would be a fool not to accept a Sunday date with a cute French winemaker. I was in *wine school*, for goodness' sake, and only an idiot would turn that down. If nothing else, I would experience more of Bordeaux and have a nice day. I told Cedric and Claire that I would see Julien the next day. They looked at each other and smiled.

After a long, three-hour car ride due to traffic, we pulled up to the chateau. I hugged them goodbye, thanked them immensely, and mentioned we would make plans for the next weekend. Of course I would see Cedric on Monday morning for work in the cellar.

After that long and lovely, fun-filled wonderful day, it felt strange to be alone again in the chateau. Because I was coming down from such a blissful weekend, when the silence of the chateau enveloped me, all my problems, struggles, and concerns seemed to come crashing down on me at once. I felt tears stream down my face, and I started to sob. I was frightened and overwhelmed by the surge of emotions I was experiencing, and I wondered genuinely if something was wrong with me. Maybe it was the emptiness of the chateau or my self-inflicted heartache; perhaps it was me adjusting to this whole foreign experience or my frustration with my own feelings. Whatever it was, it manifested itself as a heavy, depressive feeling that caused my entire body to ache. I had not expected this to come over me, and I suddenly realized that with the grandiose highs that traveling alone can bring, it can also bring shackling lows. I could feel a paradigm shift as I changed from a girl who desperately loved an imperfect man, to a girl who had to be strong because she was out on her own, and with that shift, I knew part of my identity was escaping me. Worst of all, I was completely alone, with poor cell reception and no one to help me process my thoughts. I poured a large glass of wine from a half-drunk bottle on the kitchen counter, bolted the chateau doors, and shivered as I walked up the creaky stairs to my bedroom. Despite being all smiles and laughter not even half an hour ago, all I wanted now was to sleep. I didn't want to think anymore. I was so confused and torn between my own thoughts and emotions that it forced my mind and soul to disconnect. But sleep would erase these feelings, if only temporarily. As soon as my head hit the pillow, I was out.

It was approaching noon on the day of our date, and Julien would be arriving any minute. I had thrown on jeans, sandals, and a black, fitted shirt. I was still sun-kissed from the beach and was finally feeling rested and replenished. The depressive feeling from the night before had passed, and today was a new day. I was glad I had accepted Julien's invite and told myself to drop the pressure I was inflicting upon myself. This was not so serious and didn't need to mean so much. I watched Julien pull up in front of the cha-teau. As French women are more aloof, I decided to act the same. I would wait for him to knock on the large door as to not look like I had been waiting punctually for him. Knock he did, and we exchanged bisous, a hug, and he complimented my appearance.

We got in the car, and he proceeded to tell me that he was taking me on a drive to see the hidden roads of Saint-Émilion. Then we would go to lunch at a nice restaurant he was fond of in Pomerol. We had a great conversation the whole car ride, and I enjoyed his company and the scenic drive. We arrived at a restaurant called La Table de Catusseau. Nice was an understatement; this was a beautiful place, Michelin-starred and hidden on a charming road. I would have never found it left to my own devices, but Julien said he was a regular and led me down a pathway to the entrance. I will never forget the absolutely delicious Beef dish I ordered and devoured that day. It was perfectly cooked, with buttery mushrooms and creamy, maple-glazed sweet potatoes. A melt-in-your-mouth balsamic sauce drizzled the plate. I paired this with a glass of Bordeaux and was in food heaven.

Over lunch the dreaded but much-needed question was asked: *How long since you have been in a relationship?* This was my opportunity to allow Julien to understand my circumstances. I told him that I had just ended a five-year relationship and was really at a place where I needed to work on myself and could not enter into a new relationship until that hurt was healed. I watched his face fall, and I could tell he was disappointed despite understanding this. We talked about the subject over the rest of lunch, and like a gentleman he still paid regardless of his chance to woo me being over. I was really glad I had met him and felt relieved that I would not be actively rejecting a kiss in my near future, as it was understood I was not interested in that.

After lunch he respectfully took me back to the chateau, and I did not blame him. There was no hope, and he needed to let that thought go.

This was my first experience in the French dating world, and in some ways, I really phoned it in. I struggled to communicate effectively and let the other person know I was essentially not interested in a relationship. Dating was a little different culturally here than in the States. For one thing, the French man never lets his date pay. I had also learned from Genevieve, back in Paris, that when a French man takes a woman to a nice lunch or dinner, basically it is a symbol that he is taking his pursuit of her seriously and intends to make her his girlfriend or *copine*. I remember her telling me this notion, that the formal dinner date or red roses were a significant indication of a man's level of interest. As the French are so full of tradition, these gestures should not be mistaken. Genevieve had even stated that when she had simple love affairs with men sans relationship, often they would only share an aperitif with a cigarette, never dinner. I felt ashamed of myself and bad for him. Next time, I promised myself I would not let a man take me to a Michelin-starred restaurant before that conversation was made. I did not want this feeling to be repeated, but I gave myself a break and chalked it up to a learning experience.

The next day was Monday. I had already survived a full week meeting an array of new people, participating in winemaking, navigating heavy language barriers, and living on a vineyard. I was proud of myself. One week to go. I smiled in anticipation of what the next week would bring. If it was as eventful as the previous week had been, I was in for some major fun, surprises, and a roller coaster of emotions. Cedric and I immediately got to work and reminisced about Biscarrosse.

Later that day, I had my head down, picking apart grapes at the sorting table, when I looked up to see none other than my professor, Monsieur Laurent Lavigne, standing in front of me. He gave a large smile as I looked up, and he asked how I was. He was perfectly poised and put together in black slacks and a cashmere scarf. He wanted a tour of my vineyard, my living quarters, and wanted to ask me some questions regarding what I was learning about the winemaking process. I was shocked to see him and was a bit nervous, as I was not expecting him to show up.

After speaking with me he went on a little stroll with Catherine, and I could only assume they were discussing my work on the vineyard. Shortly after, he came walking back over to tell me everything seemed to be going fine and he had received a great report on my work ethic. Phew, I was relieved. I was trying my best every day, but at the same time I was a novice. I had only hoped that Catherine and her team were not frustrated by my lack of knowledge, but apparently they thought I was great. Before leaving, Professor Lavigne requested that I contact my classmates and arrange a dinner in the town of Saint-Émilion for that evening. He said he would host it if I contacted my fellow vineyard friends and gathered a group. I was so eager and immediately got to work on organizing this. I contacted everyone, and the plan was set. Dinner in the town that night at eight o'clock. *Surprise number one for week two.*

I arrived at the restaurant at a quarter to eight. This was going to be a night of nice bottles of wine, enticing stories exchanged, and seeing my classmates with whom I already shared a strong bond over our collective experience.

All of a sudden, I heard a familiar voice. It was Pearl. "Krista, oh my goodness, how are you? Do you like your vineyard?" We hugged and laughed and exchanged short vineyard tales. Pearl was staying on a vineyard out in the appellation of Blaye, not too far from Saint-Émilion. She was with a young winemaker and his family who had just taken over the vineyard from his parents. She seemed to be enjoying her time as well.

Then there was Sarah. She was twenty-eight and from Seattle. She had seen a picture I had posted to our group chat of Cedric, Julien, and me eating oysters and had replied: *It is not fair—oysters and cute boys are my kryptonite.* I knew after that message we were going to be great friends. She was someone I felt so naturally myself around, and after just two minutes listening to her vineyard experience, I felt a sudden empathy for her. It sounded horrible. She spoke of having to take showers in a community bathroom and sleeping on a cot. The descriptions seemed closer to prison than to life on a vineyard, and from that point on, I decided I would tone down how wonderful my reality at Gaillard had been.

I gave a few more hugs and elated hellos to some of my other classmates, and then we moved into the restaurant to take our seats and start an unforgettable evening. In fact, our professor had a close relationship with the owner of this restaurant, L'Envers du Décor, and had closed the place down for us. It would just be the twenty of us dining on a delectable five-course meal. Professor Lavigne announced that he would be selecting seven bottles of wine for that evening and that we would all start blind-tasting them.

We had learned a tasting technique in school, through which the taster should be able to determine the grape varietal, the country of origin, the year it was harvested, price and aging potential, and foods to pair with it, among other things. With Professor Lavigne's statement, you could feel the competitiveness in the room grow. Everyone wanted to be able to call the wine correctly. Everyone wanted to be the best taster. Who would have the guts to take a wild guess?

As the night went on, this turned into a fun game. I analyzed Professor Lavigne frequently. He was so eloquent and perfectly intently spoken. He was tall in stature, always well dressed, thin, and well kept. Everything from his fingernails to his skin was taken care of. When he walked into a room, he demanded respect and attention just by his energy. He was downright sexy, and every woman in our class had a soft spot for him while at the same time not wanting to disappoint him. I undoubtedly had a crush on him, and Sarah joked that he and I had chemistry. She would laugh and say, "Krista, it's all about Lavigne. Like, this is your ideal French man."

This was especially true when he said things like, "Being drunk in the French culture is unacceptable. Being drunk means you equal less than nothing." He presented us with this gem at L'Envers du Décor. I had to look down at my plate to keep from laughing out loud when this was stated to all twenty of us. It was so deliberate and blunt. Everyone sat up a little straighter at that moment. I'm not sure if he realized how offensive "less than nothing" sounded in English, but whether he meant the harshness or not, it was a true Lavigne-ism. We all smiled and of course didn't want to let him down by appearing drunk that evening. I completely agree in the sense that there is a time and place for everything; having a party and letting loose is lovely sometimes, but not the place when you are dropping decent money for the pleasure and education of a food and wine pairing.

Thankfully, I will never forget this night. This was a special evening, which heavily symbolized the start of our year in wine together. We all grew closer over that shared dinner. We didn't know what was to come, but we were all on this journey *ensemble*. Laughter permeated the room, delicious wines hit the palate, and the clinking of glasses was heard as several "cheers" and "Santés" were said. In my life, I had never felt like I was exactly where I was supposed to be, not to the extent that I was feeling this way in France. There was nowhere else in the world I should have been. I had dreamed all my life of finding a tribe of people that shared my interests. I had found my people. I had found my people *in France*.

After that night, I had another five glorious days with Catherine, Cedric, Claire, and the vineyard workers. I created even more memories, such as the day the guys took me out into the vineyard with a rinky-dink car and taught me how to drive a stick shift or the multiple meals I shared with Emmanuel, Jean, Pierre, Joni, Cedric, and Thomas, laughing the night into oblivion. All of it would remain so special to me, even as I zipped my suitcase and headed north, toward Paris.

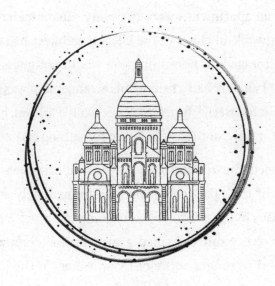

TEN

The appellation Hermitage is a single 1,000-foot-high (300-meter) hill,
with just 300 acres (120 Hectares) of vineyards clinging to its mostly
southern-facing slope. In the eighteenth and nineteenth centuries
Hermitage was France's costliest red wine.

I opened my eyes and squinted at the clock. *11:00 a.m.* A quick glance out the skylight revealed a cloudy and overcast day, but… I was in Paris.

I looked up to the ceiling to see the exposed, white wooden beams of my new attic apartment. This seemed to be the only charming aspect of the place. My new bed was a foldout black leather couch with pale blue bed sheets. Interesting to say the least, but it was not nearly as captivating as Genevieve's flat had been. This little cubby I was calling an apartment was only twenty square meters—the size of a modern walk-in closet in the US. An architect had designed it and snuck storage into nooks that you would not guess to make it liveable, but I already had a feeling this arrangement was going to be short-lived. It felt sterile, functional, not really Parisian, but it would have to do for now, until I could figure something else out.

I opened the red curtains to the half windows lining the north side of the apartment, and was immediately staring into someone else's living room. This was going to be awkward. I could watch their every move. I spied a man on his computer, eating a banana and sipping a bottle of Evian water. In the kitchen was an Asian woman cooking. Maybe that was his wife? Girlfriend? Maid? Well, I was sure to find out soon with this lack of privacy. They could see into my place as well if the curtains were open. *Oh God*. I didn't like this already.

It was Sunday, I'd just returned from Bordeaux, and the weather was dreary, dark, and gray. I decided I would stay in and have an omelet and pop a half bottle of Champagne. If my apartment was not going to feel Parisian, then at least I was drinking Champagne, which always felt very French to me.

I cracked two eggs into a bowl and turned on the burner. At least I had a stovetop with two working burners. My eyes widened as I noticed the beautiful bright orange yolks of these eggs, so different from the pale yellow yolks I was accustomed to in America.

As I sprinkled the goat cheese and thyme leaves into the eggs, my mind couldn't help but flash back to the beautiful omelet Eddie had made me that first New Year's Day we spent together. I had felt so adored, all because a man had made me a perfect omelet. I had an impulsive craving for his embrace, but I fought back the tears. I had been told people with compulsions wear rubber bands on their wrists and snap them whenever the impulse starts. I wanted to snap a rubber band on my wrist every time I thought of Eddie. It was excruciating at times. The thought of never seeing him again, as true and right as I believed it to be, also felt morbid.

All because a man had made me a perfect omelet. Now I was trying to give that to myself. Eddie and I were over, I reminded myself. I was actually starting to create a new life. Here in Paris. A fresh start and an open door to adventure.

I sipped the Champagne, letting the bubbles foam on my tongue, tasting the sweet balance of acidity and freshness while aromas of poached pears and toasted bread permeated up through my nostrils. I swallowed and anticipated my next pleasurable sip.

I was living in Paris. I was sipping Champagne and eating an omelet. I should have been jumping for joy, but on this gray Sunday, in my attic, I couldn't help but feel lonely. Anyone who has ever up and moved his or her life to a foreign country will say the same thing: It is not all roses, no matter what. You can be having the perfect day in your dream city and then be caught in a sudden squall of loneliness.

I pulled out my school documents from that week and glanced at the itinerary for our upcoming trip to Champagne. We would be getting to embark as a class on a three-day trip through the region while visiting all of the top Champagne houses. Listed were the following: Dom Pérignon, Moët, Bollinger, Duval-Leroy, Krug, and Ulysse Collin. I could hardly wait. We would leave next

month, in November, meaning I had several weeks to get reac-
quainted with Paris. I would get to explore the charming streets of
my neighborhood; flirt with the vendors at the *marché*; meet Pearl,
Sebastian, or Sarah at the hip wine bars on the Left Bank; and walk
along the Seine.

Just knowing these plans were my reality snapped me out of
my sadness. In fact, what was stopping me from living one of these
out now? I decided a long walk on the river was much needed. I
rinsed my plate, stuck the Champagne bottle back in the fridge,
saving one glass for later, and tied up my Nike running shoes. *I
live in Paris.* I loved repeating this thought to myself; it never got
old or monotonous. I could walk along the Seine admiring the
beautiful bridges and moldings of the large, romantic buildings
every single day.

As I walked along the river, I noticed everything around me:
couples walking hand in hand, boats cruising down the water with
tourists waving to pedestrians on the shore, the arched bridges
that seemed so magnificent and powerful, and then there it was,
creeping around the bend, growing larger with every step I took,
the beauty itself—the Eiffel Tower. No matter what, even as I saw
the Eiffel Tower every day in Paris, it always moved me. It was so
grand and stunning.

I took my usual five-mile stroll along the river, from Notre
Dame to the Eiffel Tower and back. Whether it was in the morning or the evening, this was a beautiful way to take in Paris. I still
could not decide if I found my city more beautiful at night or in
the daylight. I concluded it was a good dilemma to have.

As I was returning to the Fifth Arrondissement, my phone vibrated. It was a message from Sebastian on the group chat.

Bonjour! Do you all want to meet tonight and share a good bottle of wine at 5eme Cru?! It is that wine bar we talked about.

I responded with a resounding and caps-locked YES! I was so excited to learn more about my classmates.

I used to watch *Sex and the City* and envy Carrie Bradshaw. I pictured how exciting it would be to live in a big city with great friends, with everything at your fingertips. To have a full dance card of activities and to have people around who shared your common interests. I anticipated living a life close to Carrie Bradshaw's this year. Eager at the thought and for the night to proceed, I picked up the pace and rushed home to get ready.

We met at the wine bar at seven thirty. It was a tiny spot tucked away on rue Cardinal Lemoine, a famous street that Ernest Hemingway used to live on back in his *Movable Feast* days. Little did I know it would become a regular meeting place throughout the school year. With an assortment of French wines, it was the perfect spot to test our knowledge. They also had the best quiche in the city, in my opinion, as well as the most delicious pear caramel crumble dessert that was euphoria every time I tasted a bite.

The large windows from the street were lined in wood molding painted forest green. I opened the door and immediately spotted my friends at a barrel table. Each table was a slab of wood on top of a wine barrel. There were only six tables in the whole place. The walls were stone made to make you feel like you were in a wine cave.

That night we drank a bottle of Hermitage, which we found to be a delicious introduction into the Rhône Valley and the famous Syrah grape varietal. I snapped a picture of the bottle and recorded it: *Nicolas Perrin 2011.*

We were already starting to become "wine geeks." Wine was becoming a huge focus inside and outside of the classroom. I wondered if I would ever get sick of it. I had watched the *Somm* documentaries, and by the end, after tasting for weeks, they looked puffy, red in the face, physically ill, tired, and it was clear they needed a detox. But I found myself eagerly tasting wine while at restaurants in Paris and utilizing my knowledge every time, going into some sort of deep analysis.

Sarah turned to me that first night at 5ème Cru and said of the Hermitage, "This was a great vintage."

Then Pearl chimed in, "You can sense the terroir. There is an earthiness coming through."

Terroir, as I was learning, was important in wine talk, especially Old World wines. Old World referred to how they grow wine in Europe, while terroir is the complete natural environment in which a particular wine is produced, including factors such as the soil, topography, and climate. For example, in Burgundy the winemaker (or vigneron) can only grow Chardonnay and Pinot Noir grapes. Why? Because there are rules based on the land producing the best wine from those grapes. Of course, there are always loopholes, and I would soon learn the exceptions and secrets of the sommelier, such as knowing that Sauvignon Blanc, Aligoté, and at times Gamay grapes are allowed in Burgundy, but for all intents and purposes, Chardonnay and Pinot Noir are acceptable and known worldwide as Burgundy wines.

We not only shared a lovely bottle of wine that evening but also shared our life stories. We talked about everything from dating, to travel, to our pasts and even our childhoods. I opened up and shared my exit from my tumultuous relationship with Eddie that ultimately led me to Paris, as well as my ongoing love affair with France in general. I will never forget the deep conversation and delicious wine of that cool night in October 2015, in our new favorite neighborhood spot. I had made friends almost instantly, which was something I had been warned about in coming to Paris. Paris could feel very lonely if you did not have an active social life and friends to meet out in the city. I had only hoped to make a friend or two, and I had now made three friends. I felt lucky and relieved to have such beautiful people to help relieve my occasional loneliness and sadness, as I'd experienced that morning. After that night, I knew that we would be meeting weekly outside of class out in the city. I had partners in crime to explore my favorite place on earth with.

Sure enough, the next Saturday we all met at Treize, a spot in Saint Germain des Prés. The owner was an American who had brought classic brunch dishes like chicken and waffles over to Paris. The inside of Treize felt like an elegant birdcage with chandeliers and cookbooks lining the white walls. We spent several hours eating our hearts out and sipping Prosecco paired with freshly squeezed orange juice. It happened to be Halloween, and we were all going to dress up as cats and go out on the town that evening. It was so enjoyable for me to feel young and carefree again, to have friends to dance the night away with. I realized in this moment that I had traded in carefree days of curiosity and exploration for serious relationships in my younger years and that I had made compromise a big priority. Now, things were different, and I was liking this new version of me. I had finally met people that wanted to live life the way I did. I had spent so many years attached to someone else, with no real sense of being able to find myself without it affecting them. Now all I had to live for was myself, and it was the most freeing feeling.

My friends and I sat over long meals discussing the different wines we were learning about in class, talking about the beautiful French language and reciting verses to each other, and wondering if any of us would in fact find someone special in France. I wasn't sure on this last point, though I held out hope. After all, Paris so far had lived up to my expectations. I was lingering in cafés for hours, drinking some of the best wines I had ever tasted, having croissants on lazy Sundays, and frequently walking the river at night, watching the Eiffel Tower light up in one hundred thousand sparkles. I wondered when, if ever, this would get old. I could not fathom it.

In addition to Pearl, Sebastian, and Sarah, I also started to make nice with the French students in our class. I was surprised when we were invited to Michel's flat in Montmartre for a wine and cheese gathering one Saturday evening. Raclette parties were the "new thing," so Michel's invite said he would be introducing us to it. Raclette is a dish originating in Switzerland, which also gained popularity in Savoie, France. It's basically cheese heated on a flat, iron grill and then scraped off and served with bread, cornichons, and other accompaniments. Pairing it with a nice Riesling is popular in France, so this is what we did!

Montmartre was the up-and-coming neighborhood, where many Parisians in their thirties and forties lived. Michel was thirty-six years old and had that classic Parisian vibe of being nice enough but rather aloof at times. He was always impeccably dressed, and his French was butter to our ears. All the girls thought Michel was the eligible bachelor of the class. There was something mysterious about him, something elusive. From the beginning I thought there might have been something between him and Sarah. When I asked Sarah about it, she said they were just friends, but I was curious. There was definitely energy between them that seemed natural, and they were always flirting, talking, and laughing.

The Raclette dinner party in Montmartre was an absolute blast. Michel and another classmate of ours, Alan, played guitar, and we sang along to classics from our childhood like "Wonderwall."

We sang the lyrics at the top of our lungs and laughed all night. I looked around the room and realized that I had created a life here. I was in Paris, at a dinner party with friends. It hit me that night just how lucky I was, how lonely I had been in LA. Coming to sommelier school in Paris was absolutely the best decision for my life.

In addition to the start of sommelier school, I decided to take two night classes a week of French at the local Alliance. I figured I needed to start learning this beautiful language early on if I wanted to not just survive but thrive in my dream city. I attended four hours a week of basic French, going over verb conjugations and all of French's complicated spelling from 7:00 to 9:00 p.m. twice a week. At times I felt overwhelmed by my schedule, but I was so full of energy that I had decided I was up for the challenge.

Like a wet sponge you are trying to wring all of the water out of, I wanted every drop of Paris to be squeezed out. I didn't want to miss a beat.

I had a full schedule with schooling in both wine and French, I had an active social life that I adored, and I felt the only thing I was possibly missing was a personal romantic life. *Should I date French men?* Though Eddie and I had just broken up in October, I felt like I'd been distant from him since our last meeting in California. Even if I wasn't ready emotionally, I could at least date for the fun of it. The thought of meeting new people was enticing. I was so curious about the ever-mysterious French men. Sebastian had joined the online dating sites in Paris and supposedly was having luck, with dates coming out of the woodwork. He was a man dating men, though, and the gay scene may have been different than my landing a French boyfriend.

I had been told it would be nearly impossible for me to have a chance meeting with a French man. First I didn't really speak French yet, so whomever I was going to date would need to speak English. At least a little bit. Secondly, in France, you are rarely approached by a man—or any stranger for that matter—even if you are sitting alone in a café. The French respect people's privacy, keeping to themselves and their close networks more often than not; it is not like the States where everyone asks how your day is. One point in my favor, though: It was also rumored that American women had an advantage. To most French men we were seen as smiley, happy, and open girls. We were viewed as exotic, and they were instantly curious about us just based on the fact that we were from another country. (This was a concept I could

get behind, given my complete infatuation with Parisian men.…
And women.)

I decided to give it a try. *Pourquoi pas?* I joined a dating site.
I wanted to experience all Paris had to offer. I was missing one
large aspect, so a dating site it was. I set up a very basic account
just stating that I was from California and living in Paris. I posted
five recent pictures and decided to just wait and see if any French
suitors messaged me.

It was quarter to nine on a Tuesday evening, and I was nearing the
end of language class. I would be meeting Benjamin, my first ever
blind date in Paris, that night; he would be waiting for me outside
of my classroom. He had messaged that he would be wearing all
black, and hopefully I accepted that he had a dark side. This text
was sent with a smiley face of course.

Benjamin and I had started talking the previous Sunday evening through the dating app Meetic. This was equivalent to Match.
com in the States. He quickly requested my phone number and
called me, which I appreciated. He seemed like a mature, confident adult on the phone, with a charming accent, and I had agreed
to meet him for a drink. Benjamin was a full-on Parisian, which
was pretty much all I knew about him other than that he was six
feet tall and would be wearing all black. Beyond this and the one
picture he had on the site, I was in the dark. No pun intended. *This
should be interesting to say the least*, I thought to myself. I wanted

to do my best attempt at a classic Parisian look for him, so I threw on an effortlessly elegant look with faded denim skinny jeans, a black blazer, and a violet scarf; light lip gloss, wavy hair, and perfume completed my look.

He was waiting for me outside the Alliance and gave a big smile when he caught sight of the girl in the violet scarf. A grin lined my face as well, as he was cute... and tall. I felt a twinge of excitement. He wore glasses, which I found sexy and found made him look intellectual. Benjamin gave me an embrace and kissed both of my cheeks, uttering the ever famous casual *"Ça va?"* I replied with my usual *"Très bien, merci"* and smiled. He commented how my French was already improving and said that he loved my American accent. It was a nice, flirty introduction, and I knew that I was happy to be joining him for a drink.

We walked to a nearby café and took a seat. He walked on the side of the street closest to the cars, stating that a woman is never to be put on the side of danger. How charming, just as I had envisioned a French man to be. He put his arm around my shoulder, which I thought was a bit forward, but even so, I enjoyed this gesture. I felt like a lady. My heart really started to flutter when he called me *mademoiselle*, a compliment because I was technically a *madame*. A mademoiselle was more of a youngster or teenage girl.

At the café, we decided on a cheese board with baguette and two glasses of Bordeaux.

Benjamin lit up a cigarette within minutes, and I was very well aware that I would need to accept this if I was going to date a French man. The men in France were more likely than not going to smoke. He offered me one, and I had a quick, jolting moment of *when in Rome*—technically speaking, when in Paris—and received one out of his hand. I had never had issues with addiction, and I had no intention of becoming a smoker. However, at this moment I felt like having a cigarette with Benjamin, so I did.

I will never forget the look on Benjamin's face, though, when I put the cigarette out on the cheese board. He looked absolutely appalled. I said, "Oh sorry! They never brought an ashtray. Where am I supposed to put this out?"

He said, "In Paris, never on the food plates." He smiled in disbelief and told me to step on it on the ground. I laughed and felt my face turn bright red. I was not only not a regular, too-cool-for-school smoker, but apparently I had disrespected our cheese board. We both laughed and looked at the pieces of Camembert and Roquefort left on the rustic wooden board. Any chance Benjamin was going in for another bite was slim to none.

Despite this gaffe, we had a great flow of conversation, and I could not believe my date was going this seamlessly. I felt comfortable not only in a foreign city, but in a foreign city on a date with a French guy. Benjamin had lived in London for two years and dated an English girl while he was there. No wonder his English was so fluent. He was charming and very easy to talk to. I spoke more than he did, mostly out of nervousness. I quickly learned that he was as comfortable in silence as he was in conversation. He didn't always need to be speaking or asking me questions, which I found appealing.

After our cheese and wine, he said he would walk me home, which would take about thirty minutes. Before I knew it, we were strolling down little alleys that I never had taken before. I felt overcome with enthusiasm that I was with a local and having a somewhat romantic tour of Paris. It was so cliché and yet so needed for me. We stopped at a crosswalk, and he brushed the hair out of my face and gave me a sweet little kiss on the cheek. A night with a cute French man, a romantic stroll, a cigarette, cheese and wine consumed, what more could I want out of a date in Paris? I secretly hoped the kiss on my cheek was a warmup, and I would be receiving a real kiss by the time the date came to a conclusion.

We were finally outside my building. I reached up to give Benjamin a hug when he kissed me. We kissed for several minutes, and then I turned to enter my courtyard. He slowly let go of my hand, and we smiled and said good night. Once in my attic, I received a text from Benjamin:

Great evening. It was a pleasure. Hoping you wanted that kiss as much as I did.

I responded with: *Of course. I feel the same. I never do things I don't want to do.*

I was officially welcomed into the dating world of Paris. I had no clue what I was getting myself into.

ELEVEN

Burgundy is not what most people choose
to begin their journey with wine; but Burgundy is often
where many of us find ourselves at the end.

66 **T**he oak aging in the wine paired lovely with the hazelnuts in this dish. It was an obvious compliment. On
the nose of the wine in regards to aroma, there was a roundness of
dried, candied fruit and baked apricots that stood up to the rich
and savory foie gras in the ravioli stuffing. This wine also had a
beautiful, buttery creaminess on the palate that paired exquisitely
with the creaminess of the dish..."

This was my response when my professor asked me to please describe the food and wine pairing and give my opinion. It was late October, and we were attending our first of nine food and wine pairings throughout the school term. I was in disbelief that this was actually a required course because it was so extravagant and pleasurable. Basically each food and wine pairing consisted of a long, stretched-out meal with a chef preparing dishes for us and our professor selecting wines to pair with the food. That first particular food and wine pairing we dined on was foie gras ravioli with hazelnut and fried Jerusalem artichokes, followed by creamy risotto with parmesan, pan-fried langoustine, and mussels. Absolutely melt-in-your-mouth heaven, every bite.

At this point, we had become so saturated with knowledge on how to properly taste wine, it was becoming a fun game and we hoped to be called on.

The chefs and professors would randomly select someone to discuss the pairing. This was a beneficial warmup, as we would also need to attend formal, professional tastings and be able to speak what they called "wine talk." We would have to articulate our observations with confidence and the proper vocabulary used in the wine world. Otherwise, the school said they would not grant our degrees at the end of the program. This was a very important step in passing! As such, I was definitely being pushed out of my comfort zone. I could no longer be the shy observer, but in a way, finding my voice and my footing was becoming the best thing for me.

I felt my self-confidence building. I had always considered myself pretty introverted, and I was surprised at the changes happening within me since I had arrived in Paris. Not only was I feeling more self-possessed speaking in class, but I was also accepting most social invitations and found myself rarely "staying in." The past five years when I had been with Eddie were the inverse; the nights were few and far between that I would actually leave the house. We were always cuddled up watching movies and cooking dinner together. I didn't even think I wanted to be out, meeting new people, having new experiences, and feeling out of my comfort zone on a regular basis. I was learning a whole new side of myself, and I found it intriguing. I was eager to discover more.

Sommelier school was moving at a rapid pace. We were required to attend private wine tastings all over the city, almost on a twice-weekly basis. This was very exhilarating, but it interfered with my language courses to the extent that I found myself missing one class almost every week. I was frustrated that I couldn't continue with my full schedule, but the truth was I had too much on my plate. The good news was I was tasting so many wines that I felt myself becoming an expert. I could tell the subtle differences between Cabernet Franc and Cabernet Sauvignon, and I knew what a Pinot Noir from Alsace tasted like compared to a Pinot Noir from Burgundy. I was becoming obsessed with analyzing wine. I was infatuated by the history of each bottle, how a wine was made, where it was from, and the quality of it. I was learning so much about France itself by locating wine regions and the climate and topography of each region.

A typical weekday for my classmates and me was sitting through five hours of intense wine lecture, including a tasting in class, followed by a tasting out in some lavish hotel in Paris later that evening. After the professional tasting, a few of us would usually go to a restaurant and order a good bottle to share. Wine was threaded through every minute of every day. I was living and breathing wine. We could also volunteer to work wine events, thanks to Professor Lavigne's many connections in the city, and we would be sent to palaces and asked to serve wine for hours to hundreds of people in the wine business. I could not believe my life. I never expected to be able to attend private tastings in Paris where I was afforded the opportunity to taste several of the greatest wines in France. Some days we would have two events in a day, two professional tasting locations. It seemed insane, and anyone really thinking much about it would have felt immense overwhelm. I was taking life one hour at a time and showing up where I needed to be.

In addition to the jampacked schedule attached to sommelier school, I was trying to fit in nights to see Benjamin. After our first date, he had asked me out again just two days later. I accepted, and once again he met me outside of language class and we went to a café. This time he was a bit more aggressive, showing very open PDA the entire time we were at the café. In Paris, it is classic for tables to face the street and for couples to sit side by side to canoodle and kiss. I had always walked by couples in love, kissing and fondling each other openly at cafés, and secretly I hoped I could experience being coupled up in a table and two-chair setting.

Being that I was still newly out of a five-year relationship, I was not ready to actually go home with Benjamin. He also let me in on the fact that he had a roommate who happened to be a twenty-five-year-old girl. This piece of information did not sit well with me, and I am pretty sure he could feel my angst. I declined his offer to come back to his place that night and could only hope I would see him again. He didn't seem that upset, but time would tell what his real intentions were. All I knew was I wanted to build more on our relationship, and I was also not very fond of the fact that he was living with a woman. He claimed that he had no attraction to her, but it seemed a little sketchy to me.

French men, as I was learning, are much more comfortable keeping many women as friends and meeting with women one on one, even if there is only a platonic relationship. In the States this is not as common. Old friendships, sure, but in my experience this phenomenon is rare for the average American man. More often in America, there are group outings, and men and women are social in groups unless there is a romantic interest between them.

But part of the reason I was dating in Paris was because I became curious about the French culture, and this would shed light on another facet of it. The other reason was because I was so infatuated with French women, I was in love with Paris, and not so secretly I dreamed I would end up with a French man so I could stay and *be French*. Some people I spoke to said things like, "But what about the affairs? French men take on mistresses. How could you accept this?" Call me naïve, but I was determined that I could find a French man who didn't think affairs were appropriate and who shared my values when it came to love and marriage.

I often thought of Eddie, and I was tempted frequently to reach out to him. I missed him. I always thought of how much I loved speaking with him at the culmination of my day and sharing what had unfolded. However, I knew from my past behavior and patterns, it would only lead me to eventually getting back together with him. There was a part of me that felt weak if I contacted him. I did not trust myself not to go back to him. I needed to stay strong and focused on my new life in Paris. It had been a month since he had hung up on me in Bordeaux. I knew that he had felt the pain of really losing me this time, and he probably had been on a drug raid for weeks. I would have heard from him by now if he had sobered up. All I could do was say a little prayer for his protection and love him from afar.

It was a Thursday night in November, and I hadn't heard from Benjamin in a few days. I pondered sending him a text, but decided to follow the oldest rule in the book: If a guy is interested in a girl, darn it he will pursue her. It is a man's nature. Instead, I texted Sarah and made plans to meet with her at a restaurant in the Saint Germain des Prés called La Société. Apparently, this restaurant was a scene, very hip and trendy. The same brothers that owned and designed the flagship Hôtel Costes, which I had become obsessed with, ran it.

Sarah and I were quickly becoming close friends. I confided in her, and we shared many of the same interests. We were both American girls on this grand adventure in Paris, and we loved food, wine, restaurants, and traveling. Our conversations often led to the meaning of life and all of these experiences we were having as well as future travel plans, cultural differences between France and America, and of course… boys. Sarah was also attempting to date in France, but she took the dating scene in Paris with a grain of salt. She would brush it off with an attitude of *This is just for fun, something to do while I'm here.* I never felt that she resonated much with French men or Paris like I did; she took pride in America and found the men in France sort of odd.

We arrived at the restaurant at eight o'clock. We followed the hostess who looked like she had just stepped off the cover of *Vogue*. She was pin thin, with a sleek, backless black dress on; her hair was slicked back into a low ponytail, her lush lips were painted red, and a gold chain necklace dropped down to accentuate her twenty-four-inch waist. We were definitely in Paris.

La Société was very dimly lit, with black, plush couches serving as the restaurant chairs, making this fancy eatery seem more like a lounge. There were square, glass tables with roses as the centerpieces. It had a very sexy and romantic vibe and seemed to be the perfect place for a date or a fun girls' night out. We were seated toward the back of the restaurant, next to a table with two gentlemen who appeared to be in their fifties and seemed to be discussing business. The table on the other side of us was reserved for six. Sarah and I decided on a bottle of Chablis Premier Cru and got to exchanging stories from the week. When our wine was presented, the men next to us chimed in, commenting that it was a fabulous wine, one of the better Chardonnays on the list. We introduced ourselves, saying we agreed as we were in sommelier school and very particular about the wines we ordered. Low and behold they were in the wine business, and were here from Texas on a business trip.

I glanced at the bottle on their table: Vosne-Romanée. *Wow.* Vosne-Romanée, as I was intently learning, was a small appellation in Burgundy with some of the best wines ever produced.

These wines were expensive and of the utmost quality. Their bottle was listed at 425 euros. Chad and Brookes, as we learned they were named, worked for a company called Glazer's that handled wine and liquor distribution for the whole state of Texas. The next thing we knew, they were requesting glasses for us to try the Vosne-Romanée. *Thank you, Jesus.* I had been dropped in the perfect seat in Paris that evening.

The wine was the purest form of the Pinot Noir grape that I had ever tasted. It was smooth, and the aromas were perfectly intertwined to create a balanced complexity. Before we could finish our glasses, they had ordered another wine from Burgundy; this one was from the Gevrey-Chambertin appellation. It was amazing that in two short months Sarah and I easily recognized the significance of these wines. We could read any wine list in France and make a spot-on selection. In addition to the exquisite wines, Chad and Brookes also ordered the sturgeon caviar from the Caspian Sea. There are a few moments in someone's life that they will never ever forget. For me one of those moments is being fed sturgeon caviar off a pearl abalone spoon, while sipping Vosne-Romanée and Chablis Premier Cru. Chad gently scooped up eight eggs of caviar onto the abalone marble spoon, and placed that spoon in my mouth. *These types of instances only existed in the movies. Who am I?* I thought.

Sarah and I did not order one thing at La Société that evening. Instead, Chad and Brookes requested practically everything on the menu and offered us a taste of all the plates. About thirty minutes into our caviar and wine tasting, a group of men sat down at the reserved table next to us. I couldn't make out if they were French or not; they definitely looked European, but something was telling me they were not French. They started speaking another language, though I could not tell if it was Swedish or German. One of them leaned over and asked for permission to smoke. Sarah said it was fine, and they asked if we were American. Definitely Swedish, judging by the accents. Before I knew it, the Swedish guys were reaching across our table, exchanging business cards with Chad and Brookes, and Chad and Brookes were ordering more wine for all of us to enjoy as a group. It had turned into a huge dinner party with Sarah and me being the only women, seated smack dab in the middle of it all. I was feeling a bit tipsy at this point and knew I needed water. Everyone was starting to get a little rowdy. I had noticed the guy seated directly to my right. He seemed calm and cool and able to handle his alcohol. He and I glanced at each other and smiled.

We were possibly the only semi-sober people at the table of ten. We started talking, and I learned his name was Matthias and he was in the whiskey business. He was a blond-haired, blue-eyed, sweet guy from Sweden. He was in his late thirties, but I guess the Swedish have good genes because he looked much younger. He had a soft way of speaking and a very calming effect on me despite the loudness of the table. Another hour passed, though it seemed I had only been talking with Matthias for ten minutes. Our conversation was easy and flowing. He was starting to make slight gestures such as putting his hand on my leg or staring into my eyes more intently. Just as I was anticipating a kiss, the restaurant manager came over and informed us that the restaurant was closing. I looked at my watch and it read 2:00 a.m. Oh my goodness! And we were the only table left in the restaurant. One of the Swedes announced that the night wasn't over yet: we were going to a club and Champagne bar that had been recommended in the Odéon district next.

As we made our way to the club, I was definitely feeling the effects of all the wine. It took me standing up to realize I was in fact *drunk*. I remember arriving at the club to see a long line of people waiting to get in. At this point, I was curious and desperately wanted to extend my night and get to know Matthias better. I walked right up to the bouncers and asked rather assertively to be let in. I didn't even attempt to speak French. They pointed at the long line of people. Next, I surprised myself and didn't know where this ambition and absolute drive to be let into the Champagne club was coming from. Maybe it was the alcohol speaking.

"Listen, I have people here from out of town," I said. "I am a regular at this club. I am about to order a MAGNUM of Ruinart Blanc de Blancs Champagne. I would like a couch and table seating please. I will not stay a regular to your business if I do not get into this club right this moment."

I could not believe the words coming out of my mouth. *Who did I think I was?* I was acting like I owned Paris. The truth was I had never stepped foot in this club. And promising to order a Magnum of Blanc de Blancs? Blanc de Blancs is Champagne made using only Chardonnay grapes. And Ruinart?... It was my favorite and also much more expensive than other Champagnes, generally speaking. Much to my surprise this extreme assertiveness worked, and the group of us were let right in. We were led to a large, circular area near the DJ, and a waiter came over immediately. As I had promised the bouncers, I ordered a magnum of Champagne,

Ruinart Blanc de Blancs. The magnum was presented, and sparkling crystal glasses were laid out.

Sarah screamed, "Oh my *God!* Who ordered this?" I shot her a smile. She looked back in disbelief. "Krista!" she exclaimed, not understanding what I was doing.

I was in disbelief the minute the bill came. Five hundred euros. By this time, everyone had trickled out and left. It was four in the morning, I had ordered a magnum of Champagne, and I guess I was paying for my sins because *I* was left with the bill. I broke away from my make-out session with Matthias and asked him to read the bill and clarify the price. He took out his credit card and agreed to split the bill with me. I could not believe myself. I was officially wasted, making out with a guy from Sweden, in a club at 4:00 a.m., left to foot the bill of a great bottle of Champagne that I did not even fully enjoy and savor due to my drunken stupor. I felt insane.

I rolled over the next morning to see Matthias lying there. In my bed. I barely remember what happened after we left the club.

What I do remember is walking back to my place as the sun was rising over the Notre Dame Cathedral. The Seine was glistening, picking up the reflection of the baby pink splatters of light across the blue sky. I remember smelling the ecstasy of yeasty, buttery, sugary whiffs from the boulangeries and watching white trucks pulling up outside, their drivers unloading large sacks of flour.

I had definitely been intimate with Matthias, but the details were a blur at this point. I raced to the bathroom, splashed water on my face, and downed a bottle of water. I was majorly hungover. In all my days drinking wine in Paris, I had never felt like this. I had gone way overboard and was paying for it. Professor Lavigne would have been appalled with me. After taking two aspirin, I glanced at my phone to see several text messages from Sarah asking if I was safe and okay. I did not even remember saying goodbye to her. *Jesus.*

I also had a text from Benjamin.

Hello Krista, do you want to see a movie tonight with me?

I responded yes to Benjamin. I responded to Sarah and told her to meet me at our favorite brunch spot, Eggs & Co., in an hour so we could rehash what exactly had happened the previous evening. I needed toast, coffee, and orange juice desperately.

Matthias stumbled out of the room and was lacing up his shoes. We had a small exchange about how hungover we were, and I gave him a bottle of water, aspirin, and some chewing gum. We exchanged an awkward hug goodbye, and I was relieved to be shutting the door to my flat behind him.

The first one night stand of my life. I honestly didn't even want to remember the details. I knew Matthias had been a gentleman and we had been safe. That's all I really cared to remember. I suddenly noticed the empty Champagne bottle sitting on my kitchen counter. According to Matthias, I had taken it home with me for a memory. Why would I want a memory of stupidity? All I could do was laugh. I threw on a sweater, my large sunglasses, and headed out the door to meet Sarah for eggs.

TWELVE

Champagne is a solemn, spiritual place—a place of great religious and historic significance. Indeed, for all its joyfulness as a wine, the region itself has been continually town apart by tragedy, especially during World War I and II, when it was a gruesome battlefield. As a result, there's a soulfulness here that's as palpable as the dazzling bubbles in every glass you'll have.

It was November 15, 2015, a beautiful, crisp Friday in Paris, and I was in a great mood as I was preparing for my date with Benjamin. I was feeling a sense of giddy anticipation.

This was going to be my third date with Benjamin, and I felt it would be telling for which direction I would go with him. I was debating going home with him but told myself to see where the night took us. I remembered his aggressive advances from before and wanted to be semi-prepared for this evening. We were meeting for a drink at Le Hibou, a quintessential spot with a brilliant terrace for people watching that boasted a lively atmosphere and great cocktails. After drinks, we planned to see a movie around ten o'clock. I was excited to see Benjamin. It had been over a week since I had last seen him, and after that meaningless drunken night with the Swedish guy, I craved connection and meaning. I felt Benjamin and I were building something, and it was a good hunch to have.

See you at 7 pm. Avec impatience!

This text came through from Benjamin a few hours before our date. I Google-translated *avec impatience*, and learned it meant "anxiously awaiting." This put a smile on my face, and I started to feel butterflies in my stomach. I am convinced that there is no better feeling for a woman to have than a new crush on a guy. I arrived to see Benjamin, tall in stature; wearing washed-out jeans, a black, button-down, long-sleeve shirt, a typical scarf; and eyed him putting out his cigarette when he glanced my way. Scarves and smoking—there are no two more foundational pillars to being French in my honest opinion.

We greeted each other with a rather passionate kiss from which he broke away and commented that he could kiss my lips for hours. He then kissed my neck, cheek, and forehead with small, meaningful pecks, and a rush of goose bumps overtook my body.

Benjamin and I definitely had chemistry; there was no denying it. We made our way to Le Hibou in the Carrefour de l'Odéon, a square which borders the chic Sixth Arrondissement, tightly gripping each other's hands. We spent the next three hours laughing, talking, and kissing at the café over strawberry mojitos. (I think he ordered these for me to feel that Americanized cocktail vibe. It was a small detail that was sweet. Little did he know I would have preferred the best Champagne on the wine list.) I felt really comfortable with Benjamin, and I sensed his interest in me. After a slight buzz had come over us, we walked hand in hand to the cinema and I made note that this was my first movie theater experience in Paris.

Around 10:35 p.m., I checked my phone while scrunched up in the theater chair, Benjamin's hand resting on my thigh. I had thirty text messages streaming in our group chat from everyone in my sommelier class. I saw messages popping up one after the other: *Are you safe? Everyone say yes! Please report in! Oh my GOD! How is this happening? 60 people were killed. No, now it is 80! They killed the second terrorist!*

Feeling the panic seep in, I scrolled up to the beginning of the message stream: *PARIS IS UNDER ATTACK!*

WHAT?!

I reread all of the texts and told Benjamin there was a terrorist attack happening right at that very moment. He told me to put my phone away and that we would check after the movie. *Are you kidding?* I showed him the messages my classmates were sending. No one else in the movie theater seemed to realize what was happening, instead remaining entranced in the movie. Ironically the movie we were seeing was called *Irrational Man*, and now there were radical, irrational terrorists shooting people on the other side of the river.

Sebastian messaged that he was in a restaurant and that they were in lockdown mode—doors locked, all lights out, hiding in the kitchen. He was on the right bank, the opposite side of the river from where I was seeing the movie, much closer to where the shootings were taking place. I could not believe no one had come in yet to have us evacuate the theater. I felt a pang in my stomach thinking about how scared Sebastian must have been in that dark kitchen. I tried to remain calm, though I still kept my eye on the messages and couldn't focus on the movie. The attacks had been in the Bataclan Concert Hall starting around 9:00 p.m. where a concert was taking place. Also down several streets people were shot in the Ninth and Tenth Arrondissements, and there had been shootings at a handful of cafés. This was unbelievable.

The movie was over, and Benjamin finally pulled out his phone. He grew horrified as he read the latest breaking news. Officials were telling people there were still terrorists on the loose and to get and stay inside. We walked outside the movie theater to find the streets of Paris were empty. It was the most eerie feeling ever, as usually Boulevard Saint-Germain would have been packed with people.

We walked in the direction of my flat as there were no taxis in sight, and at this point Benjamin was reading his text messages and confirming everyone in his life was okay. I asked if he wanted to come stay at my place, but he declined my offer. He said he was beside himself but would make sure I got home safely. When we embraced, he seemed so far away. A cold trance had come over him, and he could barely look at me. This attack was weighing heavily on him, I could tell. I didn't blame him. It was his country, his city, and the place where his entire life, pride, and joy was.

I had different emotions due to the foreignness of it all. I could always rush back to the States, but I was currently in a foreign country under attack. It was frightening to say the least. I rushed up the stairwell of my apartment. Once inside my attic apartment, I had texts, calls, and messages from everyone in my life back in the United States. I quickly phoned my mom and dad. I also sent messages to my sister and brother. They were of course in utter panic over this and told me to stay inside and not leave my apartment. The French president was closing the border, and France had declared a state of emergency for the first time since 1985. I was scared and could not sleep that night. I had feelings of anxiety, fear, and most importantly immense sadness for the people who had been killed and the families who had been affected.

The next day I was nervous to leave my apartment. Part of me was scared that France would be at war and that every day a new attack would surface. The other side of me remained positive because they had found and killed all of the terrorists involved in the attack. I decided to venture out and stock up as much as possible if for some reason I would need to remain inside. I walked the streets of Paris that day, and tears streamed down my face. I could feel the pain the city was feeling. I had never seen Paris so quiet. There was a ghostlike aura about the streets. People were not smiling, the café terraces were fairly empty, and it made me overwhelmed with sadness for Paris. It was not supposed to be this way.

Sebastian, Sarah, Pearl, and I decided to meet that night at a café for dinner. Yes, it was only the night after the attacks had occurred, but we needed to be around each other and support one another. I had not heard much from Benjamin, other than that I knew he had made it home safely and that he had repeatedly told me how upset this whole attack was making him. Luckily no one he knew had been in the crossfire. I could not imagine people who knew someone that had been killed. My stomach hurt just thinking about it. Then my mind would venture to: Were *we* safe? What measures was France taking to ensure the safety of its people? Would this happen again, and if so, where? It was anxiety-producing not to know the answers to these questions.

The next two nights I spent with my friends. We ate in cafés and then retreated to Sebastian's apartment both nights. We talked about the attacks of course, but tried to distract ourselves with a little bit of wine talk as well. I was becoming a bit upset that I had received very little contact from Benjamin. I would have preferred him to make sure I was okay and to want to see me again despite the turmoil. It was a disappointment as I had thought he had felt more for me.

In addition, my attic apartment was having problems. This sounds like such small potatoes in comparison to a terrorist attack, but over time, these small problems gathered in force until they significantly contributed to my stress. First the washer and dryer broke, and I had to shuffle my laundry to the laundromat every week. Then the floorboards started coming up, causing such a slant in the floor that I could barely open the refrigerator door. I sent pictures to the landlord and asked for it to be fixed immediately. The final straw was when the electric toilet stopped flushing, and I had to use public restrooms and pee in the shower. *Gross!* I put in my thirty-day notice and started searching online for a new apartment. I chalked up all the problems in the attic to a major sign I was not meant to stay there. However, I was starting to realize everything takes a bit longer in France. Back in the US, a plumbing issue or floorboards popping out of the floor probably could have been fixed that day if I'd requested it. I wouldn't have gone days with slower-than-molasses responses from my landlord.

I was now experiencing many waves of discomfort. Between the attacks, Benjamin's behavior, and my apartment having issues, I was starting to feel majorly homesick. It was during this time that I also received the following email.

> *Hello Frenchie!!! I miss you. Unfortunately, I am in jail.*
> *The thought of you has brought me through some tough times*
> *during the past few months. I want to thank you for the*
> *thousand kisses that you have given me that I can still feel on*
> *my face. You loved me, and I see that more than ever now.*
> *It's hard letting go. The last time we lost communication*
> *this long you were already dating. Hope you take time for*
> *yourself. I am safe and well and working on myself. I hope*
> *this email reaches you the same.*
>
> *With Love, Eddie*

Well, there was my answer for not having heard from Eddie in two months. He must have been arrested for a charge related to drug or alcohol use. Part of me was shocked reading this email. He was in *jail*. I could not believe someone I had shared five years of my life with was in jail. This was really bad, and my heart went out to him. The email also confirmed, though, that moving to Paris was the best decision of my life at that moment. I needed to get away from someone who had such an addiction that they would end up in this predicament, a person who undoubtedly would end up on the streets, in jail, or possibly even dead. Through these realizations, I still wished that I could have fixed Eddie. Wished that I could have taken this disease away from him. I decided I would not respond just yet. I almost did not want to know more details.

In order not to feel pain for someone I still deeply loved, my mind quickly switched to the fact that I needed to pack. Despite the attacks on Paris, we would be embarking on our first wine region trip as a class the next day. We were heading to the ever-romanticized region of Champagne. This was my first of five class trips throughout France, and even though I did not know what to expect, I knew that these trips would be absolutely memorable. We were meeting at the train station the next morning at five o'clock, and I was beyond ready to welcome the adventure and get out of Paris.

Our professors told us that after some debate, they believed it would be best for all of us to get out of Paris at this time anyway. Everyone was sad of course, and shaken by this event, but they stated they would not want to put a halt on our education when they felt it was perfectly safe for us to drive an hour and a half outside of Paris.

It was early morning. I squinted and looked out to the cold, gray sky with a slight drizzle of rain coming down. Our first tasting would be held at 9:00 a.m. I figured there were worse things than sipping quality Champagne in the early morning hours.

I rubbed my eyes to fully awaken from the catnap I had taken on the train. I guess after I inhaled the pain au chocolat given to me by Professor Lavigne, I had drifted off to sleep. We had arrived in Champagne. It was late November, and the vines were bare as the Champagne grapes are harvested at the same time as the harvest in Bordeaux. There was a chill in the air, and we were told our tour bus had fresh coffee for us and more pastries. Hallelujah.

I stepped into the tour bus and quickly realized this was no joke. We each had our own plush seat, with a water bottle and storage for our things. I did not realize we would be taken around Champagne, France, in a first-class bus. Coffee was being passed around, and pastry platters made their way through the bus, with the wafting smell of baked butter and glazed sugar. I was awake!

The bus drove down a main road, and we passed the Lanson Champagne house and vineyard; my eyes widened when we passed by Veuve Clicquot. We were making our way to Ulysse Collin, an artisan vineyard with a plot of some of the best terroir in all of Champagne. Ulysse Collin was located in the town of Cogny, a commune in Champagne.

The bus stopped on a gravel dirt road. It was still lightly drizzling, and we all downed our coffee and grabbed umbrellas.

We were led into a cellar, where introductions to the Champagne makers were made. Over the course of the next two hours, we tasted eight different Champagnes, each one better than the next.

Most of Ulysse Collin Champagnes are *extra brut*, which means there is absolutely no sugar added to enhance the flavor. The land there is so good at developing complexity in the Champagnes that there is no need to manipulate the taste profile by adding sugar, also known as *dosage* in wine terms. The wine would be balanced enough from the terroir alone.

Chalk. Chalk was very prevalent in the soil in Champagne, and when you smelled the wine in the glass, if you got chalk aromas, that was a very good thing. In just a two-hour period I had learned so much. To think that this was our first Champagne house of three that day, I could only envision where my knowledge level would be when I returned to Paris.

We wrapped up the tour of Ulysse Collin and jumped back in the tour bus. We were venturing to Duval-Leroy next. I was looking forward to this, as this was a female-run company and I could not wait to become inspired. We would taste eight to ten more Champagnes and then have a multi-course lunch.

Driving in the bus along the roads of Champagne was a great way for me to be able to compare this landscape with the Bordeaux vineyards. Champagne definitely seemed more rustic, and even though there were massive houses producing Champagne in an industry worth 4.5 billion dollars, it seemed more conservative and private than Bordeaux. Bordeaux had been more picturesque, with chateaus and absolutely stunning vineyards spaced through-out rolling hills.

In lecture, we had learned that Champagne was broken down into five regions. First, there was the Montagne de Reims, which produces mostly Pinot-Noir-heavy Champagnes. Pinot Noir is the most revered of Champagne's two red grapes. It often contributes to body, texture, and aroma in the wine. Due to it being a red-skinned grape, all you need is the juice, and without skin contact, that juice will produce a white wine. The flesh is always white in the grape, but the Pinot Noir has a depth of flavor and richness that lends itself to some of the most top quality Champagnes. As such, many *tête de cuvée* (or top bottles) from major Champagne houses come from Montagne de Reims.

Secondly, the Côte des Blancs produces mostly Chardonnay. Its soil is chalk-based and produces wines with higher acidity, wines that are considered very elegant and highly sought after. Then there is the Vallée de la Marne, which produces mostly Pinot Meunier, the third grape allowed to be grown in Champagne, known for its fruity and unctuous flavors. Next, there is the Côte de Sézanne, which again has chalky soils and produces mostly Chardonnay; these wines, due to the region's frequent sunshine, are less acidic compared to the Blanc de Blancs of the Côte des Blancs. Finally, the Aube (also known as Côte des Bar) produces mostly Pinot Noir in marl soils, which tend to be aromatic wines with less acidity.

Duval-Leroy was in the Côte des Blancs, in a commune called Vertus.

After our tour of Duval-Leroy we sat down at a long conference table and geared up to compare the taste profiles of the eight Champagnes laid before us. This was a very intense hour, and I secretly hoped not to be called on. My palate was already exhausted as well as my mind. All of the Champagnes were blending together and starting to taste the same. I was relieved when Professor Lavigne called on another student, Benoit, to detect the final glass. Phew!

Shortly after, we entered a beautiful dining room where there were lovely table settings and four glasses for each seat. Over this multi-course lunch, we would actually be getting to *drink* the Champagnes, not just taste and spit them out. There was also red wine served, as the main course was a *magret de canard*. I still could not believe the treatment we were receiving between the tour bus, the lavish lunch, the private tours and explanations, and the conference table made to make us feel like the utmost professionals in this industry. The multi-course lunch was outstanding, and my belly was full by the end. We would venture next to the Jacques Selosse vineyard, another artisan Champagne maker, and then finally we would arrive at our hotel. Shortly after we would be whisked away to dinner at a fabulous restaurant. As if I could be any more in love with France, this was putting a lot of icing on my cake.

I checked my phone nine hours into this day and still had no news from Benjamin. Part of me couldn't believe he was ghosting me, but mostly I just wondered if he was okay. I thought about sending a message or even calling him, but I needed to stay focused on my class trip. I was realizing there was an eerie similarity to how I acted with Eddie here: I would feel bad about my partner's behavior, or mistreated in some way, not valued, and then somehow still care about them and want to know why. What was wrong with me that made them act like that? I placed my worth in these moments in someone else's hands. It was almost like this incessant challenge to get them to like me again or to act how they did in the beginning.

Whenever I spoke to Sarah about it, she would just be like, "Thank you, next!" She was very quick to not care if a French guy snubbed her; she didn't waste time analyzing their behavior. I wished I had that same energy. Sarah had been casually dating a French guy we had met out the night of Halloween. She was always saying how it was a fun experience to date him, but he was not really her match. She had physical chemistry with him but not much else.

She told me a story about how they were walking down the sidewalk when, out of nowhere, he started breaking down crying about some client he had, and she was so turned off. She stated, "He is like a frantic, high-energy guy that's flying off the walls making green juices. There is no salted butter from Normandy or toasted baguettes involved!"

I laughed. Then Sarah said something that I will never forget. "Krista, if he took me to brunch, I would be over the moon. But that's not what is happening. We are not canoodling in cafés and having picnics on the Seine. It's just more or less a hookup situation. My feeling is we are and will always be just a good time to the French guys, nothing more, and they are not taking us seriously."

She said this in response to my anguish about Benjamin. I didn't like this statement, and she could see it written all over my face. She was headstrong in her belief that we wouldn't actually be meeting guys with French-husband potential here, but I thought that was too general or too declarative. I especially did not want to listen to this, as in my journals I was writing about my fantasy of having a French husband; maybe I would meet a winemaker in Champagne and get married on the vineyard. When someone told me my future personal life probably wouldn't involve France, I wanted so desperately to disprove that.

Dinner turned out to be absolutely fabulous, and after that we went to a pool hall, where we shot billiards and sipped digestifs. Yes, in the little charming town we were in, you could count on my cohort to find the only bar open on the street. Some of my classmates drank hard liquor like it was going out of style, but I stayed true to just sipping something. We had consumed a great deal of alcohol over the course of the day despite the fact that at the vineyards we were required to spit all of the Champagnes we tasted. My head hit the pillow that night, and I fell into a deep sleep.

The next day we awoke and met in the hotel dining room for breakfast before we set out on the most anticipated Champagne vineyards of all: Dom Pérignon, Moët, Louis Roederer, and Bollinger. I grabbed a yogurt and coffee and spread a toasted slice of baguette with orange marmalade and salted butter. Any time I got the chance to participate in the typical French tartine for *petit dejeuner,* I took full advantage of it. I had barely spooned my last mouthful of yogurt from the glass jar when our translator motioned for us to board the tour bus. We were off for another full day of intense learning and tasting, and I needed to concentrate desperately.

Arriving at the entrance of the Louis Roederer mansion was definitely a top experience for me. I was entranced into a slice of heaven on earth. There were white marble walls and floors, with elegant angel statues adorning every slant of the room. As I looked up I was certain the ceilings could have reached the sky. Rich, deep blue velvet curtains created a border around the floor-to-ceiling windows, which looked out onto the lush garden landscapes of flowers and greenery. Rose-gold satin ties held the navy curtains gracefully apart. There was a wood-burning fireplace with elegant and intrinsic moldings and design, topped with massive mirrors that made the formal living room appear colossal. The logs burned and created a heavenly cherrywood and cinnamon potpourri that permeated the entry and living space. A large, seashell-white grand piano punctuated the entryway.

This was all captivating my senses, and then my coat was taken by one of the three butlers that appeared in front of me. Another butler, dressed in a tuxedo, came around the other side of me and greeted me with a glass of Champagne. "A glass of Cristal vintage 2006, Madame." Then another came up and addressed me with a smile, led me through the foyer, and directed me to take a seat on the plush, perfect cream sofa with fur pillows and sheep-skin blankets.

Pearl and I stared at each other as the sliced smoked salmon and gingerbread stuffed with foie gras was making its way around on platters, and exchanged wide-eyed smiles. *Was this real?* The only way I can describe this moment is to say that I was absolutely convinced I was royalty. This was the treatment of someone with great power and standing. I had never experienced anything like it.

The next three hours were spent sitting on the sofas, with butlers waiting on us hand and foot, making sure we were at the utmost level of comfort. Platters of the most delicious bites made their way around the room, and the discussion of some of the greatest vintages Louis Roederer has ever made was the main topic of conversation, along with why certain vintages were the best and what about the Champagnes being presently tasted set them apart from the others. My last glass of Champagne over this exquisite petit four lunch was a coupe of Cristal 2002. The bubbles practically dissolved into thin air on my tongue, and the aromas of ripe peaches, toasted hazelnuts, and buttery waffles put me into sensory overload. I took a bite of a wild baby strawberry tart dusted with lemon sugar and drifted back into heaven as the flames of the fire were the only aspect keeping my vision in the room we were in, here on earth.

Our next stop would be exploring the wine caves of Dom Pérignon. I absolutely did not think that anything could top the Louis Roederer mansion, but I'd been proven wrong before.

I had my souvenir bottles of Moët and Dom Pérignon in tow, along with the large, sparkly pink Moët & Chandon glass I had purchased. We were boarding the train back to Paris. I was pleasantly exhausted from our intense three-day trip in Champagne, France. Nothing could have prepared me for what we had been able to experience: visiting the wine cellar that housed vintages of Dom Pérignon dating back to 1921; sitting in a mansion at Louis Roederer being treated as royalty, which I am far from, and being served by multiple butlers; the extreme wealth of knowledge I had retained about Champagne making and this region of France in general; the superb meals and the enjoyable memories I had created with my classmates.

It was all so wonderful, and now I was anxious to get back to Paris. This is how I knew I was still in love with the city. I always felt an adrenaline rush on my way back to Paris from anywhere. Be it a train ride or a flight, I was ecstatic that Paris was where I was centered and that I was able to call it home. I never took advantage of this and was always aware and full of gratitude. It was slightly different this time, due to the terrorist attacks and the fact that we had only been gone three days. Would Paris still feel like there was a black cloud over it? During the train ride I sent Benjamin a text. I hoped he would respond by the time the train pulled into Paris.

It was nine thirty, and I had finally made it back to my flat. I took a steaming hot shower and unpacked my things. I was not in the mood to drink any wine as our trip had been utterly loaded with Champagne and plenty of food. I felt like I needed a detox after I had indulged so richly—I laughed at the thought of downing wheatgrass shots with Sarah's French guy—but it had been more than worth it. I still had not heard from Benjamin, and this was making me feel very uneasy. How could he just stop contacting me? It was shocking to me, especially since we had been building such great chemistry and had experienced the night of the attacks together. As one of my friends had said, he could never forget me now: when Paris was under attack, I was the girl he had been with. That statement didn't make me feel better; in fact it made me feel more invisible than ever. For the second time in a few days, I was reminded of the abandoned feeling I would experience when Eddie would disappear for days on end. Same feeling, different man.

Things in Paris seemed to have made a light shift back to normal, although not completely by any means. There hadn't been any attacks since, but there were armed military guards at every major monument walking around with rifles, as well as on every major boulevard. Rumors were flying around that a major tourist hub such as Notre Dame, the Palais-Royale, or the Luxembourg Gardens would be the next target attacked, so there was extra security and caution everywhere. The military made me feel safer knowing that if shooting started they would be there quickly to shoot out and kill the terrorist. It was still the oddest feeling ever, though, walking around Paris, with the thoughts that shots could be fired at any time. It took away the carefree feeling for sure. There was a looming energy despite everyone trying to resume normal life. I avoided the metro and always looked around whenever I sat down at a café, making sure no one looked suspicious. It reminded me of how things felt in the States after 9/11. The collective energy was saddened, and things changed. There was a feeling of the unknown, of anxiety and fear, even though I had been on the other side of the country on September 11, 2001. This time I had only been on the other side of the river.

The day after we returned from Champagne, I was meeting Sarah on the rue de Seine, a quaint little street in the Saint Germain des Prés. We were going to explore the charming back roads and pop into the boutiques together. The boulevards and alleys that made up the Left Bank were postcard-worthy, and I had to stop and admire this whenever I was out and about. Any Parisian dream I had ever conjured up, this exceeded my expectations. We strolled around all afternoon, popping into the Mariage Frères tea salon, bookstores, clothing boutiques, handmade jewelry shops, and finally stopped to share a platter of oysters and a bottle of rosé at a charming café called L'Atlas in Odéon.

"So Benjamin just literally never responded. That is so bizarre," Sarah said with a confused expression on her face.

"I know. I don't get it. What should I do?" I genuinely loved Sarah's opinion. She had much more experience with dating than I did, as she hadn't been in long-term relationships as I had. She had wisdom on different personalities in men and how they handle certain situations.

"I think you should text him something to get his attention. If he isn't responding to something nice, get a little feisty, passionate and angry." Sarah's eyes widened at the thought of this. "He is Latin, and they like a crazy, passionate woman sometimes."

I laughed out loud at this suggestion. The rosé also seemed to be hitting my bloodstream. I figured, *Why not? What do I have to lose? He wasn't responding anyway.* We conjured up what I should say and laughed at the thought of him receiving it.

What happened to you? I texted. *There must be something wrong with you. Don't get it at all!! What the fuck??* I pressed send and took a deep breath. I just wanted an answer; no one disappears into thin air like a ghost. At least, if they do, I refuse to accept it. Maybe he had a wife or girlfriend at home; I was suspicious of that twenty-five-year-old roommate. Sarah had stopped dating the green juice guy and started dating another man, Matthieu, whom she had met on the metro. They apparently made eye contact, and she got lightly bumped to brush his side. They realized they had the same birthday and I guess started a casual fling. She said this was interesting as, unlike Green Juice Frenchie, this man didn't speak English so well. Again her attitude was that she was not super into him; she was just out for a fun time and someone to cuddle, kiss, and have sex with.

Our next topic of conversation was the fact that Thanksgiving was coming up. Yes, we were in Paris, but we still felt nostalgic for our US traditions and we could not miss honoring Thanksgiving. Sarah had a larger apartment than I did, and we decided to have a dinner party there and actually roast a turkey, make homemade mashed potatoes, and sauté green beans. We would invite Pearl, Sebastian, and a few others from class. I was so excited to cook all day and celebrate Thanksgiving in Paris.

The day of Thanksgiving, I decided to head to Le Bon Marché, a famous epicurean department store with every gourmet food-related item you could think of. Le Bon Marché literally translates into "the good price," but that could not have been further from the truth because this store was like Whole Foods on steroids. This was a food lover's paradise, and my friends and I actually frequented their wine cave for glasses of Champagne and charcuterie plates. I wandered the aisles and picked out a good bottle of Burgundy Pinot Noir that would pair perfectly with the turkey. There would be about ten of us celebrating at Sarah's. I also grabbed a nice bottle of Champagne. Then, I made my way to the elaborate pastry case that seemed to run a mile long, and purchased a pristine apple tart that was so beautiful I didn't know if I would be able to slice it and break the perfectly fanned apple slices later. This paired with the ever famous salted caramel ice cream from Berthillon, a legendary ice cream retailer in Paris, would be divine.

I arrived at Sarah's around eleven o'clock to get to work in the kitchen. We put on Christmas music, something I always did growing up on Thanksgiving, and started preparing the meal. Sebastian was purchasing an assortment of breads from a nearby bakery as well as bringing several bottles of wine. Pearl was in charge of cheese platters and charcuterie, and everyone else was told to bring whatever they wanted. We were mixing American tradition with a little French formality, and it was going to be the perfect evening.

As I was boiling the potatoes and making a salad dressing, I couldn't help but think about the differences between France and America. It was times like Halloween and Thanksgiving that I really missed the US. These holidays, which aren't celebrated the world over, just didn't feel the same in France. I quickly felt a sense of pride for my own country, and I felt my eyes getting a bit watery as I thought about what my family would be doing on this day. Every year since I was three years old, my immediate family as well as my cousins, aunts, uncles, and grandparents would all head to the beach on Thanksgiving and rent a house in Santa Cruz, California. We would spend four to five days there and have beach bonfires, gorge on clam chowder and crab cakes, participate in daily beach walks, and go on shopping trips to the charming nearby city of Carmel. I loved and cherished those memories from my childhood. Now, I was creating a new blend of memories of Thanksgiving with French and American friends.

THIRTEEN

Above all, great Burgundies are stunningly complex.
Drinking them can be an exercise in discernment, refinement,
and delicious patience as subtle layer of flavor after subtle layer
of flavor reveals itself. Indeed, Burgundy is most certainly
the 'quiet music' of wine—not the rap.

66 I will take it!" I made this declarative statement from the living room of a charming sixth-floor flat with a partial view of Notre Dame. Yes, I could not believe it was an apartment in my price range, newly remodeled with a glimpse of the stunning cathedral. Also, it happened to be located only a block from

the Seine. I felt as if I had won the lottery. It was only twenty-two square meters, but the architect had done such an amazing job with it, it felt much more spacious than that. This apartment had tall ceilings, off-white walls, chandeliers, and floor-to-ceiling windows in both the bedroom and the living area. The bathroom and kitchen had been newly updated as well. There was a gas fireplace in the bedroom, a large flatscreen TV, and windows staring out at the cathedral. I just could not understand how this place fit within my budget. It was exactly what I had envisioned when I had pictured life in Paris. *A true dream.*

"No problem, I will not show it to anyone else." I smiled in disbelief when the rental agent said this to me. I put a deposit down and had my very own gorgeous flat that I was absolutely smitten with. I felt I must have had a good luck charm, as this was the first place I looked at. The rental agent said it had not even been put on the market, and had usually been rented to tourists due to its stunning charm. Rentals in Paris were ultra-competitive, and you were lucky to get a place, much less the place of your dreams. I signed a yearlong lease and received the keys two days later. This apartment, compared to the attic—well, there was no comparison.

Once I had moved all of my things in, I decided to throw a small housewarming party to celebrate finding my ideal apartment in Paris. I invited Sebastian, Sarah, and Pearl over, and we popped a nice bottle of Champagne, one of the bottles of Moët I had purchased on our recent trip. That night was one of those moments that I felt full of gratitude, not only for my new apartment, but also for the genuine friendships I had developed. It really made me feel that I was fully integrated in Paris and I had created somewhat of a life for myself. A happy life. To be studying wine in France was a dream in and of itself, but to also have deep-rooted friendships already, and to be living in a charming Parisian apartment that marked the very center of Paris, was bringing me an absolute sense of joy and completeness. I was starting to feel at home in Paris.

It was already December, time seemed to be flying by, and there was a lot coming up in sommelier school. Our last class trip to Champagne had been sincerely memorable, and next we would be venturing to the historic and emblematic chateaus of Bordeaux. I couldn't wait to go back to Bordeaux as I had such fond memories from October. We would also be working an event at the Louvre known as the Grand Tasting, which was rumored to be an intense twelve-hour day of work in the field of wine. We would be serving wine all day to rooms of top professionals who were analyzing it. The pressure would be on to carry tray after tray of wine glasses and not spill or, heaven forbid, drop a tray. Also, all wines would need to be kept at the proper temperature and stored accordingly. After this long event, we would be treated to dinner at a restaurant known as Le Petit Sommelier de Paris, which supposedly had an elite and fabulous wine list. I would also be going home to California for a week at Christmas time to visit my family. I could not believe it had been almost four months that I had been living in France. Already, so much had happened. So much would happen, too, but for now, I was enjoying my new apartment with dear friends.

"Cheers, santé. To an awesome year so far… and much more to come!" stated Sebastian, and with that the four of us clinked our glasses of Champagne.

"To Krista's new, amazing flat!" Pearl exclaimed enthusiastically.

"Thanks for celebrating this with me, you guys," I added, "and to new friendships!"

"Yes! I already feel like I have known you all forever," Sarah said.

Sebastian changed the conversation by sharing his latest dating news. He was in a new relationship. He had started dating a French man much older than he—closer to fifty, whereas Sebastian was twenty-seven—who was a successful attorney in Paris and a published author of several books including one on eroticism. *Interesting.* Sebastian piqued my curiosity, as I felt that, like me, he wanted something meaningful and serious in Paris. Sarah was more flippant about it, but Sebastian I felt was dating to be in something real. "His name is David," he said. "He is very wealthy; he lives in the Seventh Arrondissement." I could see the pride on his face, and the utter enjoyment he was feeling of setting down roots here. For me it was my apartment and house party; for him it was a man. We were all glued to the conversation, sipping our Champagne and passing around the cheese board.

I had picked up several cheeses earlier that day from the renowned cheese shop Laurent Dubois. We would be savoring them smashed in between pillows of heaven from Erik Kayser's boulangerie. I also had a big surprise and was anticipating opening a very treasured Burgundy I had purchased. It was from the Meursault appellation, which happened to be my favorite wine of all time. The other perk to my charming little flat was that it was located at Place Maubert, which was a small square that housed the cheese shop, a wine shop, a patisserie, and a famous butcher. I had everything I needed right at my fingertips. They say, at least we were learning in wine school, to never pair cheese and Champagne. However, sometimes we liked to break the traditional French gastronomic rules. We loved cheese *and* Champagne, and so be it, we would consume them at the same time. I was also waiting for the right time to break out the Meursault.

It was interesting learning about all the French traditions, customs such as coffee with milk only in the morning and a shot of espresso after each meal to aid in digestion. Another one was that cheese and salad come after the main course as a punctuation to the savory side of the dining experience. The salad with a vinegar-and-mustard-based dressing also sliced through any rich dish consumed in the previous course. There were reasons and awareness behind the French dining experience, and I found this utterly fascinating. There was even a saying we learned, *bon transit*, meaning essentially, "Have a good digestion and bowel movement!" If you stuck to small portions of fruits and vegetables with protein and a little bread, and were sure to add in your cleansing salad, you should have luck in the *bon transit* department.

I was trying my best to consume the typical French diet, though I was guilty of eating more pastries than the skinny Parisian woman and possibly an extra glass of wine that I indulged in daily for pure pleasure. I did this knowing I may have had an extra five pounds on me, but I was in Paris, and I didn't know how long I would be living around these French delicacies. Food had been my emotional crutch growing up, and I struggled through a chubby phase, in high school of all times. Perhaps this was why I found myself obsessed with French women. They were thin *and* enjoyed food. How was this possible? My fascination with France and food ultimately led me to French cooking school where I turned into a food snob, not a food addict, which then led me to be a chef. Snobbery embodied the French woman, but in a good way. They turned their noses up at someone not dressed well as they felt that person didn't respect themselves enough. They wouldn't speak to a stranger and guarded their personal lives unless they deemed that person important enough to tell. Back in Bordeaux, I remember asking Catherine why she wasn't eating the crème caramel one evening. She replied, "I have tasted it, but I respect myself too much. I adore crème caramel, though." I took that as: "I am more important. My health, my body's maintenance is more important, even though it's there, delicious, and everyone else is partaking." I also loved that she owned the honest reason instead of giving an excuse. It never went unnoticed, the level of respect the French not only show to themselves but to other things. Maybe this was the spark of my preoccupation with the French: the sense of confidence, respect, and the absolute element of putting yourself first.

"This comté is so high quality—Krista, did you get the one aged twelve months or twenty-four?" Sarah asked as she inhaled a slice with baguette and fig preserves. I of course had gotten the best of the best and responded twenty-four months. Comté was a popular French cheese, a newfound favorite of mine that you couldn't find in the States.

We returned to the topic of our love lives soon after that.

I still had not heard a peep from Benjamin, and my friends were astounded. How could someone just disappear? Nothing was said, and there was zero closure on why I never heard from him again after the night of the attacks. An eerie feeling invaded my body just thinking about it. I had never had this sensation in my life, of complete confusion, not knowing why someone had come into and out of my life so quickly. If this was an introduction to how French men behaved toward women, I did not want to experience anymore of it.

However, I still had my profile up on the dating site, and had been on one other date on which I had felt no attraction to or connection with the guy. It was a great conversation over a glass of wine, and then we went our separate ways. I wanted that excitement I had felt when I saw Benjamin, and I would not date a French man just to *date* a French man. No matter what country I was in, I was picky in the sense of needing a certain feeling, a feeling of being needed, I was discovering slowly, and not much else.

It was my turn. I balanced the ten glasses on the tray, then glanced down at my right hand and noticed my wrist was shaking just a hint, like an alcoholic needing a shot of liquor to calm them. I continued to focus on my wrist. *Please stop*, I told my brain… just then the curtain opened.

"Okay, Krista, on y va," Michel said, motioning for me to enter the room. I walked in a straight line down the stage. The spotlight was on me as the audience stared at the glasses, anticipating the wine that would soon be available to them to taste. I made eye contact with the first judge. I remembered to hold the circular rim at the bottom of the glass tight to the tray; this would force the tray to balance as I removed each one. I carefully set each glass in front of each judge down the row. I tried to set it directly in the ten o'clock position to their left. My last glass left the tray, and I took a deep breath. Next I had to go to the first row of the audience with that same tray and take the empty glasses from the last pour, and then one of my classmates would follow immediately with yet another tray of ten glasses. The synchronicity was highly important.

The Grand Tasting turned out to be both a success and a complete disaster. It was a success in the sense that no one in the tasting room had any wine spilled on them or any trays dropped in their laps. To the room of thirty-plus wine experts, we must have seemed flawless in our work after executing the tasting hour after hour. However, it was behind closed doors that things were really a nightmare, the ultimate challenge of working with one another under pressure. Every twenty minutes ten trays with ten glasses of wine on each would need to be sent into the tasting room. There was a team leader on every tasting, and if they did not lead the others well, it all seemed to fall apart at the seams. Though it sounds weird to say, it turned into a battle of the Asian students against the French. I stayed out of the crossfire pretty much, so to speak, though the tension in the room was dicernible.

"You really want me to just take the fucking glasses in there now?!" Jen, a feisty woman from Korea, screamed at Sandrine, one of the French girls, who was holding a tray that was about to slip from her hands.

"Yes, yes, I do. I am leading this tasting! Do it," Sandrine yelled back. I was worried at this point that the tasters could hear this nonsense backstage. All of the rest of us just kept our heads down and continued pouring wine into glasses. What was astounding to me was that our professor just let everyone rip each other's heads off screaming, and stayed calm and focused and continued to give direction. It seemed completely as if he had expected this behavior. My jaw dropped to the floor when Benoit asked Kimi, one of the girls from China, if she was stupid when he felt she was pouring too much wine into the glasses. He glared at her like he was going to pull out a knife. I could not believe the way we were treating each other—the proverbial we, I suppose, as I and the other American students were just witnesses. If I had to guess where the tension was coming from, it was the French students' innate and somewhat territorial pride over their knowledge of their country's wine coming to a head with the Asian students' eagerness to learn about French wine culture and benefit from it after graduating from the program.

The tension was intense, and this wasn't the first time the Asian-versus-French issue had arisen. The previous month it had become apparent that competition was at an all-time high. In lectures, the Asian students sat at the front of the class, playing teacher's pet and asking tons of questions. The French were subdued and in the back of the classroom, seemingly knowing some of the answers to the questions, and the Asian students' eagerness annoyed them to no end. Eye rolls coming from them were common. Agitation was paramount. It didn't help when the Asian students would walk into the classroom comparing their Hermès wallets and new purchases from Louis Vuitton. The French seemed appalled by their immense displays of wealth. They didn't seem to recognize the concept that the international students coming and supporting this institution most likely had money to spend in their country. This fact made it possible for this wine program to exist. The French economy needed the support of this global wealth. Sarah and I were determined to stay neutral the entire time. I understood the cultural differences, and I enjoyed both. I was also on good terms with all of my fellow students, and I didn't want that to change.

Annie, a girl from Taiwan, waltzed into the room and asked Sandrine, "Do you have a problem with me? If you do, fucking say it to my face."

Sandrine turned white as a ghost. "What are you talking about, Annie?" Her voice was shaking in her surprised state.

"I know you and Suzette were talking shit. We are here to learn. Grow up!" She stormed out of the back room and headed down the hallway. Hopefully she would come back and finish professionally. I had a feeling Lavigne would suspend her from the program if she didn't. This tasting wasn't necessarily receiving a grade, but we did have to attend it and work it as part of the curriculum.

Professor Lavigne was on edge and expected perfection from all of us. His name was behind this event to all the serious wine professionals of France. He would shake his head in disgust if someone messed up. The stress was disconcerting.

It was twelve hours of high tension, and there was no greater feeling than when we had sent out the last ten trays of wine. There were a few really nice bottles of wine left, out of which our professor poured us each a small glass. Everyone raised their glasses, though some people were still carrying around some animosity and the grins lining their faces were forced. The class had become divided, when the intention was to work seamlessly together. The teams were composed totally at random by Mr. Porter, but by the end the divide was clear.

After this event, I could only imagine how dinner that evening at Le Petit Sommelier would go, not to mention the upcoming Bordeaux trip.

FOURTEEN

Great wines do not have flavors that are muddled or blurry.
Great wines have flavors—whatever those flavors are—
that are precise, well defined, and expressive.

It was December 15, and we were setting out for Bordeaux. This would be our longest class trip of the year, and we would spend a total of three full days there. Our itinerary was packed with vineyards, tastings, and education. We would be lucky enough to be spending a half day in Saint-Émilion, and I was already nostalgic remembering my time spent there that past September and October.

Tension was still running high between some classmates. I was hoping that sharing meals together and bonding over great Bordeaux wines would ease the stiffness. We were about to embark on an adventure and visit some of the most emblematic and historical chateaus in the regions of Saint-Émilion, Sauternes, and Médoc. The listing was unbelievable, and I knew I was going to be privy to places most people were not.

I stared out the train window at the planes of green grass and country homes scattered in the distance. Earlier that week, I had been on an incredible date with a chef named Frédéric. We had met at a wine bar in the Saint Germain des Prés, and then he had taken me on his motorcycle, cruising over all the major bridges of Paris. We finally settled into a restaurant at eleven o'clock, and had a dinner that lasted multiple courses. I felt so carefree and alive on this date. It had been so fun and exactly what I needed after the bizarre disappearance of Benjamin and the depressive email Eddie had sent from jail. I wondered if I would ever see Frédéric the chef again. In my gut I didn't think so, and I didn't know why. I was starting to realize Paris was full of moments in time. I was starting to feel a bit like an actress. Each day was bringing something so brand new, but also something fleeting. I was smart enough to grasp the fact that the people here viewed life differently than I did. A great date does not necessarily mean anything. It is just that, a great evening shared with someone new. It was as if it evaporated, but the memory was still there. I hadn't felt a connection to anyone but Benjamin, and I feared I was going to become immune to the dissipation of moments.

Four hours later we arrived in Bordeaux. I was feeling a bit exhausted after waking up at 4:30 a.m. and was anticipating a full day. We were arriving at our first chateau in the commune and appellation of Sauternes, which is known for its sweet wines. Sauternes is a French sweet wine and is made using only the Semillon, Sauvignon Blanc, or Muscadelle grapes, unlike in the Saint-Émilion appellation, where the grapes that could be grown were Merlot, Cabernet Franc, Cabernet Sauvignon, Malbec, and Petit Verdot. Sauternes are also made from grapes that have been affected by Botrytis Cinerea, also known as noble rot. This gives the wine the sweetness as the grapes become partially raisined, resulting in very concentrated wines.

This is why appellation was so meaningful. France uses appellations to legally define and protect a certain geographical indication used to identify where the grapes for a wine are allowed to be grown. Restrictions other than geographical boundaries, such as what grapes may be grown, maximum grape yields, alcohol level, and other quality factors may apply before an appellation can legally be stated on a wine label.

Our first stop was Château Guiraud. I remember getting out of the tour bus to see what looked like a castle mixed with an old farmhouse. There were towers of yellow stucco and massive columns combined with traditional old French windows. There was a long, pebble pathway up to the entrance of the chateau. Brick fireplaces lined the outside of this enormous building. The smell of cherrywood permeated the air from the grand fireplace just through the entrance of the tasting room. We were welcomed and given a quick briefing on Sauternes and the wine style that is produced in the region. Then, cheese gougères and other small bites were passed around, with our first pour of Sauternes, perfectly matched to the appetizers and handed out by the glass.

We learned the history of Château Guiraud and then were led into a grand dining room where the private chef would prepare a multi-course lunch for us. It had a holiday theme, due to Christmas fast approaching, and there were garlands of holly at each table setting. The menu was impeccable; all courses were paired with Sauternes vintages from Guiraud. We started with lemongrass cream and oven-baked oysters on the half shell. The next course was veal shank, which melted in my mouth alongside hot, roasted winter root vegetables. The cheese course was fried Boucheron goat cheese, and finally the dessert was a honey and saffron crème brûlée. Everything tasted so well balanced, and the entire lunch was pleasurable from start to finish. Feeling relaxed and in contented bliss, we hopped into our comfy limo bus and were off to the famous and world-renowned Château d'Yquem.

Nobility that has stood the test of time, I wrote in my diary to describe Château d'Yquem. *Proudly sitting atop a rise overlooking the surrounding countryside, the sixteenth-century chateau exudes an intrinsic majesty.* It wasn't lost on me that I was standing in a four-hundred-year-old chateau. The history of where I was at that moment gave me chills.

Upon arrival, we were greeted with the vintage 2005 Château d'Yquem. Professor Lavigne always name-dropped this wine. This one and Petrus out of Pomerol were chateaus he was entranced by, and he made sure we all knew it. After a beautiful lesson on the history of winemaking, which started with Farmer Yquem going all the way back to 1604, we tasted another few vintages. Château d'Yquem is now owned by LVMH, or Louis Vuitton Moët Hennessy. Château d'Yquem was a Premier Cru Supérieur wine and was in the Bordeaux Wine Official Classification of 1855. It was the only Sauternes to be given this rating, indicating perceived superiority and deserving high prices over all other wines of its type. We were served several other vintages of Château d'Yquem that day as we got to tour the barrel room, private cellar, and walk through this exquisite property. It was breathtaking, and the most important lesson I took away was that Yquem's success stems from the site's susceptibility to gain the noble rot that is needed to produce Sauternes. They have the best land, and it's placed in the perfect terroir. Wines from Château d'Yquem are characterized by their complexity, concentration, and sweetness, which is balanced by a relatively high acidity. With proper care a bottle can keep for a century or more, and the fruity overtones will gradually fade and integrate with more complex secondary and tertiary flavors, giving the wine that much more depth.

I was starting to get a slight headache from all the sweet wines, but the day was far from over. Our next stop was Château Smith Haut Lafitte in the Pessac-Léognan appellation; this chateau was ranked in the Bordeaux classification of Cru Classés des Graves. Graves was located on the Left Bank of Bordeaux, whereas Saint-Émilion was on the right bank. "Bank," just like in Paris with the Seine, was in reference to the river that ran through the region. Saint-Émilion is known for lighter, more fruit-forward red wines with a larger percentage and presence of Merlot grapes, whereas in Graves we would be tasting wines heavier in the Cabernet Sauvignon grape.

During the longer drive to the new appellation, there was entertainment and slight tipsiness on the limo bus. The one good thing about this class trip, in the form of social activity, was that Sarah had organized a Secret Santa gift exchange. We would leave small gifts for whatever name we had drawn either on the tour bus or in the person's hotel room.

I had drawn Annie, the student from Taiwan. She had a very strong personality, and we all knew she loved very nice Champagne. Very nice as in 300-euro bottles. I had purchased a bottle of Perrier-Jouët and was excited to give this to her. As we were driving to the next chateau, Sarah suddenly announced that she had drawn none other than me. She presented me with a very lovely bottle of Hermitage, which was trending as my favorite as I had become obsessed with Syrah. She also bought me five packs of gum, as everyone was onto my gum addiction that I hadn't seemed to break ever since Genevieve pointed it out on my first day in Paris. My professor even had to write on the white board one day, "PLEASE NO CHEWING GUM." The final joke gift was three condoms that said "I love PARIS!" Everyone knew that I was the poster child for Paris and my love of it. Every person on the bus laughed in hysterics upon that last gift. I could feel everyone was starting to not be as tense, and the vibe was becoming light and fun again.

That evening we dined on a multi-course meal and were given a tasting of Margaux, which is indeed another appellation of Bordeaux known for some of the best wines in the world. The final Margaux we tasted that evening was around 800 euros a bottle, as it was from vintage 1979 and Grand Cru Classé. *Absolutely incredible.*

Over the next two days we visited the following vineyards and appellations remaining on the Left Bank: Château Cos d'Estournel (Saint-Estèphe), Château Montrose La Dame Montrose

(Saint-Estèphe), Château Mouton Rothschild (in the heart of Médoc in Pauillac). At the end of the vineyard trip to Château Rothschild we had a candlelit tasting. Standing in this piece of history—limestone cellar, dark and beautiful, which was housing thousands of aging barrels—I inhaled a breath and was conscious of doing so, indicating the experience was overtaking my body in the best way. I was told these were experiences that are not shared with tourists whatsoever. We were considered a different level and treated to some of the best vintages paired with extra touches and access to private cellars. Not to mention meals prepared by the appointed chefs of the chateaus.

I didn't think our Bordeaux trip could get any more extravagant until my professor announced Saint-Émilion, our next stop! We would be dining at the famous Michelin-starred restaurant Logis de la Cadène.

I was so excited I was getting to go back to Saint-Émilion. I could not wait! We learned why Saint-Émilion was such a sought-after region. The price for 2.5 acres of vines in the appellation was 3 million euros. And most winemakers owned seventy acres! I thought back to the four vineyards Catherine owned. I could not believe she owned *four*, and knowing I got to partake in the behind-the-scenes work for Saint-Émilion Grand Cru wine in the fall was moving. At that moment we were driving along the windy gravel road and taking in the rainbow sky hovering over the village. I gave myself a little pinch, as if to tell myself this was all real. It hadn't been just a dream. I was starting to have even more respect for France than ever before. There was a seriousness about things, a formality, and a good example was how wine is produced—with discipline, rules, quality, integrity, and immense care. I could feel this in France everyday through the attention to detail in beauty, food, winemaking, and how the French carried themselves, how stores presented their products, the flowers everywhere. I was absolutely enamored at the elegance. At that moment I wanted to stay forever.

I drifted back to my vineyard stay. I couldn't believe that I hadn't allowed Julien to pursue me. I was sort of mad at myself, thinking about what a mess I had been just a few short months ago. I remembered one evening when we had gone to a dinner party in the countryside at one of Julien's friend's houses. It was me, Cedric and Claire, Julien, and Thomas and Emilie, Julien's best friend and his wife. In true French fashion it had been outside under bistro lighting on his friend's property. Chickens were roaming around the pebbly gravel under our picnic tables, and the sun was setting over the land. We began with a course of duck pâté with cornichons starting at nine o'clock. Julien and I flirted throughout the evening, but I remember trying to force myself to do so. It didn't seem natural. I also remember thinking he was so darn cute. Confused was an understatement.

At one point he said, "Come on, let's go! I have something to show you; we will come right back." I jumped in his car, Claire gave me a smirk, and we were off to who knows where or what he had to show me. We ended up in the barrel cellar of his winery in Pomerol. He went through some wine boxes and tested the alcohol levels on some of the wine in the vats. The smell of rich red wine permeated the whole cellar; the smell of cherry and vanilla from the wine soaking in the oak was intoxicating. He was opening cases of wine as if looking for something; then all of the sudden he shouted "Ici!" which meant "Here, here it is." I turned to look at him, and as he smiled, he said, "Here, this is for you." I looked at the bottle, and it was the vintage 1985, which just happened to be my birth year. I blushed and a grin lined my face. What a sweetheart; I was taken off guard and felt so appreciative in that moment. We drove back to the dinner party not saying much, but I was in awe of this sweet gesture. Once back at Thomas and Emilie's house, we found dinner was being presented, and all of them signed my bottle and wrote me little "going away" messages like you do in yearbooks at the end of senior year.

"*D'accord à tous!* On y va," Professor Lavigne stated. I pulled myself out of my daydream as we pulled up to Château Teyssier, our first chateau visit in Saint-Émilion. It was a stunning castle, like something out of a storybook; perfectly manicured flowers went on for miles outside of the castle, with the backdrop of vines everywhere.

I noticed our translator, Mr. Porter, taking off his wide-rimmed glasses and wiping his eyes with a handkerchief. He was even brought to tears by the beauty here. This was something I was experiencing everywhere. It was so moving being in these places, and I felt emotions come over me that made my whole body flutter. Just the sheer history and beauty were able to make you sink into yourself and be so immensely present; it was an incredible feeling. Sometimes it was overwhelming, the connection, the looking back in time, to think about the work and artistry rounded out with the pleasure and care of the wines. This experience was so beautiful. Throughout the day we also visited the village of Saint-Émilion and one more chateau, Beau-Séjour Bécot. I fondly remembered when I had purchased a bottle from this winery and had enjoyed it on my terrace in LA when I made the decision to come to Paris.

How fortuitous that moment was for where I was now, even though I didn't realize it at the time. What I was undergoing in these moments made me look back on that small, scared girl on her terrace and smile. She had no clue the dream she was about to enter. I felt my eyes start to water. We would be going back to Paris after one more special night in Saint-Émilion. It was bittersweet.

FIFTEEN

Margaux are often described as being like an iron fist in a velvet glove. The soil in Margaux (appellation of Bordeaux) is among the lightest and most gravelly in the Médoc, giving the best wines in the best years a sort of soaring elegance and refinement.

I was sitting in the back of a taxi on my way to my first night working as an intern at the acclaimed restaurant Citrus Etoile. It was January, and for the next six weeks I would be doing hands-on practical work in the field as part of my curriculum. Citrus Etoile was located just off the famous Champs-Élysées, and provided a fine dining experience to the nines for its welcomed guests.

I could feel the nerves pulsating throughout my body. I was wearing a tight, black dress and four-inch heels with smoky gray eye shadow, and had spent an hour straightening my hair. Black charcoal penciling bordered my tear ducts with thick eyeliner. During my interview, the general manager, Antoine, had told me very directly, "Krista, I expect that you will dress like a glamour girl every night. By this I mean, dressing sexy and walking seductively. High heels, makeup, and tight outfits." When this was said to me I couldn't help but chuckle to myself. I was clearly in *France*. I don't think in America anyone would dare say this to a woman during an interview; otherwise they would fear being sued for sexual harassment.

But of course I was in France. Having a job in the wine world here was not just about knowledge. It was about beauty, seduction, allure, and obviously the art of selling wine had layers behind it. I had witnessed this a lot so far in the city. All the waitresses serving at the chic, swanky hotels and restaurants dressed in very sexy, formfitting attire and walked a certain way all while pouting. Working in this industry was as much about sex appeal as it was about food and wine. I had no idea what I was in store for over the next six weeks, but I was anxiously awaiting the feeling of comfort at the restaurant when I would step into in my routine. I hated my current state of intense nerves. A fine dining French restaurant in Paris... What was expected of me nightly? I didn't even speak the language. Was my level of sommelier knowledge enough to actually be of service to this restaurant? Could I help English-speaking guests select fabulous wines to complement their meals? I was pondering all this, and all I could do was remain hopeful and keep telling myself that no matter how badly I screwed up, it was only six weeks of my life.

The taxi pulled up in front of two large, frost-stained glass doors with the burnt-orange overhang and *Citrus Etoile* written over it in perfect, black cursive lettering. A man in a suit opened the taxi door for me. "Bonsoir, madame."

"Bonsoir, monsieur," I replied, my voice sounding a little shaky. I inhaled the crisp winter air and let it expand in my lungs, and allowed the valet to open the frosted door for me. *Well, I'm ready as I'll ever be,* I thought to myself.

I walked right up to the hostess podium. "Hi, my name is Krista. I am here for my internship… to work tonight. I am supposed to check in with Antoine." I said this with as much confidence as I could muster as the pencil-thin, blonde Parisian girl stared at me from the hostess stand, not giving half a centimeter of a smile.

"Okay," she quickly responded and picked up the phone at the podium to call Antoine, who was apparently in his office downstairs. The restaurant was upstairs, and all below were offices, kitchens, and storage rooms. A few minutes later, after I had stood at the front of the dining room awkwardly with staff staring at me, Antoine made an appearance. He gave me a rather close hug, grabbing my hips and kissing me on both cheeks. "Ça va?" he asked. I wondered if the staff was watching this, and if this was normal or if it was because I was foreign and not actually working there. He immediately went right into an informal exchange with me. Usually, a boss or someone in charge of me would not be so casual in an introduction, but I welcomed this energy as it calmed me. I immediately responded with how nervous I was feeling to which he told me not to worry. For the first few nights I would be shadowing him and watching what he was doing, not so much actually having to engage and exchange words with the guests. He explained that he would start by letting me memorize the wine cellar, handle water service, clean glasses in the dish room, and familiarize myself with the staff and the restaurant itself. *Phew.* This was a relief, as it meant I could get my feet on the ground for the first week.

Antoine gave me a quick tour of the restaurant and introduced me to everyone working that night. There were mostly men working in the kitchen as cooks especially, which made me very happy as the French men were all nice to me despite me not speaking much of the language at all. I could feel their eyes on me, checking me out in my tight, black dress. I would have to immediately get used to this, as there would soon be a full restaurant of patrons watching me work. It was part of my work in Paris to be somewhat of a sex symbol, I guess. After my short tour I was still feeling fairly uncomfortable, and Antoine told me to fix a plate for dinner; at seven o'clock we would have "staff meal." That night the chefs had made large platters of moules-frites for us to dine on. I filled up my plate, as the smell was luscious and I had barely eaten all day due to nerves. I headed downstairs to the room where the waitstaff was to eat. Antoine would dine upstairs with the chefs at an actual dining table. I sat at the table full of French waiters and felt like a fish out of water, as they were all speaking in French at a rapid pace. I could barely understand anything and continued to eat my meal while staring down at my plate. At that point, I wanted to crawl in a hole and hide. I felt embarrassed that I didn't speak French and self-conscious to be sitting there staring around the room as everyone spoke as if I was invisible. This was going to be a long six weeks.

"Hi, you must be Krista," a voice said to my left said. "I am Maxim. I will be in charge of your training. The next few nights at least."

Maxim was a tall, skinny, blond French guy with a British accent, and he had approached me out of nowhere. *He must have lived in London*, I thought to myself, as he didn't have the typical Parisian accent to his English. Maxim was apparently higher up in the restaurant and allowed to dine outside of this pitiful dungeon, so this was the first I was seeing of him. I quickly got up and took my plate to the dish room. I followed Maxim to the wine cellar, which was an open viewing cellar within the dining room of the restaurant. He explained to me my duties each night would include setting up the wine cellar for an hour before dinner service started, making sure we had all the bottles necessary and also ice buckets to chill the Champagne and white wine. There were only seventy wines by the bottle, which would make it easier for me to memorize the list. I was enlivened. I didn't feel much overwhelm when it came to the wines on the wine list, but Maxim had a slight arrogant demeanor, and I could tell working under him was going to be challenging. Just in the first twenty minutes of talking to him, I could tell he was a no-bullshit, work-hard kind of guy. Antoine was much more smiley with me and relaxed, but Maxim meant business.

Maxim and I had exited the wine cellar into the main dining room when a tall, blonde model of a woman waltzed through the frosted-glass entrance of the restaurant, cursing like a sailor. "Oh fuck, I cannot believe this. I have this large stain on my dress. Shit! Goodness, this never fails."

"Oh gosh, sorry. Hi, sweetie!" She gave Maxim a kiss on each cheek, towering over him.

She turned to look at me with a smile.

"Bonsoir, *je m'appelle Krista*," I said nervously.

"Um, hi, I'm Meredith. I am American, honey, no need to speak French with me. Please, I honestly need a break from it. I'm married to the damn French chef here."

"Okay. Nice to meet you," I said with a laugh and shook her hand. I had yet to meet the chef.

Meredith went to the small side mirror at the hostess podium and started reapplying her lip gloss. She was spraying her perfume everywhere and took off her floor-length fur coat. She started talking out loud to Maxim and me and anyone else within earshot.

"I need a vodka on the rocks immediately, Maxim. Can you guys get that pronto?" This woman was incredible, walking into her own restaurant cussing, looking like she had stepped off a runway in Paris, and demanding a stiff drink. I had only been at this restaurant two hours but already felt that I was on a movie set. This place was full of characters.

Meredith and I continued to speak; we discussed California as she was also from my home state. She offered me a glass of Champagne. It was a Monday night, and the restaurant was a bit slow on the bookings. She was an absolute riot, and I found myself giggling throughout the whole conversation. She was five feet, eleven inches without her stilettos. With her high heels she was more like a six-foot-two Glamazon. She had a tight, backless dress on, and her hair was in an updo that appeared professionally done. She was fifty years old but looked only thirty-five due to the work she had done: tasteful Botox, breast implants, and lip injections. Nothing was overdone but just right, and she seemed to have found a magician of a plastic surgeon.

"I have recently lost twenty pounds, due to eating one chicken breast and one yogurt per day. Yes, I pretty much starve myself, but let me tell you, it's well worth it to be the size I was when I met Gabriel." I could not believe how freely Meredith spoke with someone she had just met. I sensed the vodka and now Champagne had gone to her head. Gabriel Epié was the chef and owner of Citrus Etoile. Meredith had met him twenty years ago. She had been dining in a restaurant in LA with Richard Gere, whom she was dating at the time, and Gabriel happened to be the executive chef there. He came out to the table—well, because it was Richard Gere—and he and Meredith locked eyes. She said that she felt it was love at first sight. After that, she no longer dated Richard Gere and married Gabriel instead. They stayed in Los Angeles for several years after that and eventually moved to Paris to open Citrus Etoile. They had now been married twenty years, with the last twelve years being in Paris. Maxim came into the cellar and motioned for me to follow him.

"Okay, you will start with the water service. Whenever you see glasses on any table less than half full, go fill them up. No exceptions. Eyes on all tables."

I walked around the restaurant and glanced at all the tables. I filled a few glasses and could feel Maxim's eyes on me, watching as I did it. Once I felt I had completed that task, I went back to the cellar. I knew myself and I knew I found refuge in the cellar, as the dining room was very intimidating to me. Maxim came in immediately after me.

"Okay, so when you are filling water glasses, try not to shake as much. Also, now you will clean glasses in the dish room. You cannot hide in the cellar all night. Let's go!"

I spent the next hour running wine glasses through the dishwasher and drying them with a linen towel. I liked this, as it was a peaceful task, and the dish area for glasses was close to the kitchen line, so I was able to watch the chefs, which I loved. I eyed Executive Chef Gabriel Epié calling the line tickets calmly and watching the tickets coming in, communicating the dishes to the cooks. He was handsome and ironically resembled Richard Gere a little bit, but with a certain French twist. What a catch; I immediately thought to myself that Meredith had it all.

After cleaning glasses, my next job was taking inventory of all the wine bottles in the cellar. I would restock to the levels before service had started. This was also a task that I was comfortable with.

Antoine appeared in the cellar and asked how I felt my first night there was.

"Fine, I am a little intimidated, but I really like this restaurant. You have a great wine list," I said honestly.

Antoine poured me a glass of Château Margaux 2010 while stating that each night I would taste one or two wines once service ended. He instructed me to relax and enjoy and also take notes on each wine. With that he clinked my glass with his and exclaimed, "Santé!" It was a huge bonus for me to be able to taste seventy wines by the time my internship was finished. I sipped the wine slowly as I restocked the cellar. The wine, heavy with Cabernet Sauvignon, was rich on my tongue and had the aromas of black cherries just pitted and picked off the tree, combined with a slight smokiness, like meat on an open firepit. There was also a strong essence of blackberry jam. This wine felt like the most luxurious introduction to winter I could have.

I finished stocking the cellar, broke down the wine boxes, and took my empty glass of Margaux to the dish room.

My first night was completed, and it was approaching midnight. Antoine told me I could go and he would see me tomorrow. Meredith must have disappeared already, as I had not seen much of her since Maxim had stolen me from the cellar.

I got in a taxi and watched the Eiffel Tower sparkle in the background as we whipped through the streets of Paris. I was exhausted but proud of myself for completing my first night. My feet hurt, and I was saturated with knowledge. This internship reminded me of all my previous work in restaurants. I had a love-hate relationship with the restaurant world. I felt undeniably attached to it due to my immense love of food, wine, passionate chefs, and creating pleasurable dining experiences for guests. I hated it for the constant pressure and urgency inflicted, the long

PARIS, MY BEAUTIFUL MADNESS

hours, late nights and weekends worked, the instability, and all of the anxiety-producing, adrenaline-induced moments.

But I knew I needed to be grateful. I had gotten this internship due to a connection. Professor Lavigne had given us a list of acceptable places that would count for credits, and this restaurant was listed. He told me the girl from the program before me had a very nice time as Antoine taught her so much; she was also from California, so I had reached out to talk to her about it and learn about her experience. She then had messaged Antoine that I would be applying. It all sort of fell into place from there, compared to my classmates and friends finding internships, which hadn't gone so seamlessly. Sarah had gotten stuck in a traffic jam—the traffic was a huge and ever-present downside in the city—and had missed her first interview to work for an import company. She was crushed, and due to that, they didn't extend the internship to her. She was now scrambling among slim pickings to find something else. Sebastian found a wine sales position at the famous department store Galeries Lafayette. He had been in Paris several months before somm school had commenced, and his French was pretty good. This awarded him better positions in France, even though he had explained that the selection process for that internship had been grueling. Other classmates were floundering. Just as a train had dropped us in Bordeaux and left us to our own devices for the harvest stint, we were expected to figure out our internships here in Paris with very little handholding from the professors. We didn't have classes at Le Cordon Bleu in January or February; both of those months were hands-on, practical work within our internships, and you were to have your supervisor email Professor Lavigne a weekly report and summary of how you were doing.

Suddenly, my phone lit up; a message from a man named Damien from the dating site. *Hi, what's up?*

A French guy speaking in English slang. Hmmm. Interesting. I looked at his pictures and found he was tall, dark, extremely handsome, and appeared to be a surfer and snowboarder. He was thirty-three years old.

I responded for no other reason than that he was a tall and handsome Frenchman speaking in English to me.

Hi, just finished work, how are you?

He responded instantly. I texted back and forth with him the whole taxi ride home. By the time I entered my flat, he had asked me to meet for a drink Wednesday evening. I had to work Wednesday night, but maybe Antoine would allow me to work the lunch service instead, I thought. I would ask him tomorrow. I must have been desperate for a romantic interest in France, as rearranging my work schedule for someone I hadn't even met was my current level of owning my life. Looking back, a guy coming on so strong on the first night I talked to him was probably a red flag. I apparently was blind to it at the time.

Damien and I continued to message until two o'clock in the morning, at which point I drifted off to sleep. Our messages were all in English as he had spent two years in New York City and so was completely fluent. I fell asleep eager to meet this alluring, thirty-three-year-old French man.

The next night at Citrus Etoile was a little more intense; the restaurant was a bit busier. Meredith made an appearance again and entertained me to no end. She must have consumed a bottle of

Burgundy by herself and sat with several different tables of guests over the course of the dinner service. I could not tell if she actually knew them or if they were strangers and she was invading their dinners and feeling right at home in their personal conversations. In any case, she was hysterical. I felt weird asking Antoine so early for a schedule adjustment, especially in the first week of my internship, but I wasn't getting paid for this and I would still work the lunch service. He was so nice and agreed that for this exception it was fine. I messaged Damien that we could meet Wednesday night.

Great, meet me at 9:00 p.m. in front of Chai 33 Wine Bar in Bercy Village. 12eme

There it was. A blind date set again. I had to admit to myself I loved his suggestion and the pure confidence he gave off by nailing down a night with me and telling me where to meet. I had a good feeling about him.

It was 8:45 p.m. on Wednesday, and a taxi had dropped me off in the Bercy Village, which was basically a plaza in the Twelfth Arrondissement full of shops, a cinema, and restaurants. It was fairly new and remodeled and didn't feel like Paris to me, but I enjoyed seeing new places in the city. I was early, and I decided to go into a chocolate shop and buy some chocolates while I waited for my date.

The sales lady helping me was so sweet, and as she was wrapping my box of twelve mint chocolates, she revealed she had married an American man and had lived in Santa Monica, California, for several years. We exchanged some words about French and American culture, and she said that ultimately she divorced her American husband and moved back to France where she felt she belonged. She handed me my box, and as I thanked her, she said, "You will see. Paris is great for a few years, but you will start to miss your culture more and more. You will eventually move back. It happens slowly, but you will start to realize where you identify." I took note in my brain and wanted to argue with her statement. Instead, I thanked her for the advice and walked out of the store. At that point I felt I could not imagine missing my culture. I felt so alive in Paris. All of the French people so far had been so welcoming, and I felt a sense of peace living in Paris. I knew I would keep that statement locked in my mind, though.

Hi Miss, I am here. In front of the wine bar. Waiting for you.

I glanced down at my phone to see this message from Damien. It was 9:03 p.m. He was right on time. Impressive already for a French person, as, despite their lack of sympathy for Sarah's traffic jam story, they were usually fifteen minutes later than the time originally stated.

I walked up to the wine bar and recognized Damien, who was wearing a North Face jacket, dark jeans, and white Converse sneakers. He was standing at six feet tall and was just as his pictures had revealed: tall, dark, and handsome. *Damn*, I thought. He was even more attractive in person. I approached him, and watched as a smile lined his face. I could feel that we were both pleasantly surprised by the other person's appearance. I was wearing an off-the-shoulder black blouse with a forest green cape, and black leather pants that hugged my body. My tall, black leather boots put me at the height of about five feet, eight inches.

We gave the essential bisous and made our way into the wine bar, where he chose a comfy couch for us to sit on.

The wine bar was dimly lit and had a sexy vibe with club-type music playing in the background. He asked if I would like to pick the wine and told me to select any bottle I wanted. I picked a Viognier, which was the most affordable on the list for a decent vintage and winemaker. Damien smiled as I ordered in French from the waiter.

"*On va prendre une bouteille de Viognier s'il vous plaît,*" I said rather confidently. Ordering wine in a restaurant I had pretty much down to a tee at this point.

"Your accent is very charming," he said, gazing into my eyes.

"Merci," I said. I felt giddy as a schoolgirl inside.

For the next hour or so, we sipped wine and discussed life. There were subtle gestures of affection, and our physical chemistry was palpable.

Suddenly, in the midst of conversation, Damien kissed me. We kissed for a good five minutes. After breaking away, we looked at each other, each confirming the amazing kiss and the chemistry between us. We continued to sip wine, talk, and kiss for the next two hours.

Once it was approaching one in the morning, we both knew it was time to end the evening. Damien had to work the next day. He paid the bill and offered to take me home. We held hands the whole drive back to my flat, kissed a little more in his car before I got out, and he looked at me and said we would be in touch. I opened the door to my flat and felt a rush of excitement at the prospect of Damien. I had never experienced such immediate chemistry or felt so comfortable with a complete stranger. It had been a wonderful night, a great date, and Damien was absolutely my type. Not to mention he was basically a pro skier, surfer, and skateboarder, and apparently talented when it came to anything athletic. In addition, he was an innovation technology engineer and therefore smart as hell. Looks, smarts, and athleticism—oh, and French with a sexy accent when he spoke perfect English. Yes, well, at least it doesn't take a rocket scientist to figure out why I had become infatuated with him instantly.

I was even more excited when I received this text message fifteen minutes later.

Je suis bien rentré. J'ai beaucoup apprécié ma soirée. Bonne nuit. Bisous. Damien

I quickly typed this into Google Translate: *I have returned home. I have really appreciated this night a lot. Sleep well. Kisses.*

I smiled that night as I drifted off to sleep. I could only hope I would see Damien again. It was rare to meet someone so attractive, someone with whom I could share a comfortable, great night, one that ended on such a high note after passionate kisses. I hadn't felt a spark like this since Eddie. I also hoped my time with Damien wouldn't abruptly end as my courtship with Benjamin had. There were now two Parisian men I had felt a spark with. I felt closer to my fantasy that I would fall in love with a French man. Maybe it was because I needed that security to really make a life for myself here, or maybe it was because that was what I saw on paper for my life. I could feel myself on a mission with the dating world in Paris. I saw it as my only ticket to official Frenchdom.

It was Friday night, and I had completed my first week out of six at Citrus Etoile. It was mid-January now, and the week really had flown by. I was starting to feel adjusted and had my routine at the restaurant down. All of the staff knew who I was, and I entered the place each night and immediately got to work. Antoine had started allowing me to consume my dinner in the cellar each night so I didn't have to be in the dungeon room not conversing with anyone and feeling their uncomfortable stares. I was really learning a lot from Antoine about the wines the restaurant carried and why, and had already tasted ten of them with diligent notes. Next week, I would begin actual service and start taking wine orders, recommending bottles, and opening wine in front of guests at the table. I was nervous for that step, but felt that I was capable and believed in myself. At least I was comfortable with the restaurant atmosphere. Every Friday night was a bit of a soirée, and after service we were able to sit and drink the opened bottles of wine that were left. Since Citrus Etoile was closed on the weekends, Friday nights were a clean-out, so to speak, and the staff benefited.

Damien had contacted me and asked if I wanted to see a movie on Saturday night. I obviously agreed and was excited at the thought of seeing him again. He was coming to pick me up at my apartment around eight o'clock and the movie would start at ten. I invited him for an aperitif before the movie.

I realized I had now been in Paris a little over four months, and I was really starting to have a groove in the city. I had great friends, a flat I loved; I was dating and working at a restaurant in Paris. For just a short period of time I felt like I was greatly adjusted and almost too comfortable in this foreign city. I remembered what the French lady at the chocolate shop had told me just a few days before, and I could not have disagreed more at this moment. I felt like Paris was extending open arms and a large span of opportunity and life for me. I could not have felt better about the way the year was playing out so far. Tonight I was drinking fabulous wines after dinner service with Antoine, Meredith, and Maxim; tomorrow I was meeting Sarah and Sebastian for brunch, and tomorrow night I was going to see a movie with Damien. Life was adjusted in Paris.

That night over a bottle of Champagne, Meredith stared at my face and hair and said bluntly, "Sweetie, you need your hair colored. It is a boring brown, and we need it to look rich. I have a hairdresser who is fabulous. I will call him and make you an appointment."

I laughed as I answered. "Okay, sure. I haven't found a hairdresser in France yet. I do need a color job, though; that would be great."

It had been almost six months since I had gotten my hair colored. She was right, and instead of being insulted by her critiques, I welcomed them. She then got on her cell phone and called this hairdresser. I chuckled to myself at how insane she was; it was midnight and she was calling someone's personal cell phone to get an American girl in immediately. Was my hair that bad? Meredith never failed to entertain me.

After their five-minute phone call, in which she spoke in fast French, she turned to me. "Done. He can get you in a week from tomorrow! So next Saturday. I have a great idea: I will go with you, and then we can go to my friend Isabelle's boutique for some shopping and also have a glass of wine around. It will be a girls' day!"

"Sounds perfect and like a lot of fun! Thank you so much for calling and getting me in!" I exclaimed with honest excitement.

We sipped a little more wine, and then I ordered a taxi. I was spoiling myself a little by taking taxis every night, but I was far from home, across the river. Also, after a night of walking in heels during dinner service, I greatly anticipated my fifteen minutes to relax in the back of a taxi. I was already hungry and dreaming of brunch with Sarah and Sebastian the next day. It would be delicious; we were going to our favorite spot in the Saint Germain des Prés, Eggs & Co. Their benedicts were scrumptious, and I was famished just thinking about devouring the perfectly poached eggs.

The next morning I arrived a bit early to Eggs & Co. and was pleasantly surprised they could seat me right away. Sarah and Sebastian showed up about ten minutes later.

"Wait, so you have a guy you are seeing tonight that you really like?" Sarah asked curiously.

"Yes, you know when you have an instant spark with someone, or feel so comfortable with them like you have known them forever?" I responded intently. At the time I couldn't see how easily impressed with someone I was. It was as if as long as they were attractive and took me on a nice date, they were golden in my book without my needing to know much about them.

"Yes, exactly. I felt that with David," Sebastian proclaimed. Things were seemingly going well for Sebastian with his older businessman beau. He did share some odd things that were happening in the relationship, though. Sebastian seemed really proud of David's standing in Paris. However, he told us that David at times treated him like a servant of the house. The hired help. He had to run his shirts to the dry cleaner's; he also had to make sure David had his fresh mango and chocolate every morning to have with his espresso.

"I just really like him, though. He is so sexy. Also, I really wanted a relationship here," Sebastian stated giddily. I could relate to Sebastian; it was almost as if being in a relationship with a Parisian made us feel more officially grounded here. We all knew the school program would end, and what were we going to do in Paris then? I could tell Sebastian and I had the same love for Paris and didn't see ourselves leaving after we received our certification. Sarah voiced other feelings. She saw this more as a sabbatical and of course was entranced with Paris and the beauty here, but she was very prideful of America and chalked this experience up to living abroad.

"Will we be meeting David soon?" Sarah asked intently.

Sebastian gave a nervous laugh and said, "I am not sure he is interested in meeting my friends. He still refuses to introduce me to his friends. In fact, when there is a dinner party in his home, he introduces me as someone who is helping around the house. He is not openly gay and out about it."

"What? Wait, so was he with women before this? Before you?" I asked in complete fascination.

"Yes, he has two daughters as well," Sebastian exclaimed. "I also help babysit them."

Sarah and I looked at each other with the same face of *What the hell is happening here?* Babysitting; dry cleaning; a closeted, older successful attorney? Mango breakfasts?! David sounded odd to say the least. Sebastian was such a kind person that I just hoped he wasn't going to get hurt and that he was getting everything he wanted out of this relationship. I also realized Sebastian and I were similar in accepting things we shouldn't sometimes in exchange for the idea of what a person could represent for us. As I cut into my eggs, dripping with hollandaise, I felt a familiar sentiment. Red flags were popping up about Sebastian's new boyfriend, but at least he still had a boyfriend. A *French* one. The vision he saw for himself was overriding what was actually happening behind closed doors.

We spent three hours at our cozy table at Eggs & Co., talking about all sorts of things, and all I could think about was my excitement over my date that night with Damien.

I practically skipped home down Boulevard Saint-Germain and proceeded to pick out my best outfit. I decided I would wear knee-high, black leather boots, an ivy green short skirt, and a black blouse. I spritzed on some of my new Giorgio Armani perfume and was ready and awaiting. Just then my intercom buzzed to allow Damien in.

Damien arrived looking more handsome than I remembered him. He had on a white shirt that hugged his perfectly toned muscles, with jeans and sportive shoes. He was wearing a sporty jacket and a nice watch. He looked very well put together, and I couldn't wait for him to kiss me. I took note of how affectionate he was toward me. He was constantly touching me in some subtle way, whether it was his hand on the small of my back, rubbing my thigh, or gripping my waist. I loved all of these gestures as it felt so good to feel desired. I opened a nice bottle of Meursault, a white wine from Burgundy, and we started talking about what had transpired that week for each of us. About an hour into our discussion, we were kissing intensely and he started trying to undress me. I knew in my head this was too soon for intimacy, especially with someone I really liked. I told him I wasn't ready, which he respected, and we decided we could still catch the movie. He went to get the car, which he had parked on a side street a little bit away from my flat, and I came down soon after.

While sitting in the movie theater we held hands and were very close. We shared a few soft, gentle kisses, and I remember feeling in utter bliss. I hadn't felt so good with someone since Eddie. It felt so great to be with someone I felt a sense of connection to—natural, right, and easy. When the movie was over, we walked hand in hand down the cobblestone street toward the car. Every so often Damien would pull me in close and kiss my forehead or my cheek, or bring my hand up to his mouth and kiss it. I loved this feeling of adoration that was running through me. For the first time, I hadn't thought of Eddie. I was excited about what was to unfold for Damien and me.

Little did I know, Damien was in fact too good to be true.

SIXTEEN

The great french wines are also indisputably sensual.
For centuries they have been disputed in the most
erotic of ways, and sipping them has been compared,
among other things, to falling in love.

It was my second Friday night working at Citrus Etoile. I had completed two weeks of my internship already, and this past week had definitely been much more intense. I had made some embarrassing mistakes in my rustiness and entry into the world as a working sommelier. This was the work needed to gain practice for my service techniques and opening bottles for my final exam.

We were expected to be stars in properly opening and presenting wine come our final exams, in addition to being tasting experts.

First, there was the absolutely mortifying reality that I had failed to properly open a nice bottle of wine at a table and had to retreat to the cellar to open it. My face had turned bright red, and I had quickly escaped from the table. I had been in a rush trying to find my corkscrew and instead had to borrow Antoine's, which was rather fancy and which I had not yet used to open a bottle of wine. I could not figure this fancy tool out and looked like a total idiot in front of a middle-aged French couple trying to have a romantic dinner.

"Je suis desolée. Excusez-moi." I told them how sorry I was as I returned to the table with the opened bottle and poured a splash for the man to taste. They looked at me with a rather disgusted acknowledgement on each of their faces, basically stating that it had been unacceptable and furthermore questioning why I was even working there. The seriousness of dining in Paris.

"Bon," the man exclaimed curtly, and I poured the woman her glass and then filled up the glass for monsieur. I walked away with my tail between my legs. Antoine had watched the whole thing, and he was mortified for me. He sent the couple some savory petit fours on the house to try and console them. I apologized to Antoine, who was sweet to me and rather forgiving about it, and moved on. I had other tables to tend to. After work that night, my anxiety was at an all-time high. I kept replaying that instance over and over in my head. I was practically dreading going into the restaurant the next night, and it was now affecting my sleep.

Just a few nights later, as I was entering the kitchen with a tray full of empty glasses, the door to the kitchen swung open rather abruptly, causing my tray to shake. Two wine glasses slipped off and shattered on the floor right in front of the chef's cooking line. Again, I wanted to *die*. I could not believe my clumsiness. Two of the bussers immediately came to my side and started sweeping up the broken glass. The chefs continued to work and plate dishes and didn't seem to care, but it was still embarrassing. I was relieved when that night was over. After dropping the glasses, I was terrified to carry anything on a tray for the rest of the night.

Then there was the night when I was in the cellar opening a bottle of champagne, and it splashed and exploded everywhere due to me not opening it properly and professionally. It sprayed and splattered and made a mess, almost to the ceiling and quite definitely all over my clothes. I could not go out onto the restaurant floor until my clothes appeared dry. So, within a week, needless to say, I had made all of these little mistakes. I was being really hard on myself about it and in fact questioning if I should even deserve to be in the wine business at all. Antoine told me it was very normal, as I was not used to this work. He went on to say when you are working under pressure and need to work with urgency mistakes early on are bound to happen. I really appreciated Antoine for all that he was teaching me, but also for his calm, relaxed demeanor. Nothing seemed to make him angry, and he was very rational and remained unruffled in most situations.

Antoine and I had an interesting relationship. I could tell he had an affinity for me; even, Meredith had said, a "crush." I am sure this was why his reactions toward me when I made mistakes were pleasant. He would even openly tell me about the affairs he had

had even though he had been married to his wife for fifteen years. "C'est normale in the French culture," he said when a shocked look came over my face one night as we finished stocking the cellar.

I said with high curiosity, "But does your wife know and accept this?"

"No. It's not something that's talked about. And she has never asked. But she would leave if she knew, which is why she never asks." He said this confidently. They also had two children together.

"So then, does she cheat on you? Does she also have affairs?"

I was shocked at what he said next.

"I hope she does. It keeps things alive in the marriage as well. Keeps me on my toes. But again I don't ask." I was now onto something. The ever-rumored love affairs of the French and how it is more accepted in this culture. I was not over this topic.

I pressed for more. "But what do you do if the other woman you are seeing gets jealous and wants you to leave your wife, wants more from you?"

"I never sleep with one woman more than once or twice for this reason. I do not date who I take on affairs with. It is a sexual encounter. Because I can never develop feelings. I love my wife and children too much for that."

I wasn't sure if this admittance made me feel better or worse. He loved his wife so much, but that must have meant he had slept with *many* women she didn't know about. I got a little sick to my stomach, thinking about a fifteen-year marriage and how many women he must have been up to now that he had essentially cheated on her with. The fact that she had no idea who her husband was bedding? I couldn't understand it. Was one affair with a sexual and emotional connection worse than several sexual encounters? I wasn't sure. I really liked Antoine as a person, and it was so interesting to me how he was so caring and nice but then could be doing this to his wife. I was trying not to judge it; I just had empathy for her on some level.

The next day was the day of my supposedly much-needed hair appointment. I would meet Meredith in the Sixteenth Arrondissement for a glass of Champagne and shopping; then to my appointment we would go. It was also a date night with Damien. He told me he was taking me to dinner and that he would pick me up at eight o'clock. I was greatly anticipating the entire day ahead. I was hoping we would cross another line tonight and felt comfortable at this point going home with him. Our chemistry was so on fire, and I was so innately attracted to his take-charge attitude in life. He was uber-confident and decisive, and I found it so sexy, despite his good looks. I was looking forward to see what intimacy was like with him.

I showed up to the café that Meredith had given me the address for. She came waltzing in, wearing a leather trench coat that swept an inch above the ground, a white T-shirt under it with no bra, and dark-washed jeans. Even on days outside of the restaurant she never wore flats; she was standing tall in fur-wrapped, brown boots. She never failed to look fashionable and stunning. She sat down, motioning for the waiter to come over and hung her large Louis Vuitton Bag on the chair.

"Hi, honey! I am so looking forward to you to get that boring hair of yours done. Oh, and Isabelle is excited for us to come by and try on fabulous clothes." I couldn't help but love Meredith's bluntness. It actually made me laugh. We sat there and each drank a glass of Chablis. When the olives and peanuts were set in front of us, Meredith proclaimed, "Oh no. See, none of this we eat. Sweetie, you need to be diligent. Every little thing adds up. I don't eat any of this shit they bring." I smiled and nodded in agreement. I wanted to say, "Yes, but you drink a bottle of wine *at least* per day and a stiff drink every night at five o'clock," but I didn't. I think a few olives to offset the blood sugar rise from the wine alone wouldn't have killed me, but I listened to the beauty queen and didn't touch them. Meredith talked about Paris and how if she could have had it her way, she would have stayed in LA. I couldn't relate, as I thought her life sounded picture perfect. Let's see: marry a French chef and be whisked away to Paris, own a restaurant, and live in the posh Sixteenth Arrondissement. The dream is usually better than the reality, but with my experience so far in Paris, the reality had been even better than the dream.

I finished the last drop of Chardonnay in my glass, and then we headed up the street to the hair salon. Meredith greeted the small, Asian hairdresser with not two bisous, but four or five back-and-forth kisses. They embraced, and she turned to introduce me. He was muscular and fit but small, and had bleached blond hair that was spiked. He was wearing a patent-leather black apron and jeans with the ever-fashionable holes and tears in them. Meredith explained to him, in French, of course, that my hair was rather boring in color and that we needed a rich, deep auburn or rich chestnut brown. He nodded in agreement as Meredith was translating their opinions to me on color. He spoke zero English, so I was thankful to have Meredith there performing the translation. He ran his hands over my scalp rather aggressively and went ahead to mix the color.

An hour and half later he led me to a chair, where the adorable old lady who also posed as the salon's secretary would blow-dry my hair. I was elated to get a blowout; I hadn't gotten my hair done in ages, so I felt pretty pampered. She finally flipped my head over to reveal the beautiful color he had mastered. Meredith's mouth dropped, and all eyes on me agreed it was a million-dollar color job. I had to agree; the dark, rich brown with slight red hues went perfectly against my skin tone. He had done a brilliant job, and I felt so happy with the outcome, especially on the night of my date with Damien.

Just then I received the following text message from Damien:

I hope you are fine with Indian food. Also, tomorrow I will work which will mean we will not sleep together this night but we can spend some time in my place. Telling you that for your organization.

I reread this message a few times over. I was rather upset upon my first glance at it. I had never had a man plan a date with me on a Saturday night only to tell me that there were rules and stipulations that came along with it. I found it upsetting and bizarre.

"Honey, please tell me you are beyond satisfied with this color. It is stunning! You look upset."

I snapped out of my trance over the odd message I had just received.

"Oh my goodness, no, sorry, I was sidetracked. The color is beyond fabulous. He did such a great job. I am thrilled with it!" I exclaimed. I kissed the Asian hairdresser on both cheeks, tipped him twenty euros, and gave him three or four *merci beaucoups*. Next, we headed to Isabelle's boutique, which was ironically called *It's a Date.*

I no longer knew if I even had a date that evening; it sounded more like an arranged dinner.

Upon entering Isabelle's store, I was drawn to a gorgeous, gray mink jacket with a thick leather strap with two large antique buttons as a belt. I slipped into it and became instantly infatuated. I knew I had to purchase this. I looked at the price tag and saw 800 euros. *Ouch!* Maybe it was my new hair, or being around a former LA model, or having a girls' day in the Sixteenth arrondissement. I didn't know what had come over me, but I thought I might be buying this jacket.

"Here, I have *zee* perfect dress for you, Kreesta," said the ultra-chic Isabelle as she unveiled a jet-black Givenchy dress. I had never purchased a designer piece of anything, particularly clothing. Other than my symbolic Hermès wallet, I had never spent money on haute couture. Meredith gasped in awe and demanded that I head into the dressing room to try it on. I slipped into the dress, which surprised me as I easily was just in a sample-size

Givenchy, but it did hug my body well. It accentuated my curves, and was slimming as it was black and possessed a flattering cut. The neckline was low cut into a V, and I did not need a bra as the upper part of the dress hugged my chest perfectly while still accentuating the shape of my breasts. The dress made me feel beautiful and feminine.

Meredith and Isabelle gasped in admiration as I walked out of the dressing room.

"Oh, honey, you must purchase this. It was made for you," Meredith said.

"It *reeeally* is *zeee* perfect *feeet* for you." Isabelle came over to straighten out the back of the dress as she spoke. She studied the dress on me as if I was a painting worth one million dollars. I noticed her skin was immaculate. I couldn't see her pores, not a single blemish, and she had an entrancing perfume on.

I was in trouble. I already knew I was going to purchase the mink jacket. I had always wanted a fabulous fur, and where to buy it other than Paris? But I also knew that I felt fabulous in this thousand-euro dress.

"You should wear that tonight with Damien. You will absolutely have a French husband if he sees you in this dress," Meredith stated in a serious tone.

I chuckled, but she may have been right. I had never tried on a piece that seemed made for my body shape. I agreed to the purchase. *You only live once*, I told myself. I felt a sense of euphoria that day with Meredith. It wasn't the fact that I had purchased a Givenchy dress and a fur in a designer boutique in Paris. It was about the feeling I had being that person making those decisions. I was stepping into a new version of myself. A sophisticated version, and I liked her. I had envisioned many scenarios of what Paris would be or how I would feel sauntering through its streets, but this was an actual situation that made me feel as if heaven on earth existed.

I now had a fabulous hair color, an ever-so-perfect little black dress, and a fur coat that I could wear daily in the winter. I also had a date this evening with a very handsome, thirty-three-year-old French man. I would absolutely wear my new dress, and my hair was already perfect. All I needed was the man. He would be picking me up at my flat in an hour. I spritzed on some perfume and reapplied my lipstick.

Damien showed up twenty minutes late. This combined with his weird text message from earlier regarding stipulations for the date, and my bliss from the day was slightly offset.

"Hi, sorry I am late. There was traffic. Ça va?" He held my face and kissed both cheeks as he said this.

I took a deep breath and told myself to let the annoyed feeling pulsating throughout my body go.

"It's fine," I replied curtly. "So, where are you taking me?"

"We are going to a local Indian place next to my apartment complex."

Sounded casual and unappealing—or maybe I just had a bad taste in my mouth. Twenty minutes later Damien parked the car.

I was disappointed. Here I was in a black dress and fur, it was a Saturday night in Paris, and we had literally pulled up in front of a neighborhood Indian restaurant on the outskirts of the city.

Taj Mahal flashed in neon above the restaurant. There were red curtains and old glass doors. The interior was bright yellow, with ancient Indian artifacts and paintings everywhere. At this point, someone would have had to convince me I was still in Paris. I felt mortified that I had gotten this dressed up for a casual Indian dinner. I had at least envisioned Le Tanjia on rue de Ponthieu or Buddha-Bar on rue Boissy d'Anglas, which were trendy and international with eclectic atmospheres and a sexy date-night vibe. My fur would have been the perfect ensemble walking into these places, but instead, we were walking into a hole in the wall in the suburbs. Uncomfortable was an understatement for how I was feeling.

Damien could sense it, but did his best to make me feel comfortable. If I had a vision of places men take women they want to hide or keep a secret, this place would have fit the bill. I remember watching an episode of *Sex and the City* where Mr. Big takes Carrie Bradshaw to a hole-in-the-wall Chinese restaurant and she feels the same way. She was curious, and it made her feel he did not want to be seen in public with her.

"Here, so they do have wines by the bottle. Pick one that sounds good."

I took the wine list out of his hands. I skimmed the bottles and prices and ended up selecting a Bordeaux. I knew it was not a perfect pairing by any means with spicy Indian food, but that was what I was in the mood to drink. Damien agreed and stated that it was whatever I wanted.

Next we chose several dishes to share. Damien ordered everything and then turned to me and asked if I was okay.

"You seem quiet, like something is on your mind," he stated with an inherent trepidation. He took my hands in his. I broke from the handhold to take a sip of my wine and then returned my hands to clasp his in the center of the table.

"Well, what you texted earlier, I found it strange. I feel like you are putting rules or predetermined stipulations on the date. I would love to know why."

He looked at me intently before he spoke as if to think of the perfect way in which to respond. Then he said, "Well, I need to work tomorrow. If you stay the night, I will not be as comfortable in my sleep. I need my sleep in order to work well. I would rather not have you sleep at my place until I am very comfortable with you. It's not personal against you. This is just the way I am."

I didn't know yet if his response made me feel better or worse. Ironically, it made me want him even more. He was so formal, serious, and well spoken. He was polite and said things in a way to make me feel honored while still telling me no. It was a well-thought word of caution that I had no choice but to respect. Damien was so sure of himself that I realized it would take time to be let in or to receive his acceptance or any ounce of adoration. In a sense, he was purely unattainable. He had discipline and rules around being let into his world. I found this utterly appealing.

He went on to say, "I really want you to come meet my dog and see my place. I think you will like it. It's rather simple, quiet, and a good escape from the hustle and bustle of the city center." I responded with an "okay" and a smile.

I'm not sure I was smiling inside, though. I was hesitant to go home with him. I should have felt happy and excited, but I was instead overwhelmed with disappointment. He was apparently good with words, although I could still feel something off about Damien. That text message from earlier in the day still seemed wrong. Telling a woman she is basically not worthy of spending the night after also implying more or less that she is *allowed* to spend time in his place? It felt calculated. Or selfish. He wasn't worried about my feelings, just his own.

At the time I was willing to play with fire from an emotional standpoint in the hopes that things would turn out as I had planned. However, that off-putting text message combined with the "joint" of a restaurant he took me to on a Saturday night in Paris... Why did I want to go further and shove this under the rug? I could feel my entire being wishing that we were at a proper restaurant where I could have felt my worth, where my fantasy would have been a reality.

Paris always gave me that feeling that the reality was just as good as the fantasy. I was exhausted trying to find a man that would do the same. I had hoped that how he saw me, the image he had of me would have warranted a night of a higher standard. Why had I agreed to this? Possibly I just wanted Damien and what he could offer me: that picture-perfect look; a true Parisian; my tall, dark, and handsome French boyfriend, even though in private moments I would be disappointed. It wasn't real then, was it? It was superficial. Was I superficial? I'm not sure that is the word for it, but needing to have Damien in my life was producing an external feeling I wanted but an internal feeling I hated. I was at war with myself.

The elevator was being repaired in Damien's complex, so we walked up the seven flights of stairs to his flat. When he opened the large door, I have to say I was impressed. The flat was very large compared to most I had seen and had sliding glass doors opening up onto a balcony. He had a spacious, open kitchen with modern finishes, which also gave way to a large living area. There were exposed rock and wooden beams, which gave it the atmosphere of a wine cave combined with sleek and modern varnishes. He opened the refrigerator, which was massive for Parisian apartment standards, and pulled out a bottle of Pinot Grigio. He reached to select two stemless wine glasses from a glass cupboard. Two minutes later I was presented with a glass of Pinot Grigio with raspberries floating at the top. He also set out a platter of cookies. I appreciated this gesture; at least this was a slight step above the underwhelming Indian restaurant.

After a little wine we escaped to the balcony, and I could sense a change in Damien's demeanor. He seemed preoccupied staring out at the view. He was almost too calm, and even though I felt comfortable in silence with Damien at this point, I could feel a subtle shift in energy. I grabbed his hand and held it in mine, and I ran my fingers gently along his arm while resting my head against his body. It seemed as though, in the last fifteen minutes, he had grown somewhat closed off and cold in his body language toward me.

Nevertheless, he took my hand and led me into his bedroom. He had not kissed me since we had arrived in the apartment.

"Do you want to try the bed?" He looked at me and raised his eyebrows. I didn't know how to respond as this was starting to feel like a transaction was about to take place. Our physical chemistry up to this point had been so easy and natural, if intense. I didn't understand what was going on, but I had sensed something was off while we were on the balcony. This felt like the opposite of natural. I started to kiss Damien. I just wanted his touch, his affection, and for him to kiss me. I didn't want it discussed. What occurred next was one of the most bizarre experiences I have had with a man. When I saw the movie *50 Shades of Grey*, sure, I was as fascinated by the exploits of Christian Grey as the next viewer, but I believed I would only ever witness this kind of sex in a movie. I also never thought I would be playing the role of Mr. Grey himself.

Damien asked that my shoes remain on. He made several declarative statements as he started to undress me, such as, "I want you to take control," and, "It's a turn-on to give you pleasure, but I also want pain inflicted on me." I was told nothing is off limits, whatever that meant. After these statements were made, and I realized we would barely be kissing, I asked him what he wanted in the form of pain. I was absolutely shocked that statements like this were being made. This was the opposite of love or romance for me. This was masochism. I understood S&M and that some couples enjoy it, but this was the first time I was undressing in front of this man. This was the first time we were being intimate. For my sake as his first-time partner, shouldn't he be making me feel as comfortable as possible? I soon realised he would not be having actual intercourse with me.

213

Damien replied that he would like for me to put my feet on his face and stomp on him. To apply pressure with my heels to his throat as if to choke him, but not to actually do it, obviously. Requests like spitting on his face, and saying highly degrading things to him in English. I was extremely hesitant, but in the meantime he had managed to satisfy me orally, and I figured the people pleaser in me at least needed to try. When in Rome... or Paris.

For the next ten minutes, I did as Damien asked, and with the pain infliction and me practically demolishing him, he was in complete pleasure and bliss. Afterward, we lay in bed together smelling aromatherapy oils. Damien became very loving and affectionate then, which, infuriatingly, was all I had wanted during sex with him. During sex he had withheld any warmth, turning it into some sort of mind fuck that made me feel like I was playing a role. How was it that he was able to offer so much affection outside of sex? I kept quiet, as I didn't want to make him feel uncomfortable, even though what had just occurred was extremely odd to me. Not that I have judgments about someone's personal preferences during sex, but as I would tell Sarah the next morning over café crèmes, this was our first time together. Why was more normal sex not on the menu whatsoever?

I realized in that moment lying in bed with him that this was a man in pain, with deep-seated psychological turmoil. Sex for him was not natural, and it was attached to something happening in his mind, something highly analyzed, and certain actions would always be needed for him to reach pleasure that went far beyond the sexual.

In keeping to his word that I was not able to spend the night, Damien drove me home at almost three in the morning. The whole drive we were both silent, and I could tell Damien could sense my thoughts on what had transpired.

I woke up the next morning and lay in bed, replaying the previous night in my head. Did that really happen? *To me* of all people? Everything from the oddness of leaving my leather boots on to the pain requested, to him pouring his affection all over me after the deed was done, it felt surreal. I had basically beaten someone to a pulp last night. Did I want to laugh or cry?

I stared out at the dark gray sky clouding over Notre Dame in a haze and had to pinch myself. I felt for a minute like I was in a galaxy far, far away from everything I had once known to be true. I was either feeling anxiety creep into my bones or entering a depressive state. How could this perfect human being, this perfect man, be a… *submissive?* He was so assertive everywhere else in life. *I will pick you up. You will not stay the night. I must work.* He always planned all the details; he seemed to like being in control, confident, dominant, and organized… a true man's man. This just didn't seem to add up. Then all of those characteristics that had made me fall for him in the first place, despite his insanely good looks and stature, were snatched away from me in the bedroom. I had been anticipating this assertive, take-charge nature of his to trickle down into our intimate, physical moments, where he would take control and I would be able to surrender to this beautiful man and feel my utmost feminine self. But no. My experience had been quite the contrary.

I had to ask myself if this was a deal breaker or if everyone compromises for love. Or was it just the image of him that gave me the feeling I wanted? Being able to say that I was *with* him? I thought about Sebastian and his situation with David. We were paralleling each other at this point, the slight desperation and the need to have everything worked out on paper. These sexy Parisian men, calling them ours. At least I could relate to Sebastian, even if he felt like a servant. But Damien now wanting to be *my* servant? My brain was starting to hurt.

I decided as my thoughts were swirling to pick up the phone and call him. *No, no, and no, Krista.* A woman should never call a man when she isn't clear herself.

I ignored my own good advice and dialed his number. Why did I even want to speak to him again? The phone rang, and then the standard French voice recording switched on. I became nauseated. Was he really not going to take my phone call after we spent the whole night together? *And* I did what he requested? It was eleven o'clock; there was no way he was still sleeping.

I felt my neediness and once again gazed out at the darkness of Paris. I wished I could snap out of it, call it a weird experience and have the feeling of never wanting to see this person again, but instead this made me utterly infatuated with him, and I wanted answers. I wanted to fix this; I wanted to be the first woman that he could take control over and be the opposite of submissive with. Oh my, was he dominant with other women and I got this submissive side of him? That thought alone made me jealous. Why did I get the short end of the stick? These were assumptions, not reality, and I started to feel insane. Paris was establishing two very astounding truths within me: my absolute love and "on fire" feeling while being here, and also all of my darkness. My lack of worth, my insecurities, and my immense anxiety were coming to the forefront. Wherever you go, there you are. The paradigm was so intense. I felt for sure my DNA was changing, molecules were multiplying and creating a new biochemistry, identity, something. Maybe he had been with men? *S-H-I-T!* This was sick, twisted, and I want to know more. In my panic-stricken, psychotic state of desperation, I texted him.

Call me please.

I was entering dangerous territory and I knew it. I had become obsessed. He had hooked me. The first two dates he played Prince Charming, and then behind closed doors, when we finally embarked on our lust for one another, he played a different card. And now he wasn't answering. The feeling was all too familiar. Eddie. Benjamin. Damien.

With still no answer from him by five o'clock that evening, I was pacing around my apartment and decided there was only one thing to do: call my best friends and drink.

Within the hour, Sarah, Sebastian, plus a guy Sarah was dating, Eric, were at my door, alcohol in hand. I had now gone from obsessed psycho to crying victim, and Sebastian poured me a large amount of cabernet in a Riedel glass. I held the large glass of Bordeaux up to my lips and sipped my wine like a baby with a pacifier as I relayed the previous night's details to my friends. Their mouths dropped to the floor. No one could believe this person whom I had described not long ago as the perfect guy, my dream guy, and very soon potential *French* boyfriend, could have turned such a one-eighty.

"Wait, and you still haven't heard from him after you called and texted today?" Sarah asked with a stunned expression. She seemed more curious over his behavior than what had happened in the bedroom.

"Nope." I took another swig of wine, and Sebastian opened a second bottle. Even the Parisian guy Sarah was dating was shocked. That was saying something, as we had found, in our combined experience thus far, that French men are much more open to sexual fetishes than American men.

"We barely kissed during sex. There was definitely a coldness. It was a highly psychological thing for him. I could feel it." It had been discussed among us that, although kinkiness is not to be judged, this was the very first sexual encounter and I had only been with him once. Usually, that was introduced later, someone's fetish or preference.

Sarah even said, "Just what is with the performing arts? Like, what happened to normal penis-in-vagina sex? Why are you asked to perform theatrics on date three after a cheap Indian meal?"

Sebastian laughed, and so did I. It wasn't even the performing arts on date three; for me it was this ice-cold treatment, rudeness, and confusion, how he was handling and treating a woman he had just been intimate with. Maybe it was all my fault for even accepting this date after my intuition had screamed from the rooftops *no* after that text regarding not staying the night. I didn't listen to myself, and now I was paying the price emotionally.

"Krista, don't worry about this person. Forget him and immediately schedule a date with a new guy," Sebastian said in a caring way, knowing it was way easier said than done.

I started to feel myself getting past the point of tipsy, entering Drunken Land. I also started to laugh uncontrollably while tears welled up in my eyes and eventually landed on my cheeks. I was a mess. This whole experience had thrown me for a loop, and what hurt me the most was Damien's refusal to take my phone call. It wasn't right. We had spent three weeks getting to know each other and three dates together. How could I have fallen for someone like this?

As it approached one in the morning, I grew exhausted, and my friends told me to get a good night's sleep and drink tons of water. My eyes were puffy, and I wanted this all to go away. They each hugged me as they left, including Eric, the guy Sarah was dating. He whispered in my ear, "Seriously, forget *theeez* guy." In a charming French accent nonetheless.

If only it were so easy to follow your head.

The next morning there was still nothing from Damien on my phone. What a coward. I sent a text that I probably shouldn't have, which included telling him that he was disrespectful, messed up, and finally I really hoped he would not condone a man treating his sister this way. It worked as he responded within thirty minutes.

Hey Krista. Sorry to reply late but I have worked until night and just saw your messages now. Hope you had fun in your friends house. I don't think it is a match since you are not enough dominant with me on bed, which is a very important part for me. So hope you will find your soul mate and was a pleasure to meet you.

Reading this message gave me the chills. Was he serious? This was a next-level text to me, and I didn't know how to take it. I needed fresh air. I bundled up and headed straight out to the river for a walk and cleanse as tears once again fell down my face. I wasn't sad from the rejection alone, although that was a hard pill to swallow. I was confused and didn't understand how someone could make a statement that seemed so final based on one romp in between the sheets, especially not when I had been absorbed in finding ways to make his kink work to fit my own needs. How did he know I couldn't be dominant? How could he just write me off like this? Was I this disposable? I was upset not necessarily because I wanted to continue on with him, but because I had allowed my self-worth to be tied up in his approval. The feeling the rejection was creating was a huge blow to my self-esteem. His opinion was apparently that important to me at the time.

Later that day, as the sun was setting, I made several attempts to type a response, but I couldn't bring myself to push send. I felt numb. Instead, I changed his name in my phone from Damien to "The Submissive." That felt good enough and would make me think twice about ever reaching out to him again.

It was my thirty-first birthday. Sarah, Sebastian, and I were celebrating at the enchanting and very sought-after restaurant Kong located at Pont Neuf. Kong was Tokyo comes to Paris in a chic, 100-percent glass dome at the very top of a quintessential Haussmann building. The design had been done by famous architect Phillipe Starck and was the epitome of a refined, modern Asian-French fusion restaurant, with a music scene as well. Some of our other classmates were set to join us later that evening. I was excited for the Peking duck spring rolls, and raved about Wagyu beef paired with miso eggplant confit. I also wore my black Givenchy dress. This was an occasion where that felt totally appropriate, and I wanted to un-taint it from the suburban night of butter chicken.

It was now mid-February, I only had two weeks left at Citrus Etoile for my internship, and although I was feeling in my groove at the restaurant, all of us were sort of depressed lately. We were anxiously awaiting getting back to school, tastings, and lectures. Not to mention we were going on the much-anticipated class trip to the Rhône Valley, where we would explore the regions of Châteauneuf-du-Pape, Cornas, and Hermitage. We would also spend the night in Avignon, a sub-region of Provence. Things were about to turn around.

Paris in the winter was also a different feeling entirely than Paris in the spring, summer, and fall. This explained why there were a bunch of "resting bitch face" Parisians cold as ice on the metro. The dreamland of Paris and the American fantasy around it were seriously turned down a notch in January and February. The city was gray, dark, rainy, and cold most days. The small confinements we were living in were magnified; plus I was working restaurant hours, and things were just mundane it seemed.

Sarah was sad as she was stressed about her internship, often not feeling she knew what she was even doing or having security in it, not to mention that she and Eric had gone their separate ways. I could tell he had been the first French guy that Sarah had really taken an interest in. She felt really connected to him and would relay to me, "Krista, I found someone I can laugh with here!" I noticed this because, in all of my dating in Paris, I had been more concerned with things like: Was the guy attractive? Were they actually from Paris? Did they own or rent their apartment? All of these were nonessential attributes that wouldn't warrant a connection necessarily. That statement stood out to me, and I started to wonder if she was onto something and reflecting my faults in dating and pursuing men.

Sebastian and David were entering very dysfunctional territory. For example, that night, for my birthday, Sebastian had a "curfew," and David demanded he come home by 11:00 p.m. Why he was demanding a grown man be home by 11:00 p.m. on a Saturday night in Paris when it was his friend's birthday was beyond me. Control? A power play? Sebastian told me he would make up for it by meeting early at my favorite, the Hôtel Costes terrace, for a glass of nice Champagne as it was a special day for me. He seemed a little embarrassed and just short about the argument they had had, not wanting to put much thought into it. I appreciated that he wanted to take me for a glass of Champagne, though; Sebastian was becoming a partner in crime for me. We loved Paris, men, food, and wine. We loved to shop at the outdoor markets and cook, and also enjoyed sitting in fancy hotels and sipping Champagne. We were starting to care about each other and definitely had an emotional bond and deeply founded friendship.

After our lovely aperitif hour at the Costes terrace, we arrived at Kong. Sarah would be meeting us there. I was immediately taken by the stunning entrance and the architecture. The glass windows looking out over the city were breathtaking, especially as the lighting of the sky was turning to a deep navy blue. The DJ was at the front of the restaurant playing eclectic music, and this place was *a scene*. Leather couches lined the walls, with chic, modelesque Europeans sipping cocktails. Other tables were placed throughout the dining room, and I watched as artful plates of food were placed in front of patrons. Bartenders were shaking two cocktail shakers at a time, like a circus act spinning them in their hands. It was a symphony to see it all combined into this flow of a dining room.

"Hi! Happy birthday, Krista!" Sarah came from around the corner and gave me a big hug. "Sorry, I had a stressful day. I'm starving and glad to be here." Sarah was in a black sweater, practically no makeup, and seemed a little rushed and just in her head. I knew her well enough to know something was slightly off. I hugged her back, and exclaimed that I couldn't wait for this.

We were led to the table. I was feeling happy. It was my birthday, I was wearing Givenchy, and in a scene that entertained me to no end… in Paris. My energy wasn't necessarily met by Sarah and Sebastian, though. Sebastian started talking about David, and he and Sarah got into a small disagreement, mainly over the fact that he shouldn't need to be controlled and should just do what he wanted. I chimed in and agreed with Sarah's statement.

"Okay, you guys, seriously, look at this amazing food. I am so craving Japanese flair. And aren't these people so chic here?" I said with enthusiasm.

Sarah responded, "Krista, none of these people here are French. I guarantee it." She went on to say that French men would never take someone here and spend hundreds of dollars in a loud restaurant. She then said, "I guarantee that guy is from Norway, that couple is from Spain… hmmm, and that couple looks like they are from Australia." Basically Sarah had this way of bringing me down off the ledge of fantasy. This wasn't necessarily a bad thing, but she was starting to do this more and more frequently. Basically the only thing that would have made my night better there was, you can guess, a French boyfriend to be partaking in the delicious food, me in my dress, and my best friends at my side. Sarah was basically telling me there was a fat chance of that happening.

Sebastian then started talking about how David is this rich attorney and he makes them leave in the middle of dinners at nice restaurants sometimes because he is *tired*. What? And, he added, they are even prix fixe menus, which meant they had to pay for the entire experience regardless. Sarah said, "I told you I would be over the moon for brunch. Damien thinks an Indian hole-in-the-wall is enough, and Sebastian has to be home at eleven. What more do we need to know?"

I quickly changed the subject. I brought up the delicious dipping sauce that had just been presented with the eggrolls. I knew she was frustrated and sort of right. Our honeymoon phase with Paris had worn off, and we were seeing the day-to-day realities, seeing Parisians for who they really were. The over-the-top Kong playground for adults that evening seemed to be magnifying it.

I continued to eat my heart out and enjoy the scene, but that statement Sarah made bothered me, even if there was some truth to it. We ended up cutting the tension by taking silly photos and laughing at our expressions, agreeing we all looked tired and like we were trying to force fake smiles.

Happy birthday to me ...

SEVENTEEN

A blend does not, cannot, demonstrate varietal character.
But it should demonstrate distinctiveness. Tasting a great
Châteauneuf-du-Pape should tell you above all that this is
a Châteauneuf-du-Pape and cannot be anything else.

We had reached the month of March, and wine school was becoming more and more intense as Professor Lavigne groomed us for our final exams, which would come in a few short months. I couldn't believe that this year had flown by as fast as it had. I felt like I had just stepped off the plane at Charles de Gaulle

227

about to embark on this adventure. Flash forward six short months later, and I had mastered my life in Paris.

Some would say I was living a dream: Gallivanting through the city with my newfound tribe of friends acting as if we owned my arrondissement. Brunching on Sundays, wine bars on Wednesdays, speaking in French whenever out and about in the districts, picnics on the Seine River when the weather allowed. I no longer ever felt as if I was surviving in Paris; I felt as if I was fully integrated and *living* in Paris, even though comments like Sarah's on my birthday dinner were still constant topics: Did we really fit in here? Were French men really even that great, or were we creating a fantasy around them that wasn't there? And aside from our personal and dating lives, what was our purpose in Paris?

Thoughts started to creep into my mind such as: What next? I had just reached the top of my game in this city, was just starting to catch my groove, and then I was supposed to turn around and leave when sommelier school came to an end? This thought alone gave me a surge of anxiety. Was this it? Was Paris placed in my path for a flashing second compared to the grand scheme of life?

I had a burning suspicion in my soul that my journey in Paris was not over yet. There had to be more to it than my wine school adventure. Maybe I would work at a fancy hotel as a sommelier or help English-speaking tourists discover the city's wine shops. I had analyzed my relationship with Paris for years, though I could never put my finger on the *why*. I was certainly not fluent in the language, far from it actually. I had zero connections in France, except for the ones I was making through my training. If I wrote down the reasons for not wanting to leave on paper, nothing would add up to why I would fathom staying here, but I could care less. I wasn't necessarily looking to be rational, more looking for a sign.

Perhaps I was just so drawn to erasing my past identity, and Paris offered up a good outlet for that. Internally I was still the same girl, but Paris was allowing me to create an entirely new, autonomous self-image. I was sophisticated Krista here, sipping wine on chic terraces among other savvy Parisian women. I was worldly, meeting and befriending people from all walks of life. I felt daring and like I couldn't wait for what would unfold the next day. It was much different than the feeling I had back in the States. Back home, I knew the same people, had the same conversations, was pressured to have the same beliefs I was raised with. There wasn't much wiggle room to step out and be different. I was so fascinated by Paris due to its beauty, respect, and all things plea-surable, but also because it felt like a necessity to my evolution as a woman. I was voyaging with myself and at no time in my life had I undertaken so much self-reflection.

As far as Citrus Etoile went, I had completed my internship successfully with glowing stars. By the end I was able to open and present bottles of wine to the table with ease. Antoine unfortu-nately couldn't hire me on staff as I didn't have a work visa; I had a student visa. He suggested I consult with an immigration attorney if I wanted to work at Citrus Etoile and get paid. I considered this as a way to stay in Paris, but I really was relieved that the intern-ship was over. The world of fine dining wasn't good for my anxi-ety, even though Antoine had been the best boss ever. In any case, applying for a French work visa was also very complicated. Usually for the French government to extend this, you have to have your future employer sponsor you. This means they have to pay the

French government somewhere in the ball park of 5,000 euros as they are proving they believe in your ability that much. Antoine told me the restaurant could not afford to do that. However, he said that if I wanted to pay it, I could get the visa.

I was pondering all the hows to try and make my why justified. Time was dwindling, and I was feeling the pressure. I was clear on one fact, though: I didn't want to leave Paris. Antoine and I would stay in touch, and I could tell if I really needed him to help me he would. I pondered the thought: Would he pay the five-thousand-something euros to the government so I could work at the restaurant? I optimistically thought to myself he would if I asked him. I had told him about Damien. He listened intently one night and tried to offer me advice. I asked him, "Am I a joke to French men? Like, would any of them actually be interested in me? Be honest!"

He stared at me and sheepishly looked down at the table. "I would," he said. "But I would never sleep with you, as you are someone I could see developing feelings for. You know my rule: I don't sleep with women I know, have a friendship with, or care for."

That was sweet of him to say to validate my worth and existence, but I was also so relieved he hadn't tried to pursue me. I loved the nature of our relationship. Antoine was a safety net for me; I felt like he looked after me in a way. I could talk to him, I was comfortable, and I knew he was only trying to help me on my journey in Paris.

One night in early March, I was set to meet my friends at a wine bar in the First Arrondissement known as Ô Château. We were long overdue for a night out on the town and a gab session. School had gotten extreme, and it seemed we were having piles of information thrown at us. If it wasn't a lightning-fast lecture where we had to memorize all of the Grand Crus of Bordeaux, then it was the lecture where we learned about the rare varietals and certain appellations producing wines in the southern regions of France, the more unknown wines being made that professionals damn well better be savvy on. It was starting to feel overwhelming, and we needed a mental break and, most of all, laughter. Nothing made us more delighted than good wine, delicious food, and being out at a new discovery in the city. Our Rhône Valley trip was upon us; we were leaving in a week, but first, another night out in Paris.

I was getting into my Uber, destination bound, when my cell phone vibrated in my purse. I reached for it and proceeded to stare at the screen for a good thirty seconds.

Hello Krista. Sorry I have been so rude to you. I have some social issues I guess. How are you?

This message was from Damien, of course, appearing on my phone screen as The Submissive. Shit. Do I respond to this? I was secretly elated, as I had been thinking about him for days, and felt like I had gotten no closure on what the hell had happened between us. I didn't want to even admit to myself how validated I felt in reading this text message. Number one, just the fact that he had reached out to me was adrenaline-producing enough. Number two, he reached out to me with an apology, and number three, he admitted he had issues. Was this a prank? As I thought back on my time with him, I had pretty much considered him a narcissist weirdo underneath his incredible sex appeal. I decided to cap this and enjoy the night with my friends. At this point they were over the Damien saga. I thought I had squashed this infatuation and curiosity, and we had concluded I would let it be and move on. They would definitely be disappointed if I brought him up again.

It took all of two glasses of wine on an empty stomach before I was typing a response to his message.

I appreciate this text, Damien. Thank you.

I figured if he had an agenda he would say more. I knew dealing with Damien again could only bring questions and pain, but I *was* thankful for this text, as it brought with it an immense amount of validation in just those few words.

Within thirty minutes he responded.

Submissive: *You are welcome. (Smiley wink face.) So, how are you and what is new? Tell me.*

Krista: *Ummm, not much. Loving Paris as always. And U?*

Submissive: *I am currently on a ski trip in the Alps. But I will be back in town later this week.*

What was he getting at here? What did he want? I decided not to respond to this. If he wanted more out of this conversation, then he needed to take control and let me know that.

Ten minutes later…

Submissive: *Well, if you want to see your slave next week let me know.* (another smiley face)

"What the hell are you doing? Who are you texting?" Sarah demanded, seeing the shocked expression line my face as I read this final text.

I absolutely could not keep this in. I just couldn't. I was on the verge of either laughing or throwing my phone across the room. Who the hell says that? Even if he is submissive in bed, why is he saying this, especially when he made it very clear to me that I was not dominant enough for him? If this wasn't a mind fuck, I didn't know what was. I passed my phone over to Sarah and let her read the exchange.

"Oh my God, you are not seeing him. This is totally unhealthy. How dare he say that after sending you a text last month with 'good luck finding your soulmate'? Krista, this guy is insane." The others at the table agreed. I did, too, in the moment to appease them, but I knew myself better than that. It was just too tempting and mysterious not to see him again. I not only wanted answers that I hadn't yet been given, but I wanted his touch and the magical feeling of sparks when he knocked on my door to spend the evening with me. I was fully aware I was on the verge of becoming a masochist.

I responded two days later with a simple *sure* and asked if he was available Thursday night, to which he agreed and suggested he come by my place after work. Here we go again! I couldn't help but wonder if we would engage in another performing arts act. I didn't really know what to expect, as he had reached out to me, but I was excited by the thought alone of seeing him. I decided I was going to try and keep my mouth shut and not tell any of my friends that *The Submissive* was driving over for round two. Frankly, I think they would have been disgusted by my decision. Like a drug, the excitement overtook my rational brain, which knew better.

I tried to get through my week of classes, but all that kept flashing in my mind was anticipation of my night with Damien. We hadn't texted since we had arranged the plans, which I questioned and wondered if that was a bad sign. Maybe I didn't understand his motives, but whatever, I just wanted the night to get here. The suspense was killing me.

Bzzzzz. My intercom buzzed for me to let Damien in through the lobby doors. The night was upon us. I found I was impressed that he was right on time and that he had remembered my codes to enter the building. Even this made me feel important enough, that he had stored away a memory disc for Krista. He had memorized my address and door codes without having to ask. At the time, this really was a huge sign as to how little I had expected of a man, as long as they were French. Or as long as they picked me? It was like I just didn't want to go back to the States, where I had been with an addict and apparently all of those issues were hiding under the surface. Paris could provide plenty of men and dysfunction to aid in that familiarity. The ups and downs from my prior relationship with Eddie made anyone who wasn't on hard drugs appealing, so remembering a door code got them points. Reaching out to me got them points. Apologies got them points. It was all so sad and of such a low standard.

I felt the familiar rush that I always got when I was seconds away from seeing him. Damien knocked three times on my door, and I swung it open almost instantly. A big smile appeared on the other side of the steel door, and he immediately went in for a kiss on my lips. Wow. I didn't get the famous bisous on each cheek; no, I got his lips touching mine. Right away. Maybe he had missed me. I have to say, I went all out in a subtle "he will think it's a natural look" way. I was wearing a formfitting white silk blouse with leather pants and high black suede boots. My hair was straightened, and I kept my makeup natural with pink hues in the form of blush, lip gloss, and a dust of salmon-rose eye shadow.

"Oh, I don't get bisous? I get a real kiss? How come? Is it because I am not French?" I spoke my mind and didn't try in any regard to keep from making him feel uncomfortable.

He just gave a smile in return. It didn't need a response, and we both knew it. He made a comment that he liked my pants. Of course he did; what submissive doesn't like leather?

He then pulled out a bottle of Champagne and proceeded to open it as he coyly said he owed me an apology. I found this a nice gesture, but all I could do was stare at him and his perfectly arranged features. I took in his beauty. If he were a model, he would have needed zero airbrushing. Olive skin, the perfect shade, even throughout his face and neck; piercing green eyes; and a dark, rich, full head of brown hair. This paired with his tall stature, broad build, and classy, well-put-together ensemble? He was hard not to look at. Not to mention he was opening a bottle of Champagne for me. We sat in my salon and started out with small talk. Then I decided to go for gusto, never really having been able to contain my directness.

"So tell me, or I guess, please explain to me what happened a couple of months ago. That night, the sex... I was just, I don't know, taken back."

In usual Damien fashion, words didn't just come flying out of his mouth. He took a minute to take in my question and orchestrate his response.

"Yes. Well, I prefer this in sex. I really like the feeling of being dominated. I have been this way, or should I say, it has been what I have desired since I was eighteen years old."

"Oh," I said, stunned and disappointed at his honesty. Then I went onto ask, "With your past girlfriends, were they all this way? Has there ever been just natural penis-in-vagina sex in your relationship past?"

"That's the thing. I used to keep this to myself and not share my real desires. Sometimes weeks, months, or years into a relationship, I would keep this inside. That only led to problems, as I wasn't being myself. And that's when I would start going to clubs."

"Clubs?" I asked with trepidation.

"Yes, underground clubs where they cater to these desires. I would be tied up and have women digging their high heels into me. It was very painful but what I needed to feel aroused." He responded with such confidence and barely a flinch.

Experts say that when a man feels comfortable enough with a woman to open up about his struggles, that is a marker he feels close and bonded to that woman. At this point I didn't know any more if I was flattered and happy he was opening up to me or growing more disturbed by the second and wishing he hadn't been.

"Wow, did something happen in your childhood to provoke this desire?"

I could tell this question was the first to make him uncomfortable. He cleared his throat and looked away.

"I feel like you are my therapist now. Starting to be if we go down this road." He still wasn't looking at me. I saw the pain in his eyes and decided not to press the issue. I realized in that moment I wanted to fix his hurt. I wanted to be the woman that could make him happy and satisfied with normal sex and intimacy. In fact, I decided I would welcome the challenge. He hadn't stopped checking me out since he had entered the apartment. I got up from my chair to fetch the Champagne bottle in an attempt to top us off. As I walked past him, he put his hands on my legs, grabbing them so I would stop walking. There he was, sitting on the couch as I was standing just in front of him. He started moving his hands from behind my knee, up, caressing the backs of my thighs, and then he grabbed me. We started making out passionately, which had come as no surprise as the sexual tension in the room thus far had been palpable, and I had known it was only a matter of time.

I wanted only to keep kissing him. This was the best feeling in the world, and I knew once it progressed, I would have to take charge and I would become someone I wasn't. I was finding it hard to be in the moment of his fiery kisses because I knew what was coming next.

"Do you want to go into your bedroom?" he asked, staring into my eyes as he broke our lip-lock.

"Okay." I removed myself from him. He then got up and walked into the bedroom, where he proceeded to lie down on my bed, on his stomach with his face in my pillow. This was it. He put

himself in the most submissive state he could and left it up to me
to control the scene.

I immediately felt uncomfortable, and a sudden shift of pressure came over me.

Krista, you can do this, I told myself. *Just pretend this is a role
you are auditioning for. Suck it up and become a dominatrix. It will
be over soon.*

I was up early. I placed a pod in my Nespresso machine. We would
embark on the adventure to the Rhône Valley today. I reached into
my small refrigerator and took out a plain yogurt and ripped off
a hunk of bread from a baguette laying on my kitchen counter.
One of my favorite varietals had in fact become Syrah, which was
the prevalent red grape in the Rhône Valley. We would be taking
a train from Paris to Vienne, a major town in the French Alps
located on the Rhône River about twenty miles outside of the city
of Lyon. Sebastian was on his way over, and we would grab an
Uber to the train station together.

"So, what happened last night? With Damien?" Sebastian
abruptly asked as I got into the car.

"I'm not sure I even want to discuss it," I said quickly.

"Okay, well, I think David and I are done. We got into a huge
argument this morning. We are going to Rhône, who cares, but it
isn't the best timing for me."

"I'm so sorry. Maybe once the wine is flowing later we can chat. I just am sort of in my head about everything." I said this with truth and some sadness. I was upset at what was transpiring for both of us. Sebastian agreed and offered me a pain au chocolat. I was appeased and suddenly happy.

"Let's do this!" Alan, one of my classmates, high-fived me when we boarded the train. I had to admit I was full of anticipation. The class trips always under-promised and overdelivered, and I was sure the Rhône Valley would be no exception.

We would start with Northern Rhône and the Côte-Rôtie appellation. This appellation produced almost all Syrah as far as red wine was concerned, and was allowed three white grapes to be grown. Those grapes were Roussanne, Marsanne, and Viognier. I was anticipating tasting the whites there, as my usual go-tos had become predominantly Chardonnay from Burgundy and the Champagnes I had fallen in love with. I wanted to expand my preferences.

We approached our first vineyard, Stéphane Ogier. We were told that Stéphane Ogier produced wines from some of the most famous Côte-Rôtie areas including Lancement, Côte Rozier, and La Vialliere. His wines were sought after by the greatest chefs and most serious wine lovers around the world. Stéphane introduced himself, and I have to say, *handsome* came to mind. He was tall and very gracious toward all of us upon our entrance. This was a winery that we were privy to because of Professor Lavigne and his connections. I could tell this was not somewhere tourists visited; this was a place for serious wine professionals. We tasted an array of Syrahs once in the cellar. We were being poured Syrahs straight out of the barrel—this wine wasn't even bottled yet! A long, plastic tube with a suction was being placed in the French oak barrels, with vintages and blends no one in the open market was tasting, then released into our glasses.

Professor Lavigne stated that these were going to be wines not many get to taste ever, as they are library or reserve wines, meaning they are for private sale. That was something we would be introduced to in Rhône: private sale. This was an industry in and of itself, "you only know if you know" sort of territory. I was intrigued; it seemed elusive. I wanted an in, and apparently that day I had one.

We each bought a couple of bottles of Stéphane Ogier. Next up, we were headed to the sought-after region of Tain-l'Hermitage, to a place I had been highly anticipating: Michel Chapoutier. As in class, when we had tasted wines from Chapoutier, we were reminded of the importance of Michel Chapoutier's wines, the fact that they were constantly gaining accolades and winning awards. The Chapoutier family started in 1879, the year their first vineyard was purchased.

Unlike Stéphane Ogier, which felt sort of under the radar, like a secret gem the public didn't have access to, Michel Chapoutier had its own wine shop selling all of the bottles at the front of the vineyard. Wine lined the shelves, vintage after vintage, as we entered the tasting room through the store. We were then taken into a private room with a grand, U-shaped oak table. A plush, black leather chair was placed every two feet around the table. Whoever had designed this was a genius. This room made you feel like you were about to make a deal of some sort. Serious debate would be discussed. The room elevated the energy, and everyone suddenly stood up a little bit straighter.

We were handed a large packet of wine and tasting notes, complete with information about the vineyard and winemaking. The tasting menu would consist of eight wines that day.

We started by tasting several white wines that Michel Chapoutier produced. The first was a Viognier that was somewhat unique, although at this point nothing was to us. We had tasted somewhere around two thousand French wines by this time in the program. I liked Viognier because it was a wine typically lower in acidity, although still round and rich on the palate. Classically it had aromas of white flowers and honey, and I found it to be complex. Next we tried wines made of the single varietals Marsanne and Roussanne, the two other white grapes that are allowed in the Hermitage appellation. I fell head over heels for a 2006 vintage named Le Meal Blanc. It was 100 percent Marsanne grape, and this was what I loved about traveling through wine. I paid so much attention as we tasted this one to the soil type needed to produce this layered concoction, and I also recognized I now had a new favorite white-grape varietal. I purchased the bottle at 210 euros. The cost in a restaurant would have been tripled.

We spent the night in a quaint hotel in the small town of Tain-l'Hermitage and had a mellow night as the next day we were set to arrive in Avignon. I couldn't wait to come full circle to Provence!

We checked into our hotel in Avignon, and Pearl and I immediately opened a bottle of chilled Viognier from the mini fridge. *Santé, mon ami!* We were in Provence, and our professors gave us a travel day, which meant there were no tastings scheduled and we were on our own, free to venture out and about in the town of Avignon and do whatever we wanted. We had an intense itinerary planned for the next couple of days, so we welcomed the down time. Sarah knocked on the door, and we immediately gave her a glass. We had a girls' gab session out on the balcony of our hotel room before we would meet the rest of the group for dinner.

There was a bit of drama on the high seas between our classmates. The class had felt divided ever since shots were fired at the last large event we did in Paris, so much so that we were splitting up for dinner that evening. The Grand Tasting event back in December had really set the tone for competition. Emotions were not healed from some of the hurtful comments that had been said, the energy between the group was like a scratched record playing on repeat. Full of flaws, hard to fix, screeching sounds, you just want to steer clear. During lectures and professional tastings I didn't notice this as much; it was more prevalent when we were just hanging out. For instance that night should have been a beautiful bonding moment in a charming town. The French students I personally felt were nice, but the three girls in the class were typical— very to themselves and very cliquey. I would have conversations with them over meals, and they were gracious, but that was it; no real friendship was to be formed. I wondered if it was a challenge for them to be around such an international group. We were in their country, but any event we participated in, everyone needed to conduct themselves in English. I pondered if this secretly bothered them. We had all come to their country, and it was demanded they switch into a different language. I could see their looks of disgust when someone was outspoken or spoke out of turn or was loud; they were true to the culture's formalities. They were quiet observers, but their thoughts were all over their faces.

It was due to competition as well. We were all social, but the class was getting intense. We were all gaining confidence in the tasting world and becoming experts in wine. Blind tastings with calling a wine were now the norm in lectures; we were rarely told what a wine was. We were expected to figure that out through everything we had learned to do to detect it. We were becoming sommeliers. I had become very confident in this, and I couldn't believe it: to watch all of us attain this level of certainty regarding something sophisticated and intimidating was amazing. If someone called a wine and their declaration was way off, there was definitely judgment. At this point, you were taken seriously even by other classmates, and the message was "Please don't embarrass us as a whole by calling the wine wrong and making us all look bad."

It would be interesting to see how the rest of the year played out. We were told that one student would win the blind tasting that would be presented as part of our exams. There were many parts to the final exam day, and the grand finale was being presented with one white and one red wine to blind taste. We were going to have to stand at the podium in front of a grand jury of Parisian sommeliers, many of whom had restaurants or worked for famous hotels in Paris, and call the wine as well as discuss it and lead everyone through a tasting. Also, we had to write in an essay why we had determined the wine was what it was. We would each individually enter the same room and taste the same wines. As one person went in, the doors would shut. I envisioned how nerve-racking that was going to be, to be next in line. *Who would win?*

We were arriving at our first tasting of the day, Château de Beau-castel, in the highly sought-after appellation of Châteauneuf-du-Pape; this was about a fifteen-minute drive from the town of Avignon.

This chateau more or less resembled a large, Tuscan mansion on a vineyard. There were Roman fountains featured along the pathway, statues of angels and dragons, and large dogs roaming around the property. Horses weren't far from sight, past the vines in a pasture. There was a large Roman pool to punctuate the entrance, with more water trickling from the mouths of lion statues.

"Bienvenue," a representative of the vineyard stated as I was given a glass of crisp, white wine. I tasted it and noted it was most likely a Roussanne/Marsanne blend.

We walked through the grounds, sipping different vintages and learning about the incredible history of the region Château-neuf-du-Pape—literal translation, "the new castle of the pope." This refers to a time when the pope was not residing in Rome, but rather safely ensconced in the walled city of Avignon, away from his political enemies.

*In the remarkable vineyards of Châteauneuf-du-Pape, the "soil" is composed of large, round rocks deposited over millennia by the receding Rhône River. Barely a speck of dirt can be seen. Many vineyards are large rock beds with no visible dirt whatsoever. *Karen MacNeil (The Wine Bible)

In lectures back in Paris, we had tasted many different Châteauneuf-du-Pape wines, and we were aware of the complexity, as thirteen grape varietals were allowed in the blends of this wine. Compare that to the only grape allowed in Côte-Rôtie being

Syrah! Château de Beaucastel utilized and grew *all* thirteen grapes. This was unique to the region, as many Châteauneuf-du-Papes are mainly composed of Grenache and Syrah, with a few others mixed in for complexity.

As we were walking through the vineyards, we were all sinking into the present moment that only the South of France can bring. We snapped photos of each other among the vines, picking grapes and eating them next to the Roman fountains. We were taking in the vast amount of history in the region while also letting loose a bit. The wines were complex and bold; I could tell this was different and unique territory, and felt entirely connected to the land and what this wine was at its core. Miniature sausages with raisined cherries were being served with the next vintage. I inhaled one, and the scent of fennel combined with the earthiness of the wine was pure pleasure. We were starving. I had skipped breakfast as I knew we were going to a fabulous lunch that day, and I could hardly wait. Feeling a little buzz come over me, as well as the hot sun on my skin, I was happy when Professor Lavigne told us it was time for lunch.

In usual fashion, we had been told close to nothing about this experience in Provence, so we were all giddy when we pulled up to Château des Fines Roches, nestled at the very top of a hill overlooking Provence. There was a table set up against the backdrop of this postcard-worthy view, with beautiful china and glassware at each place setting. The waiters were in tuxedos, standing at attention waiting for us, wine on their trays as a welcome greeting.

This was actually an old castle transformed into a private hotel in the heart of Châteauneuf-du-Pape. Provençal decor was everywhere, and lavender plants and lemon trees lined the walk-ways. We took our seats among the olive trees, and I took off my blouse, letting the sun hit my skin in just a tank top. An amuse-bouche was brought out, as well as olive bread and garlic-infused olive oil. Professor Lavigne announced that six wines would be poured over five courses; he encouraged us to take notes on each one.

The tension was lower among my classmates. I think every-one gave into the pure beauty and magic happening that afternoon in Provence. Jean-Baptiste, one of the French guys in class, started making jokes about wines, which turned into a fun game of giving an image for each wine. Someone said about the wine with course three, "Oh, this is a straight Grenache; there is no blend in this wine," and Jean-Baptiste loudly stated, "Grenache is the nightmare of a nasty bitch." Everyone started laughing in hysterics. What? Where did that come from? Even Professor Lavigne turned bright red and laughed.

We were such total wine geeks at this point that sometimes making light of wine was necessary to drop the seriousness at times. We all welcomed the laughter and ease of this food and wine pairing, all while getting sun-kissed among the vines.

There was a beautiful whole white fish served, as well as a course of stew with meat falling off the bone. Everything was being presented as art; there was no family-style serving other than the bread. This only enhanced the experience and made me focus on the pairings and really tasting what represented this region in both the food and the wine. Just as I had felt at Beaucastel, I was connected here to the earth and the meaning of Provence; I could feel the culture and the history.

The next day was soon upon us. We had pulled up to Domaine Vincent in the Cornas appellation of Rhône and were eagerly awaiting some deep and heavy Syrahs. We walked into a large, industrial garage, and silence overtook the room. You could hear the echo if anyone spoke. Paintings were everywhere, on easels, hanging among the barrels, and lined up against the wine cases and boxes. A few minutes later the winemaker appeared, tall in stature, with dirty blond, messy hair, a sharp nose, and a blank expression on his face. He had a white apron on with paint splashes everywhere; he said he had been creating art as he looked down a bit sheepishly. I could tell this was a Lavigne connection, and this guy was essentially like, "I make really dope wine, but I'm an artist. I don't have time for these kids from school." He immediately shook hands with Professor Lavigne and started opening the wines. One after another, and in a very informal style, he started pouring them into our glasses, speaking in very broken English. Professor Lavigne was leading this education, as we were not able to understand the winemaker. He seemed to be running this garage of art and wine all by himself, and after my first sip of the first wine I declared him a genius in my own brain. Sebastian looked at me and whispered, "I'm literally going to buy a case of this if I can—so good."

Others started speaking up. Sandrine asked, "How long was this aged? What is the brix?" He could tell everyone was falling in love with his wines, as the curiosities had commenced. He remained sheepish and shy.

"Are these for sale? Is there a pricing sheet?" Sebastian asked.

"I do not, I *reeeeally* have not a sheet as I mainly sell these to my word-of-mouth custeemor," he stated and then said, "But I can sell. *Mais oui*, what price are you willing to pay?"

Everyone looked at each other. What was this now, an auction? Professor Lavigne smirked and decided to go with this. He blurted out, "Who will buy the 2014 Cornas by Vincent? What is your price?"

Sebastian chimed in, "I will!"

"I want that one. I will pay seventy euros," Benoit interrupted him. Others gave their best price, and now it was a fun game of who would pay the most for this artistry. Sarah and I were laughing, just one of those moments of instant entertainment. Our classmates were taking this seriously as if they were bidding on Picassos. It was absolutely comical, and it really showed what we had become. More than wine geeks, more than wine experts, we were in the Rhône Valley in a French winemaker's garage, bidding on wines now. We were wine *obsessed*.

After two more days, which included venturing to the appellation of Cornas and the following vineyard lineup, Domaine des Hauts Châssis, Faugier-Gonnet, and Domain Georges Vernay, I had definitely become sick of wine and had an extra five pounds on me from this richness of food and wine. It was well worth it, and I returned to my Paris apartment with eight bottles of wine purchased from this trip and a wealth of knowledge and memories.

EIGHTEEN

Great wine is about nuance, surprise, subtlety, expression, qualities that
keep you coming back for another taste. Rejecting a wine because it is not
big enough is like rejecting a book because it is not long enough,
or a piece of music because it is not loud enough.

—KERMIT LYNCH

After another date, I awoke to Damien watching me sleep. Given what had taken place the night before, I would have bet a million dollars against any form of adoration coming from him to me in any sense. But now he was gazing at me with tenderness in his eyes. What the hell?

I guess I must have done a good job. I felt like a cheap piece of meat or someone who had just auditioned for Crazy Horse, the allusive erotic but classy club in Paris where tickets book out months in advance, with an empty spirit. During the act I had thought to myself, watching his eyes roll back in pleasure to my heel digging into his throat, *Can you imagine having young children with this man?* I pictured the scene, sitting at our bistro table in our adorned Parisian apartment, having a lovely roasted chicken with caramelised fennel, and then, after sweet lullabies and kisses to the little ones, I would be going into the bedroom next door and beating the shit out of their father.

It just wasn't my cup of tea. It was the moments afterward, like the first time when we had taken in the calming scents of aromatherapy oils, or now this sweet morning gaze, that I cared for. In these moments I convinced myself that I liked him, and so I created a fantasy. Why was I still doing this? I was starting to get sick of myself. He left after coffee and biscuits. Paris was matching my mood; we were both weeping. I stared out at the gray sky and wondered who was messed up more: me or him? Why was I torturing myself to be with a man that wanted this? He was never going to offer me anything but pain. He was completely unavailable, and it still was all serving *him*.

Was this it? I felt like I was trying to latch onto something, anything to create a life for myself in Paris outside of school. In comparison, Sebastian and David were officially over. In my mind and heart I knew this was the best thing for Sebastian; he would no longer be controlled; he could be carefree again and able to focus on himself in Paris. He seemed pretty jolted by it, though, and said he felt surprised it had been so easy for David to just discard him like the relationship was nothing. Sarah was becoming more and more depressed each time I saw her. She would joke about the weight she was gaining and how her highlight of the day was which cheese she was getting from the cheese shops, saying she had "zero control." Aside from the jokes about her weight, she seemed really sad. She continued to make comments about how crazy amazing this experience had been, and how at the same time she didn't, *we* didn't, belong in Paris. I bit my tongue every time because if I didn't it would turn into a tense debate. I could, however, relate to the hard fact of this incredible, movie-set experience just one day vanishing. It was an unnerving feeling, a red-letter year that would turn to dust after ten months. What were we supposed to do with that impending low after all the highs?

None of us had a for sure bet on working in the world of wine. We were in another country, so we started to wonder how this program would translate in the US as well as other countries. Was this degree even meaningful outside of France? In comparison to the Master Court of Sommeliers Levels One through Four, it was not recognized in America. I'm sure on the surface level it would be. For example, in an interview, "Oh wow, you trained in Paris! Oh wow, at Le Cordon Bleu. This is interesting, *tell me more.*" It would definitely stand out on a resume, but as far as actual official identification, I wasn't sure how far it would get us.

Professor Lavigne had told us what others were doing from years prior. Some had started tourism businesses; some were food and wine writers for digital magazines; some went on to work as lower-level sommeliers in Paris. Yes, lower level, bottom rung. Basically washing glasses and stocking wine in wine caves for up to two years before actually getting out on the restaurant floor and being able to recommend and serve wine. This sounded daunting and like slave labor to me.

I think this added to all of our anxiety, as nothing was for sure. We had gone through all of this intense training, tasting thousands of wines, and then we were not even guaranteed work in this industry. I knew if I went back to the States I would immediately enroll in the Master Court of Sommeliers and at least get my Level One certification. This course would absolutely help me get there and pass that, even Level Two. Some of our classmates spoke about moving on next to the WSET course. Many of them were also trying to use Professor Lavigne for connections to restaurants in the city. Practically all of the French students would be placed due to Professor Lavigne's letter of recommendation to their future employers. His reputation in Paris was impeccable. I was of course fearful of my impending future and work status, but I also had done this for a mixed-bag reason. I needed to escape to Paris more or less; I needed a sabbatical from the US. I needed out of an unhealthy cycle of a relationship with a man.

I pulled out my itinerary for the final class trip we would be taking next week: Alsace, France. We were heading to the border approaching Germany. I had been told it was a different side of France and that we would be exploring the wine land of Riesling and Gewürztraminer.

We would be venturing to the small towns of Riquewihr and Kaysersberg. It was rumored these towns felt like you were in the storybook of Hansel and Gretel, and the homes in the village looked like gingerbread houses. I was greatly anticipating the Trimbach vineyard, as we had tasted many great wines in lectures and I had fallen in love with the wine style. I got a spark of giddiness reading through the three-day travel plan, which was under-delivering per usual, I was sure.

That evening Sarah would be happy as the food and wine pairing event we were required to attend was all about *fromage*. We were set to attend a nine-course cheese and wine pairing from six until nine o'clock that evening. Another required event would happen two days later, when we would dress in formal attire to work a sommelier event at the famous Four Seasons Hotel George V in the Eighth Arrondissement, featuring the acclaimed Charles Heidsieck Champagne house. This was an invite-only event for the top sommeliers of the world. I honestly couldn't wait for either, and needed to go on a run on the Seine desperately before the cheese tasting that night.

"That is the hottest guy I have ever seen."

Sarah said this out loud at our table of eight. She was referring to one of the owners of the famous cheese shop Barthélémy, who was presenting the cheeses that evening as Professor Lavigne spoke about the wines.

I had to agree with her; he was gorgeous. He looked so French, but had movie star Brad Pitt vibes, and his accent when he spoke English only added to his beauty. Jen, another classmate, laughed out loud and made a comment that it must have been awhile for Sarah.

We started with chèvre and a local honeycomb, which was paired with Sancerre, an appellation that grows *only* Sauvignon Blanc. The chèvre was actually made from goats around the Sancerre region, so essentially we were having food and wine grown from the same terroir. The crisp wine cut through the creamy although acidic goat cheese perfectly. It was an amazing pairing. That night I was also awakened to Sauternes paired with Roquefort, a deep, rich, and creamy blue cheese. The sweetness of the wine paired perfectly with the creaminess and richness of the cheese. There were other standouts like the Comté paired with *vin jaune* or yellow wine, which is an almost oxidized wine from the Jura region similar to sherry, as well as the Camembert and Meursault pairing. There were fresh, hot-out-of-the-oven breads baked minutes before by Le Cordon Bleu's patisserie and boulangerie students. It was the most scrumptious evening.

"Krista, I dare you to get his number after this. I feel like you look cute and could swing it." Sarah was absolutely fixated on this guy. I gave her a smirk and told her I would think about it. I was entering a point, a phase where I took weird risks in the city daily to see if something would stick. To look for signs. What was I willing to say yes to? This would be another one of those.

There was this subtle awareness as if I were watching myself from a tree branch above, noting the batshit and at the same time rooting on this audacious, fearless girl. That was the thing about living in a foreign country: there were moments where you did things you wouldn't normally do in your hometown. For me it felt like this constant, invigorating feeling of autonomy, and it was as if I could reinvent myself, be anybody I wanted. Especially in Paris, there was so much life force and energy vibrating through the city that anyone could pick up on anything. I knew this was a major reason I had dreamed of living here, and I think many American women do for the same reason. Paris is such a feminine city, full of art in every way; you just sort of unleash parts of yourself that were always there, but that you hadn't met yet.

After the cheese tasting, even though I felt bloated, I took a bite of a chocolate petit four, a swig of our final wine, Premier Cru Champagne, and approached the cheese man. I told him how much I had enjoyed his presentation and said, "Here is my card. Can I also have your contact info?" He obliged and smiled. I entered him in my phone as "Cheese Hottie."

The next evening we were in the Eighth Arrondissement. I always loved it when I was called over to the famous avenue of the Champs-Élysées. I noticed I tended to stay on the Left Bank more often than not, and like a true Parisian I only left my neighborhood when I had something going on. Once you are in the groove in Paris, you start having your spots. Whether it be your butcher shop, your cheese shop, you start to personally know all of the fruit and vegetable vendors, and of course your favorite cafés.

The Four Seasons/Charles Heidsieck event was successful, although tiring. My favorite part of all was standing in this grand hotel, taking in the vastness and the pure luxury, people-watching and observing the French dining experience, and being immersed in this underground food and wine world within the greater French culture. I always loved being the observer, and it connected me to why we were studying what we were. The food and wine culture of Paris was magical. It was an art, it was taken seriously, and I took immense pride in understanding it. That evening was a synchronized event, almost like watching a performance in a pool. Once every dish was placed on the table, we would waltz over with a bottle of champagne and pour, ladies first, clockwise, and repeat. This event lasted five hours not including setup and cleanup. It was a presentation with speakers at podiums, all speaking in French about the different vintages of Charles Heidsieck we were pouring. A formal dinner to the nines, and we were along for all of it.

After being on our feet all day and most of the night, Sarah, Pearl, and I decided to snag a table in the lounge of the hotel. We plopped down on fabulous, forest-green leather chairs and admired the bouquets and overall ambience. That night we ordered fancy cocktails with roses floating on the tops of them, and also the joke of the evening: spending twenty-five euros each on cups of *chocolat chaud*.

"Yummy, this cocktail is hitting the spot. Okay, I know the next month is going to be grueling after Alsace, with studying for the certification exam, so we need to plan a graduation trip somewhere amazing," Sarah blurted out after the waitress set down the *frites* we had just ordered. They came with a delicious aioli dipping sauce that looked addicting.

I was starving. *"Excusez-moi, je vais prendre un croque madame s'il vous plaît, pour partager,"* I said to the waitress. The ever famous hot ham and cheese sandwich drenched in creamy bechamel sounded great split among the three of us.

"I was thinking that as well. My vote is for Italy, or the island of Corsica," Pearl happily declared.

"Being that we are about to study Corsican wine, why don't we aim for that! I have been told by a few French people it's *the place* to vacation." I always wanted to be in France; Italy and Spain were of course appealing, but I just wanted to see other parts of France as much as possible, even ones off the coast of Italy.

Sarah said, "Krista, I envy you and Paris. You are your best self here. I don't feel the same, and would be so excited for a city to light me up that way. The way Paris lights you up."

Pearl agreed and started talking about running out of money and how she also loved Paris and could see herself staying if it weren't for a financial issue.

Sarah chimed in pretty declaratively that she wanted to go back to the States.

I was dying to stay in France. Leaving Paris felt like I was losing my arm: I just couldn't imagine it. She went on to say she didn't feel taken seriously. She felt like a joke. In dating, American girls were simply a "fun time" to men; in the working world, forget about wanting to be on this tax system; finally we didn't speak the language. I understood all the points she was making rationally, but there was something so much more than that for me. My soul was somehow connected in a way I didn't understand. I could just feel it in my bones. I knew my time here wasn't up. A psychic once told me that I had lived a past life running a vineyard estate for my wealthy father in Bordeaux. I wouldn't dare question that. Who knows if we have past lives? Paris made me question it and lean toward believing it.

We turned to other topics like dating and what the current status for each of us was. I was continuing to go down a rabbit hole of not feeling good about myself after I would see Damien, and I knew I needed to cut it off before I got really hurt, but I kept this to myself. I wasn't sure what would be more of a challenge: my final sommelier certification exam or not seeing Damien again, as I would be saying farewell to the one source of my external validation and self-worth.

NINETEEN

Alsace is one of the rare wine regions in the world
devoted almost exclusively to white wine. More than
seven different varieties are common and, with few exceptions,
they are whites rarely made in other parts of France.

"**K**rista! *Oh my God*, Krista, it's Julien from *Somm!* He is here! Remember, from the Alsace vineyard in the documentary?"

I could hear Sarah yelling from outside the tasting room, where I was purchasing my very worshipped bottle of Clos Sainte

Hune. Clos Sainte Hune is a three-acre plot of land exclusively planted with Riesling grapes, located in the heart of Rosacker Grand Cru in Hunawihr. It was pricey, but for our final class trip I wanted something memorable. We had just finished a tour and tasting at Trimbach, an iconic winery specializing in Riesling with many Grand Cru vintages.

Everyone stared at Sarah as she came barging into the room, the messy bun on top of her head bouncing around, showcasing her excitement. "Sorry, you all, I am, like, a bit starstruck. I love the *Somm* documentaries, and he is here."

I started laughing.

"Hang on, did you talk to him, or is he in the distance?" I asked as I signed the receipt, and did a double take at the price I was paying.

"He is outside and said hi, probably wondering who and what this crazy American woman dressed in all black is yelling about."

"Let's get a picture with him!" I declared and instantly felt like we were idiot tourists and our wine class tribe was going to disown us very soon. I didn't really care; Sarah and I lived for stuff like this, and I wanted to condone her enthusiasm.

I believe it was in the second documentary where they interviewed a winemaker and his son from Alsace, and Julien was this nice young guy who would be eventually taking over the entire vineyard. That encounter with the *Somm* star was one highlight of several for me in Alsace.

It was May and we were on our final adventure as a class.

We had arrived the day before and settled into the town of Riquewihr. Historically, this town served as a wine hub and trading center for Alsatian and German wine. It was one of the only villages not badly damaged in World War II. It was charming as all get out, with its cobblestone streets that were interlaced with half-timbered winemakers' shops and tasting rooms. There was a stunning backdrop of mountains through every slanted angle of the town as you looked down the rows of alleyways and Renaissance-era homes. Ruins from the thirteenth century outlined the village, serving as its walls.

That evening, after resting at our hotel, recuperating from several wine tastings that day, we were going to Flamme & Co., a famous restaurant in town that specialized in the Alsatian flatbread known as *tarte flambée* or *Flammekueche*. Out of all of the trips we'd taken, this was the first one that felt pretty foreign to Paris. Yes, we were still in France, but being so close to the German border, there was a huge cultural influence. You could see it not only in the architecture and hear it in the accent when people spoke French, but also experience it in the smell and taste of the food.

Everyone was pretty sentimental about it being our last class trip and was getting along for the most part. All twenty of us slid into a long, family-style table with a red-and-white checkered tablecloth. The mood was light and fun, and it was becoming clear that Paris was feeling heavy. Sarah was laughing and flirting with the waiters; even the French girls scooted down the table to hang with Sarah and me. Sebastian was telling stories about hot German men he had met in our hotel lobby, Michel was pretending he was American in ordering and making everyone laugh out loud, and the whole vibe was jokester city. Maybe it was the feeling of being in another land, maybe we were not trying to take this experience for granted, I wasn't sure, but in that moment Paris felt like a dark cloud and I knew it would be hard to leave the mountains and the fairytale towns of Alsace.

Professor Lavigne started selecting the wines we would pair with all of these hearty Alsatian dishes. I couldn't wait! I honestly was a little sick of the Rieslings, being that we had tasted them all day long, and was in the mood for red wine, but I did want to get the full Alsatian experience, so more white it was—my life wasn't that terrible considering they were all Grand Cru. We ordered several different tartes flambées, and they were served family-style down the center of the table for us to all dig in. My first bite of traditional Flammekueche—crème fraîche, crispy bacon, and caramelized onions paired with a crisp Riesling—was a culinary orgasm.

The next day, after popping into the famous store known as Féerie de Noël, a sought-after village shop that sold Christmas decorations the entire year, we boarded the tour van and headed to the town of Kaysersberg, which is German for "emperor's mountain." In fact, this town was at the edge of the Vosges Mountains where Switzerland and Germany bordered France. This village was said to be one of the most beautiful in the country. Our hotel had a view of the mountains, and we all had balconies staring at them. We could wave to each other from the balconies and chitchat before all meeting down in the hotel lobby. Our final meal would be at the Michelin-starred restaurant Au Relais des Ménétriers, but first we were heading to Domaine Josmeyer for a visit and tasting. I was excited because the winemaker was an uber-chic French woman;

I had looked her up when Mr. Porter had told us Josmeyer had a female winemaker.

We walked into the vineyard's tasting cellar just as the rain had started to fall onto the cobblestone pathway. The sky was gray, the smell of wet rock was prevalent, and we were all in our jackets and trench coats, trying to squeeze inside as quickly as possible. I noticed right as we walked in, everyone catching their breath and trying to take their place, that the tasting cellar was lined with barrels holding wine, which all had chalk drawings of them. There was beautiful chalk artwork of lions, horses, flowers, stars and moons, and abstract items as well. Josephine the winemaker introduced herself and said with her beautiful French accent, "On dark days like today I must amuse myself. I consider myself an artist both in making wine but in life. So I also do chalk drawings as part of my day, all while being in the dark cellar. It brings a sense of joy." Also written on the barrels were the alcohol levels and notes about the fermentation. After a brief introduction to the vineyard, we sat down for a formal tasting that included almost every grape varietal allowed to be grown in Alsace. We would be departing from purely Riesling and tasting wines made with Pinot Gris, Pinot Noir, Gewürztraminer, and Sylvaner.

Somewhat moved by the art Josephine had created on the barrels, I thought back to all the tours we had taken throughout the year. It had been a mixed bag of experiences and observations. Some were grand and royal, like the Louis Roederer mansion and the castles in Bordeaux; others were obscure and artisan like Domaine Josmeyer; and some felt like you were part of a bizarre and exclusive club, like the auction in a lone garage at Domaine Vincent in the Rhône Valley.

"You know, I think I should go into business with Vincent from Domaine Vincent and sell his Cornas to businessmen in Hong Kong," Sebastian said rather assuredly. "I think I could make a killing on that."

I knew he had dreams of exporting French wine in Asia, specifically in Hong Kong where people had deep pockets and were willing to pay several hundred dollars for good bottles of wine. Sebastian, like me, had fallen in love with Paris, so he wanted to eventually split his time between Paris and Asia and work in the world of wine export. I thought it sounded perfect for him, but the legality and licensing or whatever was needed to make that a reality seemed a bit far-fetched. I knew he had the vision, but it was hard for all of us, in anything we wanted to do in the wine world, to see how that job would come to be. At least when it came to continuing on in French wine.

"The foie gras, madame." I was intently listening to Sebastian's wine goals when this highly distracting concoction was placed in front of me at Au Relais des Ménétriers.

Tiny rimmed glass jars sat on a striking white plate. They were filled with coddled eggs, mixed with herbs and cream and topped with thick pieces of pan-seared, beautiful foie gras. The smell was intoxicating. I stared down the table to make sure everyone else had gotten their dish, then took my first bite. The crispness of the foie gras edges combined with its buttery texture, plus the cream and herbs, was divine. I took a sliver of the most perfect brioche toast point with yet more butter soaked in and topped it with my second bite of seared fatty duck liver and eggs.

"You know, my father has a hotel in India, and he wants me to run the wine program. Not only select all of the wines, but hold tourism events centered around food and wine pairings at the hotel," Pia chimed in after eavesdropping on Sebastian's statement.

"That's so great, you guys. Sounds like you have these entrepreneurial goals and wine is the niche back in your home countries," I said enthusiastically, not wanting to put my fork down just yet.

I couldn't relate, as I didn't feel anything exciting was waiting for me in my home country. I was from California, which was a wine capital as well with Napa and Sonoma in the north pinned as destination wine regions. Bringing wine knowledge there wasn't needed, and people already had import businesses, tourism businesses, and so on. I hated my safe thoughts around what I could actually do. Be a wine sales rep for a distributor, be a server? Work in a little wine shop? Nothing seemed riveting enough to blow my socks off. I just really liked wine, I liked France, and I loved Paris.

We really were just coming to terms with the fact that our diploma from Le Cordon Bleu was not some officially recognized certificate in the somm world. To actually be considered a sommelier would require us to go through WSET or the Master Court of Sommeliers. Did that even matter? Did I even want to be a sommelier? If nothing else existed, and the roadblocks were cleared as far as legality and visa establishment, my ultimate dream would have been a wine tasting business for English-speaking tourists, where I offered masterclasses pairing French wine and food. These classes I envisioned in chic apartments in Paris with grand balconies. The start of the session would be welcoming my guests with an aperitif of Champagne and then having everyone take their seats, where I would educate them on everything I had learned at Le Cordon Bleu. I wanted to turn all of this knowledge into an entrepreneurial endeavor. If only money wasn't the issue, or the fact that I wasn't a French citizen…

Just then we were interrupted. Professor Lavigne placed three wine bottles down on the table with linen napkins around them so we couldn't see the labels. It was declared we would do a blind tasting and that whoever called the wine correctly would get a bottle of Grand Cru Trimbach courtesy of Professor Lavigne. I was excited by the challenge even though I had just dropped half a month's rent on Alsatian Grand Crus. I was essentially a wild child splurging on wine and food, eating and drinking in excess, though primarily, I believe, because of my anxiety over *what the hell I was going to do next!*

TWENTY

Northern Rhône wines are tempests of wild flavor ...
and for those of us who love them, the wilder, the better.
In particular, the daringly intense Syrahs here have no equivalent
elsewhere in the wine world. Falling in love with them
isn't easy at first, but it is a right of passage.

"Madame Krista Bender." My name was called; this was it. I was led into my first of many tests on the final day of Le Cordon Bleu's Wine and Management program, the sommelier exam.

I sat down at the desk in the room. I was given five glasses; each glass had two ounces of wine in it. A spit bucket was in the upper right corner of the table.

"Voilà, okay, madame."

I was trying to concentrate as I looked around and observed the room. It was just me and the white walls. Roberta, one of my classmates from Venezuela, sat in the first row. She was also being instructed. I was at the last table in the room.

The instructor continued to say, "On this sheet you are to taste wines one through five and state for each what the varietal is, where it is grown, the vintage, if it is aged in oak, and how long it can potentially age for. Below you will give the estimated price at cost. Do this for all five in writing. When you are done, bring it up to the podium. You have twenty minutes."

This was supposedly the easy part, when we just got to observe, taste, and come up with conclusions without having to speak. The next sequence of the exam would be practical, and I would be standing up with judges staring at me as I analyzed the wine. This was the least stressful part.

Wine number one—I immediately smelled apricots, then honey, like dripping honeycomb on a cheese board, and some lemon zest sprinkled around. My initial thought was Viognier, but then I tasted it. It was crisp but not nearly round enough to be a Viognier. The alcohol level was lower too. The peach and lemon notes on the palate sealed the deal—this was a Chenin Blanc. I was nearly 100 percent certain. In fact, I had most likely tasted a hundred by now. I called Vouvray as the appellation, region, the

Loire Valley, and wrote, *30% oaked in French oak, vintage 2013, not too old based on the color on the edge when held against a white sheet of paper.*

Next, light red. This wasn't Pinot Noir out of Burgundy; it wasn't nearly complex enough. I smelled it several times. Floral, earth, rosemary. Gamay. It was close to Burgundy; Beaujolais was the region. I was 95 percent certain. The price point was much lower; I pegged it at thirty euros.

Ooh, this was getting fun. Wine number three was definitely a twist. It was Pinot Noir, but it wasn't from Burgundy either. It was from Alsace. Pinot Noir was the only red grape allowed to be grown in Alsace. I could remember the exact difference of the tastes between Alsace and Burgundy pinots, and this had it—and thankfully we had just tasted several in Alsace. I guessed the vintage was 2010, similar to that of the ones I had experienced in those lovely mountain towns.

Fourth wine? Definitely Bordeaux. Definitely Médoc—Left Bank; the gravel and graphite gave it away in the aroma. Tons of fresh green bell pepper aromas meant this was at least 65 percent Cabernet Franc. Sure, there was Cabernet Sauvignon for the rest and maybe just 10 percent Merlot to round it out. Dry. Very dry. Still young, tannins were still tight, and my mouth was puckering. Merlot may have only been 5 percent, so I adjusted my answer. There was not much fruit; it was herbaceous. Another ten years in the bottle, even fifteen, and this would be so smooth. This was a 2014 Médoc. Price point? Seventy euros. It wasn't nearly Grand Cru status or Classification 1855.

Fifth and final—I sampled it—was a Syrah. Bold and heavy... appellation Saint Joseph. Not as meaty as its cousin Cornas, but definitely Rhône style—definitely a Syrah, definitely a hot climate. Still young but getting smoother, bloody and meaty, I was suddenly craving *steak au poivre*. I would price it at 150 a bottle.

I saw the female adjudicator approaching again as I scribbled down *Vintage 2012*. Just in time, I was done.

"C'est fini?" she asked with raised eyebrows.

"Oui, c'est facile pour le moment," I said.

She gave me a half grin. "Bon. Now you will take the hundred-question test please, before you leave the room and head to practical applications, consulting interview, or decanting. Voilà, you have sixty minutes. *Bon courage.*"

Exactly sixty minutes later, I had turned in my written test, and I exited the room. I saw Alan and Michel standing there waiting to go in.

"How was it? Were the wines a hard call?" they whispered, but there were faculty all around and it would have been cheating to tell each other any details. We had been severely warned.

"No, I think you will do well. Which did you guys just complete?"

"The decanting. Someone spilled, not going to say who." Alan looked down as he said it, indicating his own shame and embarrassment.

"Aw, it's okay. I'm sure it doesn't count as a huge percentage," I said, trying to reassure him. For the past two weeks we had all been practicing opening bottles in front of each other. We not only had to open it properly, we had to decant it into a long, glass pouring vessel with a candle lit to it, showing that we were in fact removing the sediment from the bottle. Then, we had to properly carry this in a small wire basket to the table and present the bottle perfectly, stating everything about the wine and giving the perfect pour. This was the service aspect of the exam. I thought back to all of my service at Citrus Etoile; I was secretly glad for that in retrospect because it really did prepare me for this.

Ten of us had been at Sarah's two nights before with candles lit, opening bottle after bottle. We had stocked up on five-euro wines from Franprix, a grocery store chain in Paris, so we wouldn't have to be limited in our practice measures. It also helped to take the nerves out of being watched as you opened a bottle of wine. We wanted to get very familiar with being watched so as to remove some of the intimidation we had heard about with this exam.

I waited for my turn to be let into the decanting room. My palms were a little sweaty, and my mouth was dry from the previous wines in the blind tasting analysis. I needed water. I thought about what would happen if I didn't open the Champagne bottle correctly and it made a pop sound, or if I spilled the wine or broke the cork. Butterflies formed in my stomach.

"Madame Bender?" A man opened the door as Jen, one of my classmates, walked out past me. She gave me a hopeful look.

Three men in suits were sitting at a table staring at me with still faces when I walked in. I was told to begin my wine service.

I took the serving tray. I took a brief glance at the wine label. Then, based purely on muscle memory, I started to place the necessary components on it: the ashtray, two wine glasses, one smaller glass for me to taste a small sip, the candle, the wire basket, and finally the decanter. My wine key was in my pocket, I hoped, I prayed.

I smiled and placed the glasses in front of the gentlemen, and I put the tray down on the side table next to them. I heard Professor Lavigne in my ear: *Always keep the wine in a horizontal position in the basket, with the label facing outward.*

I approached the "clients" with the wine. My hand was on the verge of shaking, but my brain was fighting this impulse.

"Bonjour, monsieurs. Château Beaucastel 2016."

They nodded in agreement. Already my brain was fogging up; they were watching my every move, but I had to act completely calm the entire time, like this was normal. *Shit. What the hell is the very first step now? Pull out my wine key? Open the wine? Right. Candles, something with the candle.*

That's right, it came to me—the very first thing after the presentation is lighting the freaking candle. I was scared the match wouldn't catch—we could not use a lighter as this was formal service—but fortunately it did. I remembered to strike the match toward myself and not blow on it, as Professor Lavigne said all of these details would be judged. Next, my wine key. *You can do this Krista,* I said to myself. After opening hundreds of bottles of wine at this point in my life, I still got nervous with people watching my form. It was uncomfortable. These Parisian judges were giving off the energy that we were in open heart surgery, and I was the physician with my silver tools; they were waiting to watch me cut the chest open.

I knew I couldn't remove the bottle from the basket and would have to open it perfectly all while the label was still facing the client and the bottle wasn't moving. I would also need to put the foil back on the bottle after decanting the wine in case the client wanted to take the bottle home as a souvenir. I remembered the tips Mr. Porter had given us on making sure you cut the label really well using the knife of your wine key so the foil isn't damaged. They were still staring at me intently. I thought about how different it would be taking this exam in America. I could have bet the judges would have made the student feel at ease, not intimidated the hell out of them. The linen napkin—*shit, I had already screwed up*—I had forgotten to grab the linen napkin that would gently wipe away the drips of wine after pouring. Oh well, hopefully this wouldn't be a huge dock in points, but just that alone set me off kilter a bit.

Ten minutes later I had completed both the presentation of the red wine and opened the bottle of Champagne. The Champagne oozed out of the top a bit, but at least I had twisted it from the bottom and it hadn't made a peep, a super no-no in opening Champagne professionally. Yes, the pop and explosion are fun when you are celebrating with friends, but in France it's an embarrassment if the bottle makes any noise or explodes. I concluded that my deductions would absolutely come from the linen napkin, the Champagne bubbling out of the top, and I'm sure there were a few other minor errors. All in all, I felt pretty good and was two for two. I had done the written part, the presentation part, and now… now was the true test: blind tasting one red, one white in front of the rumored *five* professional Parisian somms. There was no telling what we would face in there. We had been advised we could even be poured a non-French wine to determine how sound our judgments of French wine and the New World versus Old World wines were. Beyond all that, Professor Lavigne, being an accredited sommelier, was set to also be at that table behind the elusive door. I was very nervous, to the point of feeling as if I was going to pee my pants.

I saw Pearl in the hallway.

"I just completed it," she said. "Ugh, I hope I called the right wine. That was nerve-racking for sure."

"I'm sure you did; you have one of the best palates in the class," I responded truthfully. "Do you have one more room to attend?"

"No, I think I'm done. Champagne and pastries are being served down in our old classroom. Once you are done, come down there! Phew, it feels good for this to be over!" I was instantly envious she had completed everything. Just then someone grabbed my shoulder.

"Krista, I'm having anxiety, like I don't know if I will pass this whole course." It was Sarah; this was the first I was hearing that she harbored these doubts.

"Oh my gosh, you will! Don't think like that or else it will become a self-fulfilling prophecy," I quickly stated. I could tell she was actually nervous; it was hitting her that this was do or die. Neither of us had gone into the blind tasting yet.

Suddenly, the door swung open. Pia walked out. She reached out, gave me a half hug, and whispered, "Krista loves these wines."

An instructor came out; alongside him was Mr. Porter. Mr. Porter looked at me, and his face had a few sweat droplets right under his hairline. I remember looking up at his blue eyes through his wide-rimmed glasses, those same glasses he had removed to wipe his tears in Bordeaux. "Krista, let's see what we have learned," he stated with confidence in his voice, confidence in me and my ability to call the wines. I instantly didn't want to let him down. Not only did I want a good grade, I wanted to win. I wanted to call these wines and describe them to perfection. The student who won this final, judged blind tasting was supposed to receive a writeup in Le Cordon Bleu publications, as well as all kinds of special invites all summer long to professional wine networking events in Paris. I wanted this so badly. I wasn't worried I wouldn't pass; I wanted to pass with flying colors.

I entered the room. The first person I saw was Professor Lavigne in a striking gray suit that he had paired with a black-and-lavender tie. His shiny, gold sommelier pin was flashing against the gray. He looked up and seemed pleased that I was approaching the podium. Next to him were five others, four men and one woman, for a total of six judges.

The instructor started to speak.

"Ladies and gentlemen, this is Krista Bender. Please write her name at the top of your sheet.

"Ms. Bender, Mr. Porter will pour you the first wine. This is the same wine that all of your other classmates have been and will be poured. The label is covered with a linen napkin as we would like you to be able to tell us what this wine is. Please analyze this wine in front of us, telling us all of your observations and conclusions. Please explain how you are coming to those conclusions. Please lead us through tasting this wine. And remember, you are an expert now. Don't second-guess yourself; we believe in your abilities. The judges may ask you questions as well. Please remember this is a timed tasting and you do not have time on your side to answer. Answer quickly, perhaps your first impulse. Your intuition. Mr. Porter, please proceed."

I was shaking; I felt sweat dripping down my spine.

The wine splashed into my glass. It was golden yellow with straw-like hues. My first thought was… Chardonnay.

I stood up straight as I slowly allowed the glass to approach my face. Before I swirled the wine in my glass, I wanted the first aroma to have zero aeration. I saw Lavigne write on his sheet of paper. He must have given me a point for that. Most forget how important it is to smell wine before the classic sommelier move of swirling the glass and allowing air in. I ruled out Chardonnay immediately. There were no butter notes, no oak notes. Purely fruit.

I took the wine away from my face and now swirled it in the glass. I watched it move intently. I had said nothing yet. I knew I would have to start speaking; I just wanted to gather some thoughts to myself first. I stared at the wine, not the judges; wine was calming me on all fronts at that moment. I took it up to my nose again; this time I was able to identify which fruits I'd smelled. The smell of apricots was overwhelming, also fresh, juicy peaches, like a basket full from picking them up off the grass in a countryside landscape in France. There was also a minerality, a chalky, mineral note coming through. I swirled it once more. This time I got an overwhelming whiff of Acacia honey, but there was also a crispness coming through. A green-apple essence.

I secretly thought to myself, *Chenin Blanc*. I didn't want to call it yet, and that was also the wine I had called as number one on the written exam earlier that day. Shoot, would they really pour two Chenin Blancs? Maybe the one from earlier had been a Viognier, or maybe this wasn't Chenin, or maybe they did this to trick us? I remembered what the instructor had said when she told me not to second-guess myself. I also knew it had been at least two minutes and I had yet to say a word. I needed to change that immediately.

"Upon sight, this wine is golden yellow in color. I initially would have pegged it as a Chardonnay due to its golden and potential oak influence in the satiny straw shade, but upon my very first smell sans aeration I picked up no oak. I have also ruled out it being a Chablis, which is typically Chardonnay unoaked due to the specific fruit aromas that came through after aeration." Two of the judges nodded as if in agreement and wrote something on their paper.

"I do not believe this has oak aging based on the fruit and mineral notes. If it was in oak, it would not be able to be unmasked, but I am coming to the conclusion that the golden hues of this wine are due to sunshine on the grapes, and that leads me again to an appellation where there tends to be a warmer climate, possibly south of Burgundy, which again is where I rule out Chardonnay. This is no doubt a wine made in France, and the determinant on that for me is honestly that I have tasted several very similar wines to this, all made in France, not another country, and so that call is made purely out of memory and embedded recollection."

"The first aromas I picked up on were very fresh and ripe stone fruits, white peaches and golden apricots, fallen fresh from the fruit trees. I imagined them on the ground and me picking them up and placing them in my wicker basket. Secondly, I smelled an overwhelming aroma of acacia honey." I brought the wine up to my nose a third time to draw any final conclusions.

"Yes, apricots and honey plus a hint of mineral always leads me to one of my favorite white grapes, and that grape is Chenin Blanc."

Professor Lavigne looked down, and before he could camouflage it, I saw a miniscule smirk line his cheeks.

This boosted my confidence instantly. I said a few other sentences about the wine, noting it was from the Loire Valley, guessing the age, price point, and offering a complementary food pairing of exotic apricot chicken or a tartine that was topped with lightly fried chèvre rounds with a light spread underneath of quince jam.

One of the judges looked up and asked, "Do you believe this wine went through malolactic fermentation? If so, please explain why you have come to that conclusion."

Malolactic fermentation was a second fermentation done based on the winemaker's decision to reduce acidity and bring on a creaminess in a given wine. It was done by converting the malic acid to lactic acid, which was common in most Chardonnays, many red wines, and some other whites as well to add a layer of depth and fattiness on the mouthfeel.

"I tasted the wine, and yes, I do believe this has gone through partial malo. There is a richness after the initial acidity. It coats my tongue just enough, and in my opinion, this winemaker made a good call there."

The judges seemed satisfied. The instructor appeared again from around the corner.

"Okay, Ms. Bender. We are onto the next wine. This will be a red wine. Here are some crackers and water to cleanse your palate."

Mr. Porter came toward me with the bottle of red wine wrapped in a black linen napkin. My nerves had subsided somewhat, but a rush of butterflies invaded my stomach, and I felt goose bumps like a slow wave go up my arms. I better call this one correctly. I thought back to what Pia had whispered moments before: *Krista loves these wines.* If that was any indication, I figured it was going to be a Syrah. I was certain I had called the Chenin Blanc correctly. Everything from Professor Lavigne's facial expressions to my glimpse of that smirk, to the astounding aromas all led to a heavy persuasion that it was Chenin Blanc. I hoped this one would feel as slam dunk as the white wine had.

It was ruby red, red plum in color. It was slowly being released into my glass, and I had tunnel vision on sound. Nothing else in the room existed. Just the splashing of the wine. Mr. Porter gave me a nod.

I tilted the glass slightly, to see if the color would lighten at the edges. There was a subtle difference where the color was approaching magenta, but not much give on the intensity of the concentration. That told me the wine was fairly young, a recent vintage.

I smelled it.

Meat. Blood. Earth. I decided to say my thoughts out loud this time, fairly immediately.

"This wine is a recent vintage. Before I make a determination on the exact year, I want to taste it. Also this is Syrah."

I swirled the wine vigorously; the judges watched my glass. I brought the glass up to my nose. "Aromas coming through—white pepper. There are also now herbs such as rosemary and thyme. Originally I smelled meat, like a peppered salami on a charcuterie board, and now secondary aromas of dark, rich fruit like blackberries and black plums. Also an element of fried bacon."

Professor Lavigne seemed to be pleased with my description. He started writing on his sheet of paper with a confident nod.

I tasted the wine. The sides of my mouth started to pucker like I had just sipped a cup of tea that had steeped too long.

I quickly gasped in some air to open up the flavors on my tongue. This was very common in professional wine tasting, to take in air with your sip and immediately close your mouth. The effect air has on wine is like magic. It will open everything up, change flavors, change things.

There was something so familiar about this wine. I had tasted something like it very recently. I thought back—it was at 5ème Cru with Sebastian. *Gosh, what did we order that night? With the cheese board.* I tasted the wine again, hoping it would come to me.

It did.

Côte-Rôtie. This was a Syrah from the Côte-Rôtie appellation in Northern Rhône. I knew it, with the pepper, the violet now coming through. A quick thought of *I can't believe they are pouring Côte-Rôtie on the exam! So pricey!* and then I started speaking again.

"I am now picking up some violet, this is herbaceous, combined with the rich meatiness and the black fruit. There is great complexity here despite the wine being young; that was also just confirmed when I tasted it and realized the tannins haven't relaxed yet. This wine is very rich, very elegant, a lot going on here. I mentioned this is a single-varietal Syrah; I will now say it is from Northern Rhône. There has been decent sun exposure, but the fruit is not baked; it's just ripe, which is my indication it is not Southern Rhône. The sunlight would have shown me baked plum tarts, the fruit would have been caramelized. These plums are however fresh off the tree."

I saw the female judge smile to herself. Either I was spot on or she enjoyed me talking about plum tarts.

"All right, let's see, so we know it's Syrah, Northern Rhône, and I am calling the appellation as Côte-Rôtie."

"Madame, how did you come to this conclusion? Côte-Rôtie?" one of the judges asked pointedly.

"To be very honest, after determining it was the Northern Rhône, I thought back to many Syrahs I have tasted, and this parallels some I have tried from that appellation. There are too many similarities for me to call another appellation. I would say that in confidence purely from muscle memory. I am also ready to call the vineyard and winemaker.

"This is Guigal. I know what his wine style is. I am very happy you all are letting us analyze this wine. Merci." Guigal was highly sought-after and usually a minimum of 100 euros a bottle. Professor Lavigne must have gotten a good deal on a case or something.

"Vintage Madame?"

"2013."

"Finally, what are we eating with this wine?" the female judge asked. I knew it was those plum tarts. She wanted more food descriptions; she must have been hungry.

"Simple. Lamb shank. Make sure there is a lot of rosemary in the braising liquid. Yes, falling-off-the-bone lamb with some beautiful roasted parsnips."

"Bon. Merci, Madame."

"Congratulations, Ms. Bender. You have completed the exam. You may join your classmates in the classroom for the post-exam Champagne toast."

Slam dunk.

TWENTY-ONE

The persistence of wine on your palate,
even after you've swallowed, is called the length or finish.
The better the wine, the longer the length.

"The sparkling froth of this wine is the
dazzling image of us, the French." —VOLTAIRE

It was graduation day. We would walk across the stage, shake hands with the president of Le Cordon Bleu, and there you have it, signed, sealed, and delivered straight to you from Paris—a French Wine consultant and sommelier.

It was June, and the air was muggy and hot. I had five weeks until my apartment lease was up, and I needed to figure out my next step. Would I continue to rent this apartment through the summer? Would I move? Would I spend the summer in California and reassess? I had completed the program I came to Paris for and was unemployed, with my savings being chipped away at weekly. Sarah had already booked her flight back to the States. We would go on our graduation trip to Corsica, and then she was going back, back where we *belonged*, at least according to her.

I took a sip from my aperitif; I was sitting at Café de Flore by myself, watching the Parisians go about their daily lives. After I calmed my nerves with my Aperol spritz, I would take a taxi to the ceremony, which was being held in a beautiful old museum in the Eighth Arrondissement across the river.

No one from my family was able to come to my graduation. Sarah and Sebastian's parents had flown into Paris for the event. Despite Sarah's anxiety she did end up passing the certification. Everyone did. We were all graduating from Le Cordon Bleu today. I understood my parents had to work and had been at all of my other graduations, but it still made me feel a slight depressive feeling to not have them there. There was something about this whole thing that didn't feel celebratory at all. It felt sad, like the ending of a beautiful chapter that I didn't want to stop reading.

As I brought the large, soup bowl of a glass to my face, I thought about my conversation five months before with the lady in the chocolate shop.

"You will see. Eventually you will move back. You will come to realize where you identify." I kept repeating what she had said in my mind.

Would I move back? I didn't want to. I felt so certain that I wasn't meant to leave Paris. *You will come to realize where you identify.*

"Mademoiselle, *je vous puis offrir un autre verre?*" The waiter interrupted my train of thought. I looked at my watch. I'd better not; I needed to be able to walk across the stage.

"Non, merci," I stated despite the temptation of wanting another.

Here. I identify here. Can everyone I love just come here?

I came to the food and wine capital of the world, Paris. I felt I had been trained for positions *out there,* but this, this was my only chance to be right here, to make it in Paris. I couldn't imagine parting from my sixth-floor flat with the windows staring at the Notre Dame Cathedral—mere years, I couldn't know yet, before its roof and upper walls would tragically burn—my vegetable vendors, the sweet man at the boulangerie below my apartment that sold me my daily bread. Even the cheese shop workers at Laurent Dubois knew my favorites and always had something new to recommend. What would I do without these things I had come to love? I couldn't let it all vanish.

Sebastian had landed a job at Galeries Lafayette, the huge department store where he had his internship, in the wine sales department. I was happy for him. He was the only other person other than the six French students that was staying in Paris. I was glad he was. Then, there was me. I would have to get a job here if I wanted to stay. An au pair, an English-speaking teacher, something? I needed to figure it out.

My mind went to my failure to secure a French boyfriend. I had stopped seeing Damien after I realized I couldn't sustain his demands and after he had begun treating me disrespectfully once again. At a certain point, I just stopped caring. I didn't expect to hear from him, and when I did, I knew I was an afterthought and therefore would decline his invitations to meet. I was proud of myself for at least being intuitive enough to know that I deserved better. I had become aware of my conscious exchange of picture perfection for private problems. In that relationship I was okay with the exchange, in what would look good as an image while deep down I was in darkness. I would experience beauty and joy and the pure highs of Paris and good friends, and then in my romantic relationships it seemed I would experience complete dysfunction and sad moments. There was no stability to them, and grasping onto a sliver of good moments and hiding the bad wasn't working for me anymore. The extreme contrast Paris had brought me was the only way I was able to see the light. To see that there was better out there than a mundane, average life. I had needed to set my comfortable world on fire, and now I needed to start to erase the darkness. Underlying trauma, that was what attracted the other side. I had been broken when I came to Paris after my traumatic relationship with Eddie. I was still the same person inside, but Paris allowed me to define that person as clearly as an X-ray: the underlying issues, the codependency, the need to find a person who would value me.

The graduation was bittersweet. It was in a beautiful museum, stunning, full of chandeliers and French moldings. Nice Champagnes were served, and we definitely felt pampered. I was sort of in a daze. I still had that depressive, shocking temperament. I socialized with my Champagne in hand, met my friends' gracious parents, but I felt disconnected to the entire day. It was odd. Even Sarah noticed. She pulled me aside and asked if everything was okay. I told her I had a slight headache; I didn't want to open up just yet because I knew she wouldn't entirely understand. I also wasn't sure of what I was doing and trying to sort through these thoughts myself. One by one we were announced and walked across the stage to get our diploma. We were asked to stand at the podium and say what we intended to do with our new and fresh wine degree. When it was my turn to speak, I said something disingenuous. I am sure my energy was read.

"I will be implementing luxury retreats in Napa focused on the education of French wines, comparing French wines to Californian wines, and sharing everything we have learned this year with Americans in California." I walked off the stage.

While a good idea in theory, it couldn't have been further from the truth. Not one ounce of me wanted to go back to California. I was afraid I would feel like a fish out of water in the United States. At that moment I realized I would rather do *anything*, even if it meant not working in the world of wine, anything to stay in Paris. This was a sacrifice I was willing to make. My body started trembling as Pearl was giving her speech. I looked up at the stained glass windows and the intrinsic beauty of this historical museum. I took several deep breaths. I looked at the servers pouring and lining up Champagne for when the ceremony concluded. I saw mini cheese trays lining the back buffet table. I stared almost in a trance at the grand chandelier in the center of the room. Sparkling light, glowing, beautiful. It was stunning. I was very present.

I started to feel at peace. I started to believe I would be staying, and that thought alone calmed me. I gazed around the room; I looked at my classmates and said a happy thought about each one to myself. I loved this entire experience. I adored this bond I had formed with them, and this could never be taken away from me.

Alan was my final classmate to walk across the stage. He was from Armenia, and supposedly the world of wine was up and coming there. He was looking forward to capitalizing on the fact that he had been in Paris and adhered to the fact that there would be endless opportunities for him in Armenia.

Finally, it was time for the president of the school and Professor Lavigne to announce the winner of the final exam's blind tasting. The week prior, the administration had emailed all of us and asked for a headshot, as the winner would be announced by having their picture being blasted across the stage's backdrop.

Professor Lavigne gave a closing speech about our class, about how proud he was of each and every one of us, and about how sad he was that it was over. He wished everyone well and told us to keep in touch with him, and said he would be a reference always. Then, drumroll please…

The president of the school approached the podium.

"Ladies and gentlemen, on behalf of Le Cordon Bleu, I have to say we are pleased with all twenty of your performances regarding the two wines you were poured during the certification and asked to analyze in front of the six judges. There is a winner of this tasting. With that being said, eighteen of you named the correct varietals. The grapes were Chenin Blanc and Syrah. Eight of you named the appropriate and correct appellations; five of you were correct with the vintages; however, only one of you guessed all of the above combined correctly. In addition to that, the descriptions and tasting were perfect as far as the judges were concerned. It was a professional analysis to the utmost. This student will receive a loaded itinerary of professional tastings and events in Paris this summer and fall. This is an absolute honor for us to extend this. And without further ado, the winner is Jen Gwan of Korea."

Lights flashed to the canvas, and there was Jen's picture. She gasped. "Oh my goodness," she said as her hands covered her mouth in disbelief. She was smiling ear to ear, and her face was red.

"Jen, please do us the honor of coming and getting your special medal."

She walked up to the podium and said a gracious few sentences about how much this meant and then posed for photos. I looked at Benoit, one of my French classmates, and he looked down with no smile. The French girls stared straight ahead.

But I was happy for Jen. I watched her getting her picture taken and felt the glee she must have been feeling as everyone watched. I was secretly disappointed I hadn't won. I knew I called the wines correctly, and I am pretty sure I guessed the appellations right. Maybe my vintages were off. Well, the course was over; what was done was done. We all met for Champagne and dinner afterward at a restaurant. Sebastian had rented out an entire room and terrace so students' families could also join in the festivities. Sebastian gave a toast that made me cry. He was a very kind, beautiful person, and I had also learned he tended to be poetic and sentimental. He was the type of person that would listen to sad music when he was sad, really feel the emotion he was going through and magnify it.

He stood up in the front and center of the room with a glass of Champagne in his hand and said, "I love each and every one of you. I feel that you are all a Grand Cru wine from an outstanding appellation; all of us are unique and were all meant to travel this journey together. May your light shine wherever you go in this world. May this year be the best harvest of your grape ever. May the memories that were nothing but remarkable stay with you from our time here in Paris. In France. Santé."

With that we all clinked our glasses.

With the saluting of my glass to theirs, it was as if the year of memories flashed before my eyes in a fast-paced reel as you would see on instagram.

My brain had the images swifting through quickly, a play-by-play. At that moment, I vowed to myself I would not loose the option and determination of making life extraordinary. Not good … not even just great. *Extraordinary.*

EPILOGUE
July 2016

It was storming in Paris. I was walking along the Seine, and the top of the Eiffel Tower was engulfed in a thick cluster of fog. I could only see the bottom two thirds of the magnificent monument. It was eerie, and I felt the goose bumps crawl up the back of my neck.

The rain was coming down, harder and faster. Sometimes I relished these moments, ones where I could be alone with the city. Thanks to the storm, there was not one other body on the boulevard for miles to see. It felt exhilarating. I didn't care about being drenched, uncomfortable, and cold. I found these circumstances essentially my private, intimate dates with Paris.

I'm that weird person; when everyone else wants to go inside, I head outside. I do the opposite to have my own escape. When I was a kid, I always pushed the envelope right there to the edge. Like the time my mom found me in the back of a schoolyard with an injured crow. My preschool teacher put her hands up with a sigh as she led my mother to the edge of the playground, where she would see her daughter holding a large, jagged, dirty stick with a black crow on the end.

"Only Krista," as she would say. Another "Only Krista" was the fact that I was becoming obsessed with securing ties to Paris.

I was racking my brain any and every possible way to stay. I was about to hit my one-year mark living in this city, and the very thought of me having to go back to the US, to California, led to the full feeling of anxiety that I wouldn't even recognize myself anymore. It was entirely part of my identity.

I needed to get back to *mon petit pied-à-terre*.

I couldn't believe what I was about to send. *Just do it, Krista. You have nothing to lose.* These were my last thoughts before hitting the send button on my iMac computer's keyboard. I remember my hand was shaking; I remember listening to the rain on my window; I remember a force greater than anything I'd ever experienced in my life making my finger drop on the send button. As if fate was ushering me into the next chapter in life...

Bonjour Delphine,

I spoke over the phone with Simon about renewing my lease. I was first wondering if you are aware, and if not can you ask the owner if they would be at all interested in selling the flat at this time?

I love the apartment and am also looking to buy property in Paris now. If you know of other properties for sale that would be great as well.

Please let me know, and then secondly we can discuss the lease renewal after this answer.

Merci beaucoup,
Krista